Reminiscences

of

Captain Phil H. Bucklew, USN (Ret.)

U. S. Naval Institute
Annapolis, Maryland

Preface

    This volume contains the transcript of nine taped interviews with Captain Phil H. Bucklew, USN (Ret.). They were all held at his home in Fairfax, Virginia during 1980.

    This is a fascinating account of the development of the Navy's Special Warfare from its inception in World War II down through Vietnam. Captain Bucklew's own career spans the time from the invasion of North Africa in 1942 to Vietnam in the 1960s. He participated actively in such operations as TORCH, HUSKY, SALERNO, NORMANDY, the CHINA THEATER in World War II, KOREA and VIETNAM. The reader will find it not only an adventure story of the first magnitude but also an authentic (but little known) account of what is accomplished by some of the U. S. Navy's most daring and able men.

    Captain Bucklew has corrected the original transcript. It has been re-typed and an index has been added for convenience.

                                            John T. Mason, Jr.
                                            Director of Oral History

                                            Annapolis, Maryland
                                            March, 1982

BIOGRAPHICAL INFORMATION ON

CAPTAIN PHIL H. BUCKLEW, USN, HEAD, SPECIAL OPERATIONS BRANCH, STRIKE WARFARE DIVISION, OFFICE OF THE CHIEF OF NAVAL OPERATIONS.

CAPTAIN BUCKLEW IS A NATIVE OF COLUMBUS, OHIO. HE IS MARRIED TO THE FORMER HELEN NAGEL OF COLUMBUS, OHIO. A VETERAN UNCONVENTIONAL WARFARE AND NAVAL INTELLIGENCE OPERATOR, HE HAS BEEN EQUALLY PROMINENT IN COLLEGE, PROFESSIONAL AND SERVICE ATHLETICS AND COACHED FOOTBALL AT XAVIER UNIVERSITY, CINCINNATI, OHIO AND COLUMBIA UNIVERSITY, NEW YORK CITY DURING THE 1940's. IN 1961, HE WAS NOMINATED TO THE SILVER ANNIVERSARY ALL-AMERICAN FOOTBALL TEAM OF SPORTS ILLUSTRATED MAGAZINE.

DURING THE PERIOD JANUARY 5 TO FEBRUARY 20, 1964 CAPTAIN BUCKLEW LED A STUDY TEAM WHICH WAS TASKED WITH INVESTIGATING THE COMMUNIST INFILTRATION PROBLEMS IN SOUTH VIETNAM. THE TEAM TRAVELED THROUGHOUT SOUTH VIETNAM, PARTICULARLY THE DELTA REGION, OBSERVING AND GATHERING, AT FIRST HAND, INFORMATION CONCERNING INFILTRATION AND WATER-BORNE COUNTERINSURGENCY PROBLEMS. THE COMPILED REPORT BECAME KNOWN AS "THE BUCKLEW REPORT". THIS REPORT WAS AFFORDED THE GREATEST ATTENTION AT THE HIGHEST LEVELS OF GOVERNMENT AND BECAME THE BASIS FOR ACTIONS NOW BEING IMPLEMENTED TO ASSIST THE PEOPLE OF SOUTH VIETNAM TO MAINTAIN THEIR FREEDOM.

DURING WORLD WAR II CAPTAIN BUCKLEW WALKED ACROSS CHINA TO OBTAIN RECONNAISSANCE ON BEACHES, PASSING HIMSELF OFF AS A CHINESE COOLIE. AT ONE TIME DURING HIS ADVENTURE, HE WAS CONCEALED IN A HAYSTACK WHILE SURROUNDED BY JAPANESE.

BEFORE THE INVASIONS OF AFRICA AND SICILY DURING WORLD WAR II, HE RECONNOITERED THE BEACHES. HE WAS ASHORE IN NORMANDY SIX MONTHS PRIOR TO THE INVASION AND WAS ON THE BEACH ON D-DAY. ON ONE OCCASION, CAPTAIN BUCKLEW WENT IN TO AN ENEMY BEACH TO BRING OUT A BUCKET OF SAND WHICH WAS TESTED AND

ANALYZED AS ESSENTIAL INFORMATION FOR INVASION PLANNING.

CAPTAIN BUCKLEW's PREVIOUS COMMAND WAS COMMANDER, NAVAL OPERATIONS SUPPORT GROUP, PACIFIC, WHICH CONSOLIDATED UNDER ONE HEADQUARTERS AT CORONADO, CALIFORNIA, SEVERAL OF THE PACIFIC FLEET AND AMPHIBIOUS FORCE COMMANDS RESPONSIBLE FOR COUNTERINSURGENCY AND SPECIAL WARFARE. THE GROUP INCLUDED UNDERWATER DEMOLITION TEAMS ELEVEN AND TWELVE, BEACH JUMPER UNIT ONE, SEA AIR LAND (SEAL) TEAM ONE AND BOAT SUPPORT UNIT ONE.

CAPTAIN BUCKLEW WAS RECENTLY AWARDED THE LEGION OF MERIT. HE IS HOLDER OF SEVERAL OF THE HIGHEST MILITARY AWARDS INCLUDING THE NAVY CROSS WITH GOLD STAR (SECOND AWARD), SILVER STAR AND JOINT SERVICE MEDAL; THE CROIX DE GUERRE WITH PALM (FRANCE), THE ULCHI MEDAL (KOREA), COMMENDATIONS FROM THE REPUBLIC OF CHINA AND GREAT BRITIAN, AND THE NAVY LEAGUE MERITORIOUS CITATION, WHICH IS THE HIGHEST REGULAR NAVY LEAGUE AWARD WHICH CAN BE MADE TO UNIFORMED PERSONNEL OF THE DEPARTMENT OF DEFENSE.

DECLARATION OF TRUST

The undersigned does hereby appoint and designate as his (her) Trustee herein, the Secretary-Treasurer and Publisher of the United States Naval Institute to perform and discharge the following duties, powers, and privileges in connection with the possession and use of a certain taped interview between the undersigned and the Oral History Department of the United States Naval Institute.

1. Classification of Transcript.

    (X)a. If classified OPEN, the transcript(s) may be read or the recording(s) audited by the qualified personnel upon presentation of proper credentials, as determined by the Secretary-Treasurer of the U.S. Naval Institute.

    ( )b. If classified PERMISSION REQUIRED TO CITE OR QUOTE, the user will be required to obtain permission in writing from the interviewee prior to quoting or citing from either the transcript(s) or the recording(s).

    ( )c. If classified PERMISSION REQUIRED, permission must be obtained in writing from the interviewee before the transcribed interview(s) can be examined or the tape recording(s) audited.

    ( )d. If classified CLOSED, the transcribed interview(s) and the tape recording(s) will be sealed until a time specified by the interviewee. This may be until the death of the interviewee or for any specified number of years.

2. It is expressly understood that in giving this authorization, I am in no way precluded from placing such restrictions as I may desire upon use of the interview at any time during my lifetime, nor does this authorization in any way affect my rights to the copyright of my literary expressions that may be contained in the interview.

Witness my hand and seal this 3rd day of June 1981.

Phil H. Bucklew

I hereby accept and consent to the foregoing Declaration of Trust and the powers therein conferred upon me as Trustee:

Interview No. 1 with Captain Phil H. Bucklew

Place: At his residence in Fairfax, Virginia

Date: Wednesday 19 March 1980

Subject: Biography

By: John T. Mason, Jr.

Q: Let's begin this talking biography in the proper way by having you tell me where you were born, when you were born and something about your parents, your background.

Capt. B.: I was born in Columbus, Ohio, and lived there until I went to college in Cincinnati, Ohio, Xavier University.

Q: You were born on what date?

Capt. B.: December 18, 1914. I went through public schools through the elementary and the junior high school; Northwood Elementary School and then Indianola Junior High School, which prided itself on being the first junior high school in the land - it was a little old too; and then to North High School.

Q: What did your father do?

Capt. B.: My father was a streetcar motorman. My parents were originally both farming folks. I had an interesting circumstance a couple of years ago; I had never previously known much history of my father's background, although I knew his father was the sheriff of Coshocton County and my father was the deputy under him. He came to Columbus to join the police force. It was at a time when the first electric streetcars were coming into being. I was told this story by a man who was helping him join the police department--my father became intrigued with this electric machine and he said he could run one of those. The man said "If you can, I can get you a job there," and my father worked there for the rest of his life.

Q: That is very interesting. What is the background of your family name? Is it English?

Capt. B.: Bucklew is English. I have recently been learning some of the circumstances of that. That's why we went to Coshocton. Helen, my wife, has been bugging me ever since "Roots" came out that there was so much that I didn't know of my background. There is a long history apparently; they came to the United States after expulsion for supporting Mary, Queen of Scots, and back in the 1600s landed in New Jersey. I haven't fully analyzed all the things they gave me at Coshocton but they were farming folks. I didn't get much on the move from New Jersey. In the navy I never met another Bucklew and I have never until recently, here in this area, met anyone with the same spelling of our name. I thought there were very few but I learned in Coshocton that there were six thousand branches in the country and all scattered from this New Jersey landing way back when.

Q: Obviously they didn't move out into the middle western area at that time when the family first came; that was Indian country still and they must have stayed on the eastern seaboard.

Capt. B.: Many settled around in Virginia, they branched out and into West Virginia and I think some of the West Virginia tribe moved up into Ohio. My father told me very little but it intrigued me as a boy that, at the age of 12 he had gone to Kansas with his father and he used to tell me stories about riding the range and shooting coyotes; then he returned to Ohio from Kansas. His mother had died at an earlier time. I couldn't find much on her background. My mother's family was of German extraction, her name being Hinkle. They were farming folk from Bellepointe, Ohio, which is about 20 miles from Columbus, though a long way then. There were several branches of the Hinkle family but I believe all have died. I have always considered myself as an end of the line. I do have a surviving niece as I had an older brother who was quite a character. He was the youngest living veteran of WW1; and was in France for two years after joining the Marines at fourteen.

Q: Adventuresome too?

Capt. B.: Well, he was a big kid! He got into the service and the folks couldn't get him out.

Q: He must have misrepresented his age to get in?

Capt. B.: That was the story. I did see some interesting letters from President Wilson. The folks were trying to get him back, fourteen is pretty young.

Q: Were there only two of you?

Capt. B.: My brother really never did return home. He came back but was soon married after WWI. He died at the rather young age of 47 as a result of some of his WWI experiences, he was gassed there, he was with the Marine Corps. He got into out-of-door work due to his lung problem, became a fireman and was later assistant State Fire Marshall of Ohio, then went into safety work. He received the first Safety Degree in the country, an academic Bachelor of Science degree at Ohio State; this, while he was in the fire work. Actually his terminal illness came right after WWII when he was working here in Washington, setting up Veterans Administration hospitals.

Q: His illness was connected with the lungs?

Capt. B.: Yes, complications occurred; he died in 1951.

Q: Tell me about your education. What was your goal and did you have an ambition at that point?

Capt. B.: I am afraid I was rather single minded in that. I

wasn't very strong, I was a tall, skinny kid and my family lived just off the campus of Ohio State where I became imbued watching their football and practice, enthusiastically following every detail. I think all I wanted to do in those early years was to play football.

Q: You had a good model in mind certainly, Ohio State was pretty strong.

Capt. B.: Well, I wasn't physically built for it then but it worked out that I was ultimately accepted. I also played basketball in junior high school and high school but the coach (who incidentally is still living and we are going to have the 50th anniversary this year of our 1930 team which was a pretty good one--Helen and I are going back) refused me even a uniform. He said "You go to track, you have long legs." Well, I knew the football manager, a neighbor, and through him I got a uniform - this was in the Spring as I had come into the high school in February under the semester system - and instead of running me off the field the coach let me go ahead. I was lucky as can be, I must have made five or six tackles--boom, boom, boom--and he adopted me. So, I was in football and, after some time, started my first game in my first year; they broke my ribs, they knocked me around, they did everything. Thereafter, the coach took me under tow and worked with me, but I was a substitute for the rest of that year. The following year I was more successful, I was All-City and later, captain of my team. But I was pretty young, as a senior I was sixteen and though I wanted to go to Ohio State, Ohio State wanted me to go to a prep school and get more matured. My folks objected strenuously to that in that they wanted me to get through college--this was Depression time, 1930 and 1931--and they couldn't approve that prep school bit.

Q: Ohio State didn't have the funds to help?

Capt. B.: They had the funds but my folks just wanted me to get through college.

Q: They wanted you to get the education?

Capt. B.: I had won an athletic scholarship award that year--one that a local men's club gave to each of the high schools--and at the dinner I was approached (I had been approached by several colleges) by Xavier University, Cincinnati. Clem Crowe who was at that time assistant coach, later the head coach, and later a professional coach--a lot of things--he talked to me and I explained to him, "Mr. Crowe I am going to Ohio State," and I made clear my intent though he said, "Why don't you come down with us for a while?" I said, "Well, if its agreeable with you that I come for a year and then come back," and he said, "Fine, think about it."

It wasn't quite that easy. It turned out that little Xavier University was aspiring to be a second Notre Dame at that time.

Q: Is it a Jesuit school?

Capt. B.: Its a Jesuit school. Instead of outright assistance and scholarship, when I got to Xavier there were 200 others there - for a try-out. There was a lot of pride at stake then and though I had been in athletics throughout my life I think those tryouts were the most strenuous, prideful struggle ever. I would have felt disgraced had I come home being turned away. But it worked out and I stayed all four years. As a matter of fact, I coached there afterwards.

Meanwhile, I had joined the Naval Reserve, stretched my age about four years then, but I got in the Naval Reserve back in 1930.

Q: What impelled you to do that?

Capt. B.: I suppose the pay as much as anything. We were paid $1.20 a drill and in those days that was pretty good. One of my neighborhood friends, a little bit older perhaps, and several others from our neighborhood, all stretching our age, joined the Naval Reserve. I was six feet two at that time.

Q: Had you put on any weight?

Capt. B.: I was just beginning to. I had no real problems in joining; I had some problems right afterward though. I argued with my Dad, we didn't have to get things like parental signatures but I was getting my parent's approval, and explained that this entailed no obligations, it was just a good way to make a little money and its an interesting thing.

Q: And a summer vacation too.

Capt. B.: Oh yes, but the folks weren't too convinced on that part, so I didn't play that up too much. My father was more concerned that I wouldn't be like the National Guard--standing guard over miners that were striking. Out in Ohio this was a very sensitive subject to the working people.

Q: A labor conscious state?

Capt. B.: Very much so. I assured him that "No, that's the National Guard. The navy doesn't get into such things." I hadn't been in for more than two months when the Ohio Penitentiary fire occurred (a very tragic event) and a navy man came around to our door, telling my mother for her son to report to the armory immediately for duty at the penitentiary.

Q: The penitentiary being in Columbus?

Capt. B.: My mother said, "Why he's just a boy," and the chief said, "Madam, he is in the Naval Reserve." So I was in the penitentiary for 30 days, and that was quite an experience. It was a time when many of the reservists were fearful and concerned not to lose their jobs. It was critical for them to have this dual responsibility, so, as a high school boy they kept me all the way through the emergency.

Q: How did your parents resolve this, how did they feel about it?

Capt. B.: They recognized there wasn't much choice after it was done. I suppose their objections were due somewhat to my brother's background. There was no real problem, although it was a hazardous situation and the public was very conscious of the tragedy. As I recall, there were over 280 casualties (deaths) resultant from the fire, so it was quite a dramatic thing and quite a personal experience for me. A revelation too. The effect was a little maturing I think.

Then came the cruises, which were at that time on the Great Lakes. We started from Toledo, Ohio, and went through Chicago, Detroit, up through Mackinac and the Straits.

Q: And you got up to Superior?

Capt. B.: Yes, I enjoyed them very much.

Q: What did you do on a summer cruise like that?

Capt. B.: I was a seaman, I qualified for first-class, then I was a boatswain's mate striker but I never got the rating, I was a coxswain on one of the motor whaler's of the old type, but by that time I was in college so I couldn't get enough drills to make my rating promotion. I worked mostly on deck force and always ended there regardless of whatever other thoughts. My neighborhood buddy was a pretty good angle shooter and would size up those easier jobs. He ultimately became a Chief Storekeeper in the wartime navy. He didn't care for the deck force and one time got me to be a pharmacist's mate striker, which sounded great as pharmacist mates slept in sickbay bunks, rather than in hammocks, as did the other crewmen. I lasted a couple of days there and the chief bo's'un mate came in and said "What in the hell are you doing in here--back up on deck." So I ended up with the deck gang and my buddy became the storekeeper.

I was then having some success at football and high school athletics and the reserve officers, Naval Academy graduates, wanted me to go to the Academy. I was for that and, although I didn't realize the necessary preparations, the Reserve Unit arranged that I receive entrance examination.

Q: Scholastically you must have been pretty good in high school?

Capt. B.: I failed the Naval Academy test the first time. I had to take the whole six subjects; I wasn't eligible coming through the reserve to take the condensed exam. I took it without any preparation and I failed ancient history, which I would probably fail today; I thought nothing of it though, and I expected to take it again the next year when I was a little more ready for it. But as events occurred and then college, I never got to the Naval Academy. I wanted to go during my junior year at college but the coaches talked me out of it, and the age factor was coming up--I think it was age 20 at the time--and at the university I still had this football bug.

Q: The Naval Academy could have used you too, Slade Cutter was there about that time.

Capt. B.: Well, Rip Miller had been at Xavier. He left Xavier the year I came in and went to the Naval Academy - so there were tie-ins on that, but the Xavier people said well, rather than go to the Naval Academy we can send you to the Army, West Point, and you will get four more years of football.

Q: You mean, go to West Point?

Capt. B.: Yes, to West Point, the age limit was a year higher and that was a little incentive; they said if you will come back for your senior year (I guess I was never really sincere with them) and so I went all the way there.

Q: Did they have a good team? Were they really achieving something?

Capt. B.: We did very well; too well. We had an outstanding year and rather than it developing as they had hoped, their schedule for the next year was cancelled. We beat Indiana, Carnegie Tech did beat us three to nothing and then beat Notre Dame the next week. Things like that happened and our schedule for the following year people cancelled. We were to play Harvard, we were to play Northwestern and we ended up too small a school. The larger school has everything to lose and our schedule dwindled away.

Q: I suppose they were scheduling you early in their season were they? Then if they lost this was a black eye?

Capt. B.: That was the usual way. Back in those days, you may recall the story of Little Center College and Bob McMillan. They came east and they beat everyone--Harvard and around the circle--that theme was occurring in the minds of many of the small universities, the Catholic ones, the Jesuit ones, hoping to be another Notre Dame and make lots of money; though it doesn't compare with today, scholarships were a very sensitive subject then.

Q: It was the hey-day of collegiate football as contrasted with today.

Capt. B.: I graduated at Xavier and was asked to coach there the next year.

Q: What about West Point?

Capt. B.: I was a month too old by then. I became 21. Gar Davidson was the West Point coach at the time; he wrote me a very nice letter which is someplace in the bottom of the trunk and said, "We've miscalculated, you are going to be a month too old." So that was that. I was next going to law school.

Q: Xavier?

Capt. B.: No, Xavier didn't have graduate schools then; I was going to University of Cincinnati law school and although I took the coaching job at Xavier, was going to start law school in February--another thing I never accomplished. When we came to the end of the football season Xavier asked me to become the graduate manager in charge of scholarships and funds and to continue as assistant football coach.

Q: They weren't going to let go of you?

Capt. B.: I accepted the offer, but the following Spring my father died--you couldn't live in two cities and support two homes. Mother's home was in Columbus and I didn't make enough money at Xavier to support both. Meanwhile, I had played what you would call semi-professional football in Cincinnati during this same season--a group of us from the same college teams, Xavier and the University of Cincinnati, and we did very well. We had an undefeated season and we played several major teams-- Chicago, St. Louis, Louisville and teams of that nature, and out of it I got some professional offers. First from Chicago and that was very enticing, but the more I thought of it, why not something a little closer. Cleveland had just come into the National League.

Q: What were they called in those days?

Capt. B.: They were the Cleveland Rams, they were later sold and became the Los Angeles Rams. The Cardinals were actually the ones that gave me my first offer, but Cleveland responded and I signed and played there for the next two years. Then I came back to Cincinnati to play with the Cincinnati Bengals, another outstanding independent team then before they came into the National League, and I coached at Xavier again. I was still you see, floating, with home in Columbus.

Q: But the law went down the drain?

Capt. B.: Always it was going to be next semester. So the following year, 1939, I was going to give pro ball one more fling. I found it very difficult in the off season to get any reasonable job. There were jobs available if I would say "I won't go back to football," - rightfully so, and it was still in that post-depression time - an employer didn't want to invest in you for six months.

Q: And football salaries weren't comparable to what they are today?

Capt. B.: No. I had a good contract--$125.00 per game--and many of my friends, high draftees, one of my friends was all-professional with the Chicago Bears and it was five years before he got over $100.00 a game; so I had a good contract, comparatively speaking, but still not much money. The problem in professional ball in those days was your off-season and in building up to something that had a future. But, I planned to give it one more whirl and I signed with Detroit Lions but then some friends asked me to investigate--getting a team for Columbus, Ohio, into what was forming as the American League. They financed me and I went to the meeting in Louisville. I found it was possible to get a franchise and did my job, but by the time I got back to Columbus there was a headline in the sport page that Columbus was to have a professional team and it was going to be coached by me. I was in a rather embarrassing

Bucklew #1 - 15

situation.

Q: Did that come out of the Louisville meeting?

Capt. B.: That came out of the meeting as part of an Associated Press release. Well, the only thing to do was to do it.

Q: Was this the intention of this publicity, do you think?

Capt. B.: I think it was, at least, to pressure Columbus' acceptance of a franchise. I had to round up the capital to get it started, as well as the players--rather hurriedly as this was mid-July--for the coming season. But we did it.

Q: Was it difficult raising the money?

Capt. B.: It was a struggle, week to week. Fortunately, I was approached by the father of a boy whom I had known in college, who had a packing company in Columbus, named Frederick Schmidt of the Schmidt Packing Company. He had read this newspaper article and called wanting to know if there was any stock open. Everything was open, and because his son's name was Frederick Schmidt, same as the packing company, he said "I would like to get my son in a sort-of man-around-town position. Maybe if you could make him an officer of your football club I would be willing to make an investment." We were glad to make him "president" and did.

Q: Was he effective?

Capt. B.: It was in name only. His father put up five thousand dollars and we were probably one of the best financed teams in the whole American League, as it developed.

Q: What had you been thinking of in terms of money? How much did you think was absolutely necessary to get under way?

Capt. B.: We incorporated for $11,000.00, and had we had that much as operating capital, I think we would have been a tremendous financial success. The money came in by dribbles, there wasn't enough and we were always fighting to meet payrolls, but we met them and paid all bills. I had an idea that worked for three years--I'll get ahead of myself and say we won the league championship all three years up to World War II. Coming from the National League, I knew a lot of players, some on their way up and some on the way down, some could be going back to school at a place like Ohio State and/or completing a degree. I rounded up a very good team at about half the going prices, where I said $125.00 had been my salary, for about $60.00 I got some of the better National League players but we played twice as many games--on Sundays and on Wednesday nights, and, having done this myself with Cincinnati,--which was great excitement in those pre-WWII days--I promised them a trip to the west coast and arranged a barn-storming trip. You know in those pre-WWII days it was quite an event to go to the west coast.

Q: By train wasn't it?

Bucklew #1 -

Capt. B.: The first trip was by train; we played three games there and did very well. The players did better on that really, we operated on a barn-storming split of the gate receipts and would make maybe $100.00 a game and expenses, see California and the west coast. It worked. But the problem was holding the league together because there just wasn't enough money behind it. In those days the National League was having the same problems. It might be that a city was on the verge of collapse and with that your whole scheduling system collapsed. It was a critical matter to help one another out.

Q: What sort of base did you have in the town.

Capt. B.: We had a baseball park stadium of a nice size for then---about 15,000. It was the Columbus Redbirds Baseball Stadium, owned by the St. Louis Cardinals, as a farm team. That was a good situation except for the well-established Ohio State and Columbus is dominately a college town, a university town. We had reasonable success, some of it rather spectacular in the course of three years; I had the best ball club in the league. We played in New York to over 40,000 when we brought in Tom Harmon and John Kimbrough to play, and some of the names of the day. It was patterned after some of the earlier days of football when they brought Red Grange out and barn-stormed him. We were never on a solid financial basis, although we expanded the League in the west to include Los Angeles amd Hollywood, and in the east--Boston, Buffalo and New York. The same organizations that after WWII became the All-America

Conference.

Q: How did you manage the transportation, was it still by train?

Capt. B.: We moved by train until in the third year I had a new backer who was an automobile dealer, and he provided us with station wagons. We traveled coast to coast, much more economically! The players really enjoyed it and we saw the country and went up and down the west coast.

Q: Was it a problem scheduling your time?

Capt. B.: We had to make some changes. We did very well if the schedule was firm. As I programmed it, if we were going to the west coast when I left Columbus I would arrange a game in St. Louis on the way. When we got to Los Angeles we would have two games there, Los Angeles and Hollywood. In 1940 we had an all-star game in Portland, Oregon, with 17,500 people; outdrew the National League that time and against an all-star team. The same promoter wanted us to play over in Seattle and there we had 1,000 people! So it was an up and down situation, but you could arrange your guarantees through promoters so that your hotel accomodations and meals were taken care of. It was a gamble at times, some times we won and some times we lost on a dollars and cents guarantee or on a percentage of the gate. You get a little selfish at times, and we'd feel the publicity and crowd interest looked very good and take the percentage. I remember playing for a percentage in Seattle in a driving rain before 1,000 people and we lost that gamble!

Q: What did people pay for a ticket for a game like that in those days?

Capt. B.: A dollar was the yardstick. You always had to have a dollar seat in the bleachers. It was what you could get out of the grandstand and what type of city you were playing in. Some were very responsive; you learned a lot the hard way. Buffalo for example, is an industrial city and is as enthusiastic as can be over professional football as opposed to college football. They don't support the college but are enthused for professional play. A factor of that is playing on Sunday.

Q: When they are not at their jobs?

Capt. B.: When they are not at their jobs, and there are many people who could never see a Saturday afternoon game, particularly the blue collar worker. New York City is much that way. Later I coached in New York and worked for the professionals in scouting, I coached for four years at Columbia under Lou Little. I was going to graduate school then - that was post-war, so I am ahead of myself - but the professionals always out-drew the colleges there; New York is a Sunday town, as it is today with professional sport. They pack them in at 70,000 today, though we couldn't quite do it then.

Q: Out there in the meadows they really do pack them in.

Capt. B.: Then came the war. We were playing to a full stadium in Los Angeles, full being about 17,000--the field has since been made into a housing project. We were playing on December 7th when war was announced over the loud speakers: "The United States has declared war." I had four contracts in my pocket, San Diego the next week, which was impossible, and back up the coast, San Francisco and Oakland; we just tore them up; all of us came into military service.

Q: The whole bunch?

Capt. B.: There was a funny incident there; I wish I had the opportunity to meet the man--it was one of the cleverest things--We, the team, all got together down in the bar of the Hayward Hotel in Los Angeles on the night of December 7th. Some I was sending back to Columbus.

Q: Did you complete the game?

Capt. B.: Yes, we lost 17 to 16. That kind of ballgame and the crowd started to leave after the war announcement.

We were down in the bar and someone said, "Let's all join the service." I expressed a preference for the navy.

Q: Had you kept up with the Reserves?

Capt. B.: No, I completed my four years and got out--I was in college and just let it ride. So we sent a telegram to the Navy recruiting office saying we had (whatever number then) twenty athletic type people available for your service.

Q: Was this the recruiting office back home?

Capt. B.: No, we sent it to the Los Angeles office. We got a cable back next morning that said, "Our doors are open twenty-four hours a day. Thank you." I thought that was wonderful!

Q: Some of these fellows must have had families, did they? Or, were they all single?

Capt. B.: The majority were single; some married we would have didn't make the west coast run. They would play through the season and go back home. Being single and the incentive for travel was a part of the same circumstance really. To many, there wasn't enough money in it, but playing professional ball was a new experience and a temporary vacation to others - before you got serious, I guess.

Q: The League came to an abrupt standstill at that point?

Capt. B.: Yes; with the war it was discontinued. Following the war which I finished out in China, I went back to Xavier.

Q: What year did you go back?

Capt. B.: In 1946 and I had a very poor year, and a disagreement with the school on general principles. We only won three of ten games but we had only high school boys, and at that time the GIs were our competition, which was rough. Teams like Kentucky--Bear Bryant was there at that time and he fired more people every week than we had all season. We had a poor season and I had disagreement with the university and put a choice on the line of to either reduce our level of competition or to let me recruit sufficiently to produce a competitive team. First of all I hadn't really wanted the job--to come back to it--they went through the navy to my commanding officer in Shanghai who gave me a dispatch one morning and asked what my answer was about coaching at Xavier-- this coming via BuPers.

Q: They really wouldn't let go of you, would they?

Capt. B.: Well, they did after that year. I hadn't even heard from Xavier in four or five years, and my C. O., Capt. Andrews, said why don't you take a couple weeks leave and when you get back home put in for an extension and I'll give you a couple more and at least resolve this thing. He said, "You've been out here a long time and it will do you good."

So I did but I liked being home again and I married Helen, and chose the coaching over return to Shanghai. One thing, I didn't realize the changes that had taken place; I was pretty naive about it, the coaching. It was different from when I could go out and get my people in pro'ball; the college players didn't come into it in the same light, with the same enthusiasm, as when I played there.

Q: It was a watershed, you were now on the other side.

Capt. B.: I was definitely on the other side. As the season neared an end I felt the pressures and resented them. I had my old friend, the college president, but he was hesitant and he was building the university, I was offered much money, one man offered me $50,000.00 for athletic scholarships, so I put it to them, "There are three alternatives that I see, we either go out and get a ball club if we are going to play this type of competition, or we reduce to the level that we can meet in smaller colleges, or you had better forget it." That's the way I had seen it then. The president, F. Steiner said, "We are not going to reduce the level of our competition because that will reduce the gate." (We had broken attendance records in 1946 even with a poor team!) And, he said, "If people will offer you that kind of money to build a football team I can get the same money to build buildings. I won't go along with either thing." I said, "Well, I won't have unconscious boys on the bench." So, we parted company.

Back to the pro-ball; the St. Louis Cardinals wanted me to bring a club back to Columbus, reactivate where we left off in 1941, and their investment would be the stadium, which is really quite a bit.

Q: Their participation had been held in abeyance during the war too, I suppose?

Capt. B.: Oh yes, there was nothing there. This was the American League again and it was forming up what was called the All-American Conference. I was afraid for it in this sense--Paul Brown had been at Ohio State for a number of years and then at Great Lakes; he received considerable financial backing from the Hertz people, automobile backers and then came into Cleveland, a far different situation, with a 70,000 stadium and an unlimited bankroll and he was buying the top players with heavy salaries and previously unheard of inducements. I advised the St. Louis Cardinal people--with the size of their stadium they couldn't possibly make it--17,000 against 70,000, the expenses involved, the city play, even if they expanded their stadium they would be competing against crowds of 40,000 to 50,000 at least. About that time I was thinking about going back to graduate school, I had become quite imbued with the Chinese during my time there, and I was also thinking of going into Foreign Service type work. So I decided to go to Columbia. I had an offer of a job at the Maritime Academy to coach in New York and I thought that would be a good combination. A friend of mine in Columbus was the Big Ten Football Rules Commissioner and was also on the college rules committee with Lou Little. I was at his house one night and told him what I thought of doing and he said "Buck, if you are going to go that way and you want to go back to Columbia; wait a minute..." He went to the phone and called Lou Little at his summer home and told him, said "He's a friend of mine, he's done very well in professional play and coaching, and he is going to go to Columbia, I think he ought to work with you." Lou said, "Okay, send him over."

Q: You hadn't known Little?

Capt. B.: I had never met him. So I went there without any understanding about pay and went back to graduate school and worked with Lou for four years. I was recalled to the navy while at Columbia. In my last two years, 1949-50, I taught NROTC, and coached.

Q: You were a busy fellow?

Capt. B.: And, I also scouted for four pro teams and went to school so I was quite busy.

Q: What were you studying, international affairs?

Capt. B.: International affairs and political science.

Q: Was Lindsey Rogers there?

Capt. B.: No, not at that time. I know more of the Columbia college people than I do of the graduate school.

Q: Was Adolph Berle there?

Capt. B.: No, I was in Far Eastern studies; I had a hell of a time there though, I had to unlearn all and any Chinese I had learned--I spoke fairly good GI Chinese you know. I might have handled it if it hadn't been for the written language. That was just too much for me, at that age and...

Q: You being how old?

Capt. B.: About 32, but as I say I was doing a lot of other things. I finished my doctorate points but I didn't do the dissertation for several reasons, I did fairly well and I had a B average doing it and I didn't work too hard. I had the theory that going to graduate school--and I still think it goes--if you are more mature and you go to class and listen, you don't have to read as much. Making grades is not so difficult, but as I came to know, this was not really giving me the complete academic background that you would expect from a degree.

Q: What were your languages, Chinese was one of them?

Capt. B.: Chinese, though I threw in the sponge on the Chinese after a year and took my language tests in French, I had had French in high school and college.

Q: Did you have a second language?

Capt. B.: No, you just needed one. The system they used at Columbia in International Affairs was that you choose an area specialty, for the Far East it would have been Chinese or Japanese. I was interested in China. I took every course that they offered. I still can't recall who was the director on that. I know it was becoming pretty _Pink_ at that time.

Q: Yes, in the post-war era they became that way and remained that way.

Capt. B.: Meanwhile I was recalled to the navy, at Columbia for NROTC instructor duty. I told them that in the spring I had already signed a contract for football and the Navy said, "That's fine, that will be good Public Relations, knowing that football practice at Columbia does not start until five in the afternoon. So I came back on active duty in their NROTC program.

Q: You headed up their program?

Capt. B.: No, I was a lieutenant commander and an assistant professor. This was coming on to the pre-Korea time. I had 200 students-(when I now read about the optimum in a class, which is 35 to 40)-we packed them in. There were many that were obvious draft dodgers coming to the program hoping for deferral from the draft. I had the freshmen in Naval Orientation and History. All the first year people and you take all the way through, so I had three sections a day, three days a week, then the fourth day you have lab and field drills and the like (tours of ships, naval bases, etc.).

Q: In addition to doing your graduate work?

Capt. B.: I was cutting down but I was still going to class and doing these other things on the weekends, and football. I don't think Lou was very happy with me that year as he was the type coach that liked to have you sitting in the office in the morning at eight and on hand until you went to the field. He went along with me on it, I think partially because he thought I was taking care of some of his boys that might otherwise be drafted, by having them in the program. And I did, later in the service I must have had at least 20 of my former Columbia boys on active duty. A lot of them stayed in career-wise too.

Q: How did you manage your personal life, it seems to me you must have been 24 hours on the campus? You were married then weren't you?

Capt. B.: The first year Helen and I both went to school.

Q: Was she doing graduate work too?

Capt. B.: No, she was doing undergraduate work in the General Studies School. We commuted together and had lunch together, then she would pick me up afterward at the football field. I did a lot of scouting, both for Columbia and several pro teams, and some of the weekends she would go with me. It was a hectic period--no doubt about it, but I gradually excused myself, I think in all honesty I would have to put it that way, asking myself, do you really want to complete this academic work? I pretty well convinced myself that the navy--the overall military--was more important in foreign affairs than was the foreign service, which at that time I believed to be true. I was getting more and more annoyed with some of the things that I heard in class, gritted my teeth rather than speaking my mind, but as I say, Columbia was getting pretty "pink" and tensions of a political type were growing. Then, with the Korean war coming on I was expecting my orders. The commanding officer took me to Washington one day planning to get me extended, because I had these 200 students and he needed me.

Q: You must have been an exceptional teacher.

Capt. B.: We did pretty well. The BuPers detailer, however, pointed out that we were going to re-activate some of World War II programs in the navy, which the computer said I was the only person from World War II in that category still on active duty. Captain Pat Moran didn't quite buy that but to me it was fine. From Columbia, in June 1951, we went to Norfolk, to Little Creek and back into the navy the rest of the way.

I never really took the navy seriously until I had been in service almost 15 or 20 years. I always felt it was temporary, though I enjoyed every experience and assignment.

Q: Because you had that dual career, you had the athletics in the backgound.

Capt. B.: I bumped into that right away at Little Creek, I coached there for four years as an extra duty to my command. Spike Fahrion (Admiral Frank George Fahrion) was a football enthusiast, a great leader and wonderful person. We both enjoyed the football and we talked about it a lot.

Q: Do you want to go back and make some comments on NROTC?

Capt. B.: Columbia is an unusual school, very high in their academic standards, and about 50/50 in their motivations--the patriotic and dissenters too. I don't question that among my 200 students you would have classified many as draft dodgers and the other half as highly motivated as you could ask for. But 90% of them were academically stronger than your average college student by far. Columbia College--I had occasion during the summer cruises to make comparisons with students from other colleges and I am convinced that academically Columbia had a stronger type and, based on their comparative scores (BuPers had uniform tests they put out each year), my boys did very well. In that sense they were very good. They operated under difficult circumstances with New York City and the Columbia GIs that heckled and pooh-poohed them as if they were boy scouts. The GIs would hang on the fence and heckle when we had close order drills and such public training we had to do--that's a hardship really. It was the beginning of the build-up that New York had and there were a lot of students in Columbia that were just avoiding going to work and were using the GI bill as unemployment compensation. The times were rather unusual, but of these NROTC students, after I activated and commissioned a unit at Little Creek I later had five or six Columbia athletes that had requested assignment to that duty. It wasn't just in knowing me, I may have instilled a little bit of special operations thinking in their minds, but they served at least four years through the Korean War period. I met a boy here recently, a Marine flyer and a Colonel now, he played football as well.

Q: At Columbia?

Capt. B.: Yes, a participant shall we say, and a good one-- not a first stringer, but I was able to help him out. You know you go through waves of physical "hobbies" in the navy and he was caught on "mal-occlusion." Some doctor decided his teeth set out a little bit, but I got him in the Marine program which was less critical at the moment, physically, and he is a Colonel today.

Q: Yes, we went through that mal-occlusion state, I went through it myself.

Capt. B.: I had another boy who was an intercollegiate fencing champion and the navy turned him down because his arches were too high! Not flat footed. We wrote many letters about that. We got into the racial thing too. I helped a couple of boys in after they were first turned down. I don't know what has happened to them.

Q: Now, shall we turn our thoughts back to WWII? We were interrupted by the outbreak of war on the 7th December in 1941 and you immediately joined up with the navy.

Capt. B.: I found I wasn't the answer to the service's hopes in a lot of places. I think the first recruiting office I went in was for paratroopers and I got as far as the sergeant, an army sergeant; he took one look at me and said we could take two instead of you. I guess I weighed about 235 at the time.

Q: You had improved from your high school days.

Capt. B.: Yes, it was a long way from there--140 to 235. I received an appointment to Navy training in 1940 - but they wanted me to weigh 185 lbs. So I skipped that! I read in the newspaper of Gene Tunney's program on physical education and thought, as I had been in coaching, this was a logical place that I might be qualified for.

Q: Were you back in Ohio by this time?

Capt. B.: No, I stayed on the west coast. Tunney was coming on a recruiting trip to Los Angeles and I wrote a letter and received an appointment. At the time, with my own thoughts in the matter and not that it was required, I also wrote back to Ohio to some of the newspapers sports editors and various athletic people with whom I had been in association and asked them for any comments they might make in my behalf. I received a few letters of that type and had them in my pocket when I had my appointment with Gene Tunney. He was very brusque and cut me down pretty well, saying, "You are nothing but a football player, I want physical education people, trained in it." I responded that I had coached college and professionals, football, basketball, track, and had run swimming schools; though I did not have a degree in physical education, I felt that I had versatile qualifications.

Q: Nor did Tunney.

Capt. B.: We didn't discuss his qualifications at that moment. He said, "I'll keep your name but you needn't count on anything."

By that time I was pretty irritated and said, "Commander are you interested in these or shall I throw them in your wastebasket?" He said, "What are those?" And I said, "They are a few letters on my background, written by people back in Ohio." He said, "Why didn't you say you had letters of recommendation?" And I responded, "I didn't realize you were running a political program." He assigned me to the program. We had no more exchange at that time.

I didn't really meet with Tunney again until after Normandy. We had quite a sociable evening together and dinner at the house of one of his friends on the strength of a few martinis I repeated the story to him which I don't think pleased him too much. Everything was fine there however; as a matter of fact during that period he took me to see Secretary Forrestal and gave me the red carpet treatment. I was one of his boys, in each place I almost repeated the story because he would say, "HE is from MY PROGRAM!"

Q: Did you have anything to do with Tom Hamilton and his program?

Capt. B.: No.

Q: That was largely for recruiting flyers, I guess?

Capt. B.: Well, they had a good physical training program but I think it ultimately worked out to my advantage. I had an opportunity to come into the Hamilton--as you know they were all officers. I, in my peculiar sincerity, felt that the way to come is to get back in shape and your promotions would come. Lynn St. John, then the athletic director at Ohio State was recruiting for the Hamilton program at the same time that Tunney was recruiting for his. I declined help from Columbus, with my thoughts on it, but after I was enlisted for about a year I wondered about my decision. It wasn't quite as easy to get a commission as I had at first thought.

Q: Well, you got into the Tunney program then, how did this develop?

Capt. B.: I completed the course and was held over as an instructor in the program for a couple of weeks.

Q: Were there any developments that you had not known beforehand?

Capt. B.: No, but I was becoming disappointed in the program in that it was primarily a calisthenics drill for boot training, and I had anticipated a lot more. However, soon after I became assistant chief to an on-coming training class, during the course they called for volunteers for what they termed "amphibious commandos." There were not too many of us to volunteer (I can't recall how many) but I have jokingly said I was one of the first to get out of the Tunney program. I was selected to that group--there were ten of us.

Q: Had Dieppe taken place by that time?

Capt. B.: I am not sure of the timing--approximately the same.

"Amphibious commando" was not as the name implied, however it was the best training I ever had in the navy. We moved from Norfolk to what is now the Patuxent Air Base. There was very little there; a small boatyard--not on the Patuxent side, on the other side. We lived in a private house that had been a small commercial boatyard, the ten of us from the Tunney program, and we had approxiamtely 100 seaman that were brought in straight from boot camp. They weren't volunteers, they were just assignees from boot camp. This was really the assembly point of the first landing craft the navy had and the purpose of it was, that as the transports would come up from Norfolk or from wherever they embarked the Marines, and came up the Chesapeake Bay, we then would come out in landing craft, come alongside, debark the troops that came down the nets and land them ashore. This was the training for the Marines for amphibious assault, as well as a period during which our ships were being rigged with davits to carry landing craft, which they had not had before. There was no way to lift them (the landing craft) that's why we had to operate them from the shore base. Of course we hadn't operated boats until then, but we were under four Coast Guard chiefs who were tough, knowledgeable and good! It was the most practical training that I experienced. The whole program was to "go out and do it." They gave us a boat--to go out and try anything you wanted with, beach it, come alongside a float--whatever.

Q: This was in '42.

Capt. B.: In the Spring of 1942. I came into the service in March of 1942, so this was around May when we were into this program. The whole theme was - if you smashed up a boat or the engine quit, all the chief said was, "Fix it!" I recall one time I said, "Well, chief, its not working so well, after chow I'll be back down." He said, "No, you'll have chow after you fix it." That was the theme of the whole operation and I think I learned more then in practical training than possibly any other phase. By Fall, we had rumors of a coming amphibious invasion, somewhere in Europe. But we also had rumors that we were all going to become instructors--the original ten--after the coming operation. This didn't set well with us and much scheming developed to offset this plan. I convinced someone that a future instructor should have combat experience and pushed myself enough to become the first of our group to be deployed.

Q: Were you of similar backgrounds?

Capt. B.: All from the Tunney program with athletic background. One of my closest buddies was Big John Tripson--John had been an all-pro tackle with the Detroit Lions, played in college at Mississippi State; Buck Halperin was from Notre Dame, and so on down the line. Each of us had college background and we had come out of the same squads in the Tunney program. Jerry Donnell, who was later killed at Anzio, played pro ball for me in 1940; he was out of Oregon State. We were the first ten of the Scouts and Raiders and there was this threat of becoming instructors, so I used a little salesmanship and said, "Now, if we are to become instructors and there is going to be this operation in North Africa, I suggest it would be the best for an instructor to get some operational experience and I want to go." So I was assigned.

Q: To North Africa?

Capt. B.: I was assigned to a transport--that didn't know where it was going, it happened to be the LEEDSTOWN, it was a former Grace Line ship, the Santa Lucia, and she was commissioned as the USS LEEDSTOWN.

Q: Let me divert you and ask you if you had any contact or any relationship with a group training on the west coast at San Diego under Admiral Rockwell who were preparing for the Aleutian campaign--that was almost simultaneous?

Capt. B.: None whatsoever. We didn't know what was going on on the west coast, only what we observed as ships would be rigged with davits and landing craft. The ship crews themselves had no idea as to what they would be used for. As a matter of fact, when I was first deployed and I took eight men with me aboard the LEEDSTOWN at New York--they had 28 landing craft on board. I went not as a commissioned officer but with a letter of authorization from Commodore Felix Johnson. He had written a letter on my behalf that I had special qualifications with landing craft. Upon boarding the LEEDSTOWN there was not a man, including the captain, that felt they were going to use those 28 boats they had on board, they thought they were delivering them some place in England and turning them over to our allies. So, the exec was happy to put me in charge of boats, and wanted nothing to do with them--at that time!

Q: There was some validity in that because most of the boats we were building went to the British.

Capt. B.: Yes and no, as it turned out. In any event, this letter of qualification put me in charge of the boats as a Chief Boatswain's mate and with my 8 men from Patuxent Training we managed but had considerable struggles keeping them secure in heavy seas. We had very little cooperation because the ship's crew wanted no part of those boats, either for operation or for security or for custody.

Q: This was in advance of the flotilla going over?

Capt. B.: This was September of 1942.

Q: Were you in a convoy?

Capt. B.: We went over in convoy, a battleship, the New York, full convoy and it grew as time went on. We went first to Belfast, Ireland, then over to Scotland where we picked up British commandos and a different aspect came into view here.

Q: They had a different approach, didn't they?

Capt. B.: Yes they did. We thought, if these commandos are embarked and there are troops in every passageway, we must be going someplace ourselves, and we were. We joined other convoys.

Q: Were these Lovat's outfit? He was the one in charge of the Dieppe operation--Lord Lovat?

Capt. B.: I don't know the British command. There was not that much communication really. There was little known aboard that ship until after we passed Gibralter and were going into the Mediterranean that things came to light. There were a couple of battle conferences, one of which I was sent to to represent the LEEDSTOWN and I was stopped at the gangway and told this was for officers only. I was quite offended at that and did not attempt to explain. The Captain of the LEEDSTOWN had sent an officer with me and he didn't say a word. When I came back I went to the Captain and said, "I have turned down discussions of a commission before, but I am now ready to do it." I was humiliated, but actually I had enjoyed myself so much as a chief. We had a great time and until then I had no concern or ambition for commission status.

Q: But it didn't open all the doors? As a chief?

Capt. B.: Well, that door I had slammed in my face and it hurt my feelings. In any event we came on into the Med and the battle conferences, pre-battle, occurred, we had the commandos to be landed at Algiers and went on in.

The other U.S. task force--the Kirk Task Force (under Admiral Kirk) came direct from the U.S. for landings at

Casablanca and Arzew and Oran. The forces were deployed throughout the area as you know.

Q: Was Arzew one of the places?

Capt. B.: Right. We landed our commandos near Algiers. My job was not very important; I had command of the lead boat. We had been trained in beach identification and carried the commando commanding officer.

Q: What was your mission on this occasion?

Capt. B.: Only, with the lead boats, to put these commandos in a specific target area, which had been outlined to me through beach silhouettes, charts, sketches, such as we had been trained on in the Chesapeake.

We landed the troops and upon returning to the ship there was one hell of a mess. Of the forces there, boats were scattered to the seaward, many of these inadequately trained boat crews had gone to the seaward instead of to the beach. They had no compasses, there was very little understanding of where or what should have happened. After spending a night trying to round up seasick soldiers and lost landing craft, many of which had run out of fuel, having gone miles to the seaward, I got back to the LEEDSTOWN and the following morning we came under air attack.

Q: German planes?

Capt. B.: German and Italian both. They didn't come very close to us but we had all hands topside, those not manning guns, and watched the bombs fall, but didn't really have any near misses. However, unbeknownst to us a German submarine came up and sank us while we were watching the air attackers!

Q: That's why I remember the LEEDSTOWN.

Capt. B.: On the first day, a torpedo bomb carried away the steering gear on the ship and the next day they came back and finished us off.

Q: Had you been under attack from the German planes out from the Bay of Biscay enroute down?

Capt. B.: Yes, but not to any major extent. It was a huge convoy and nothing came very close to us. We had the big fat transports in the middle of it and were troop loaded.

But they did sink us. I left the ship with the captain and the chief engineer. We were the last to leave the ship. I had been throwing life rafts over the side. I was in a raft with Captain Cook and we were picked up by a British destroyer.

Q: How far off the coast were you?

Capt. B.: Within sight. After the first hit on the steering gear we anchored. Before that we had landed all of our troops without any major casualties other than a few lost boats. As I say, I had been rounding up boats throughout the night. I had just gotten back aboard ship in time for the first hit.

From the British destroyer they took us ashore and put about twenty of us on a British transport headed for India, survivors of the LEEDSTOWN. However, before that ship got underway, the powers that be got us squared away, somehow they identified us and we were transferred to the USS ALMAC, an AKA that was going back to the States. We rode that ship for several days until we got just outside of Gibraltar and we ran into a nest of submarines. They sank three ships.

Q: Was this in the Atlantic?

Capt. B.: Yes, we were just outside of Gibralar. They sank one British carrier right in front of us--it looked like a cigar exploding. I don't think they had more than 10 survivors from that. But there wasn't radar or the detection gear and other such defensive equipments on any of these ships at that stage. The ALMAC took a hit in the engine room; we lost several days at anchor. This was rather tense since we were crippled there, with no steam or power; but a Norweigan destroyer finally came alongside and took us off, took us in to Casablanca.

Q: The landing had been made there already?

Capt. B.: Yes, things were settling down. This was in December. At Casablanca I brought my small group--I think I had about 20 people at that time--survivors from the LEEDSTOWN and ALMAC. I was the Chief Bo's'un Mate, so that made me senior petty officer although I didn't explain to anybody about Tunney Fish Ratings. Chief Bo's'un Mates were a little different but I was a full-fledged Chief Bo's'un Mate by now! The executive officer at Casablanca however, wouldn't listen to me that we were survivors off the LEEDSTOWN and that we were really being sent back to the States. He said, "Yeah, that's where we all want to go. What have you been doing?" I answered, "I've been in charge of boats, small craft, landing craft boats." He said, "Can you operate a crash boat." And I said, "Yes, sir." He said, "Fine, we have two and we have submarine problems here and I'm going to put you in charge of these two boats on submarine patrol." "In a 45 foot crash boat?" He said, "Absolutely, I'll give you a 50-calibre gun." Though we didn't run down any submarines, and we weren't exactly looking for them, we did serve as admiral's barges and run messages, assisted on salvage operations and a lot of service of that type.

Q: Do you mean in an out of Casablanca?

Capt. B.: In and out of Casablanca. A couple of days after Christmas a message came through calling for all survivors of the LEEDSTOWN to be returned to the United States.

We had lived on these 45-footers and on any food we could scrounge from ships that we passed, K-rations, C-rations and that sort, and I had one very talented Jewish boy in my crew who, by whatever story he told, got us a cherry pie for Christmas.

Q: You were going to tell me about beach silhouettes.

Capt. B.: While we were working in the Chesapeake Bay, one cold night in the middle of the summer, I was in a rubber boat off the Nansemond Hotel at Norfolk and I suppose we were a half mile offshore. In the boat with me was an army captain named Pettigrew. He had been instructing us in tactics and identification techniques, while we were waiting in the cold to demonstrate this phase of landing to some V.I.P. naval officers who were watching from the roof of the Nansemond Hotel, we shivered in our rubber boat. I asked Captain Pettigrew how, as an army officer, how did you get into this with the navy. And he said, "Its very simple. For many years prior to WWII I was a rum runner. I operated out of Canada and throughout the New England area. When war came along I applied to the navy saying that I have as much knowledge of shoreline silhouettes and identification and of landing undetected as any man you will find. It is proven by the fact that I have never been arrested or caught. The navy turned me down cold. So I told them the same story to the army and they commissioned me a captain and sent me over to train naval personnel."

Q: That's a lovely story.

Capt. B.: Its the truth.

Q: It shows the application of common sense.

Capt. B.: In the course of many years since, I have met

Pettigrew; I met him in India in the Burma fighting; I met him in Korea when he was advisor to the ROKA chief of staff. I think he retired as a colonel.

Q: He was still using his knowledge; gained illegally but useful. So you came back to the States.

Capt. B.: Yes, I can't think of the transport but we came in to New York. I had a little problem there. It was about 20 degrees below zero when we came in and I had just dungarees and a foul weather jacket, a beat up Chief's hat that somebody had given me. I came ashore at Pier 92 receiving Stetron then which was rather a controversial place. I didn't know at the time but there were many problems there with the Captain (Captain Pashley) and his wife, who ordered shaved heads, commanded a salute, and did various things, harsh and questionable. I was there over night and the following morning, Saturday, there was to be personnel inspection. I went to the division officer and told him I had no uniform, that I was very anxious to get one and if I could be excused I would get over to the supply depot and, as much as anyone, would like to get in uniform. He said, "I can't excuse anyone, I'm sorry but you are going to have to stand inspection as you are." We stood out in the cold for at least an hour at which time the Chiefs would come and put their coats around me. Even then I didn't realize that there was a little politics involved, but the C.P.O.'s were trying to keep me warm and I was appreciative because it was very cold! When the inspection took place and the Captain came to me he gave me a real chewing out for being out of uniform. I tried to explain that I had just arrived, a survivor, and he said, "I don't care for any of those stories, I just want you to understand you won't get by with it here." It all passed. He was the same captain that Walter Winchell made quite an issue about: Captain Pashley, I should never forget him; there were other incidents. After the inspection I got my uniform and I was awarded 30 days survivor leave. However, my crew, I had one boy with lots of wavy hair, who had his head shaved and he didn't want his leave--Mrs. Pashley had directed that.

Q: What did she have to do with it?

Capt. B.: She commanded a salute on Pier 92 and if she didn't get it there was punishment. I had three boys with shaved heads; after their experiences, as I say, they didn't want to go home. So I was a little embittered there. But, we all took our leave. I came back from leave and my commission papers were in; I was commissioned at Pier 92 with orders to report to the NEW JERSEY. However, a phone call from my Scout and Raider buddies whom I hadn't seen since September '42-- they meanwhile had gone with Admiral Kirk's group landed at Casablanca and returned to Norfolk. They had now moved from the Chesapeake Bay down to Fort Pierce, Florida, and were the forerunners of setting up a base there. They had been a little curious about what had happened to me too. They got my orders modified immediately and I was to report back to the home outfit instead of to the NEW JERSEY.

Q: This was along in 1943.

Capt. B.: February of 1943. I got orders modified for the rest of my crew, got the whole gang together and kept those kids together for four years, by hook or by crook.

Q: You were not going to allow their dispersal again?

Capt. B.: So we went to Fort Pierce, Florida. We were there about a month. It was just getting organized; it was to become the largest amphibious training base on the east coast, but the Scout and Raiders were an independent outfit, a little snobby in our select activity. Having gotten there first, Scout and Raiders had taken over what had been a gambling casino and had the best situation on the island, so to speak, the rest of the base was a tent city!

Q: What was your rank at this time?

Capt. B.: I was an ensign, just commissioned. I must tell you an experience in New York City. After being commissioned and getting a uniform with one gold stripe, (there was nothing formal about being commissioned other than signing a paper) I walked down the street in New York, expectantly, and finally it happened. A little Wave saluted me--that was the first and I don't think I was saluted again for a month or so. I had it made, I thought.

Q: Talk about the Scout Raiders a little bit--under whose aegis were they sponsored, they were growing up like Topsy in a sense?

Capt. B.: Yes. From the original title of amphibious commandos, I don't know how the titles came about--we had come to the Patuxent area as amphibious commandos. We became Scout and Raiders for the African operation and continued until after Normandy under that title. The training was basically the boat training that I described at Patuxent. I had later training with, what was known as "Combined Operations" with the British, during my next deployment in April '42. That was for the reconnaissance of Sicily beaches and for this we operated from Malta with the British and from their submarine base there. Training was not formalized at the time our original group of ten, plus our enlisted crew men, was brought together. In experience, we picked up many things as we went along, changes, the varying requirements of the operations, from the handling of weapons--the 50-calibre types, the small arms and demolitions, and when we later worked with the commandos we picked up more, the rope tricks and assault tactics. We gradually converted to rocketry, and before Normandy went through demolition work with the initial U.D.T. groups that were to deliver and cover during the Normandy operation.

Q: Sort of an ad hoc thing for them wasn't it, at Normandy?

Capt. B.: They took tremendous casualties there you know.

About 40% casualties. Theirs was a very difficult task due to the obstacles on the beach and the clearance of them, under heavy mortar fire and the various problems that occurred. That came a little later. Then the transition of Scout and Raiders. When I returned some time after Normandy they were forming new units that were known as "Amphibious Roger" and these were to be jungle operators for the Far East. (The names were building up under the same Scout and Raider command headquarters.) It is difficult to say who was responsible in a training sense. The first officer in charge at Patuxent was a Commander Royal, a navy commander, whom I never met afterwards. Following him, an Ensign John Bell. This incidentally involved a problem on our commissioning. When they recommended us for most of our ten people were a little bit older and our first commissions came through as Lt. JGs, but since John Bell had been there ahead of us and was an Ensign he sent our commissions back and changed them to Ensign.

Q: So he would be senior to you?

Capt. B.: That wasn't a very popular thing in our minds at the time, but he sent them back. He was the officer in charge, so he could do that. Of course you got promoted every three or six months in those days and it didn't really make much difference in the long run, excepting that he remained senior.

Q: Was there any feed-in from the Marines? They had some experience with amphibious operations.

Capt. B.: Not directly in training. We worked together as coordinated training at places like Fort Pierce. The Marines that we worked with in the Chesapeake were being trained as landing teams, in coming alongside the ships, in embarking in the boats, and in movement procedures ashore, and they went over land back to wherever, to--Norfolk or wherever. In coordinated training as such, no--this did not at this time occur. We worked more closely with the U.D.T. people in England prior to Normandy, in really living and working and fighting together-- we fought at night when we used to gravel quonset huts on each other and that sort of thing; we were friendly rivals. We worked together there and then back at Fort Pierce we were even more coordinated. Admiral Kauffman (Rear Admiral Draper Kauffman) was at Fort Pierce then and I think he assisted in coordination a lot at that time. He was a Commander at that stage.

Q: Just beginning to draw them into a unit then?

Capt. B.: So throughout WWII Scouts and Raiders were the type of outfit that just grew; the expedient of the moment. There were many things that happened that I will come to. My next move, I left Fort Pierce with a fellow officer, Poss Johnston and two four-man crews. We went, a very enjoyable trip, on a hospital ship.

Q: Relatively safe, or supposedly so? Was it lighted at night?

Capt. B.: We traveled in convoy, it was troop loaded as well as nurse loaded. We had more of a social junket, the only one

I have ever experienced. That ship took us into Oran and this was in 1943, April '43. We went overland from Oran to Algiers (which is one hell of a ride in the back end of a truck). From there, a flight out to Malta. It happened we had the first unescorted flight going into Malta; we were buzzed a couple of times, which my Texas friend and fellow officer, Poss Johnston, quite a humorous character, was very much impressed and concerned about. We joined the British at Malta, as part of their Combined Operations Group to perform submarine and beach reconnaissance on the coast of Sicily.

Q: Malta was a pretty hot spot, wasn't it? for raids?

Capt. B.: There wasn't much food, there were problems and there were a lot of air raids but mostly on the submarine base (we didn't live at the submarine base, we were in a separate training and security area out on the point and relatively safe.) The submarine base was bombed continuously, but it was underground and the raids did very little damage; blew in some windows and I had an embarassing experience there a little later. We spent our time with the British Combined Operations who were tasked with the job of reconnaissance on Sicily. We were really participating with and under them. I think mainly, though it was a part of a joint effort, the British were trying to encourage our accepting their equipment and developing it better with U.S. construction—navigational equipment, radars, diving gear, midget submarines and the like. They loaded me with equipment when I did leave there and I was briefed: "Please ask your people to work this stuff over. We know you can do a better job with it than we have."

Q: The British had the top command in the Mediterranean didn't they, with Cunningham?

Capt. B.: Yes. Back to Poss Johnston, after a few weeks Poss became sick. Meanwhile we had made a couple of runs in the small submarines. The British were tasked with submarine responsibility in the Mediterranean. Their favored type was of medium size, about 150 feet in length, more maneuverable and, for Mediterranean use, a very practical assignment. These were also used for reconnaissance purposes as well as for attack--of going in to the beach, releasing the Scouts in kayak canoes to go on in shore, make the beach recon and then homing to the submarine. We had made a couple of runs and Poss didn't like submarines. Don't misunderstand me, Poss was one hell of a boat operator and willing for any assignment. He had a single gold tooth right in front and was very Texan in speech. I had a little bit of problem in translating and interpreting between Poss and the British, who were more of the Welsh type. For example, Poss always talked about those 'bummers' and the British never understood who the 'bombers' were. Poss became sick and asked me to go with him to the British captain, to whom he explained, "There is something wrong and I hate to let you down but I don't think I ought to be doing this." I knew he had difficulty (he died later, I think it was cancer of the stomach). He had a problem and I knew that. I will never forget his audience with the British captain. He explained, "Sir, they took me in an airplane and brought me here to Malta. They took me in a submarine to show me Sicily. Now Captain, before this I ain't been higher than picking apples and I ain't been lower than digging potatoes. Aside from that I'm sick." The captain didn't know what to make of it; he sent him back to Algiers and later he was sent back home and poor old Poss was sick. But Poss had a way of expressing himself that not only amazed me but really confounded the British.

Q: In the reconnaissance of the beaches in Sicily, what sort of data were you supposed to get? What kind of opposition did you meet or did you meet up with any?

Capt. B.: Minor opposition, although there were several British men lost on similar missions.

Q: This is on the south coast?

Capt. B.: Yes. How they were lost? Though you couldn't pin this down, when a man doesn't return you don't know why unless you can see firing ashore, but operating from a kayak canoe is not the most secure method and whether they were swamped or beached and didn't return from that, or were captured by sentries without gunfire, we didn't know but they lost several people. They did not, during my stay and participation lose any men. Most of the work involved determining beach gradients and changes in the beaches--as you came to Normandy later, there were obstacles and demolitions and the like. It was a differnet picture and most of that was initially detected by photography. On physical reconaissances in the Mediterranean area, the main objective was looking for shoals, taking soundings and making any sight observations and specific checks. We worked with the British until I was returned to Algiers, I can't recall the date but probably about June. This was prior to Sicilian landings. From there--in Algiers I was assigned to Admiral Richard Conolly, COMLANCRABNAV, at Bizerte, where the troops had just come in and Bizerte Harbor hadn't yet been cleared.

Q: Pretty much of a mess wasn't it?

Capt. B.: It was--ships sunk or on their side, the channel was pretty well blocked. Commodore W.A. Sullivan had to come in and do a lot of explosive clearance--never did get all of it cleared while we were there. There was a large lake inside the Bizerte Harbor and it was ideal for landing craft with the exception of during air attack when it was pretty well bottled. There was no place to go, but there was fairly good protection and we didn't have too much problem from the air--occasional attacks.

At Algiers I was assigned to a private home for a billet, I was only there overnight--what it amounted to was just a bunk in a basement. About the middle of the night this big fellow came in, he had a bottle, he was shaking me by the shoulder saying, "What's the matter don't you drink?" I had never seen him before but he said, "My name's Fritz Gleim." He was a commander. Our conversation was not very clear but he several times insisted, "I'm going to take you to Bizerte with me." And I said, "Fine." I didn't know at the moment, I found out the next morning that I was going to Bizerte and I don't think there was anyone more surprised than Fritz Gleim when I walked into headquarters there and met him again. He had been there about an hour ahead of me. He was the communications officer for Admiral Conolly. Later as an admiral, I know he had Key West during our problems down there a few years ago. He was a great help in the forming of a new force (the first actual landing ship force). He was a strong believer and voiced it in defense of reserve officers. He would contend you professionals are expected to do things, these men you have on landing craft are inexperienced but they are the people who are doing the job. He voiced that often and naturally was pretty popular among these landing craft landing ships. He was very supportive as well on equipment which was hard to obtain. He had been a tackle at the Academy and he was pretty well liked.

Q: By this time the ships were improving, were they not? I mean the types and all the rest.

Capt. B.: Well, for this type operation, Sicily was the first-- at least for the Mediterranean, I can't speak for the Pacific on timing--landing ship operation, under Radm. Conolly and with Captain George Dyer as chief of staff, were a new experiment with a small staff headquartered (they were back and forth, afloat and ashore). They had an old plane tender, the BISCAYNE, but also had headquarters ashore, where organization, training and planning was accomplished. There, I had with me one of my original ten group--Rip Howe, who was later killed at Cassino, Italy--we got our boats together on my arrival and with a nucleus of crews from our Scouts and Raiders, commenced building a new outfit. Rip had come in from the States to the little port of Karuba, a couple of miles down from the Bizerte headquarters that had been the old French naval base. It had been bombed and shot up badly. Rip and I made a real strike there. We found a former BOQ available to be taken over and Rip and I getting there first, and browsing around in this shell torn rubble that was heaped five and six feet high, touched a faucet with running water, we said, "Ah, this is for us." We got a couple of shovels from some Seabees and shoveled out this room and secretly had the only running water in Karuba! When we left the base, captain was in line to take over! We rigged mosquito netting over a four-foot wide shell hole and lived in luxury. How or why we didn't know, but we had running water!

We trained our people there and Admiral Conolly gave me a pretty blanket back-up, on how many men we needed--how many men I should get. We sent out calls for volunteers from both army and navy. Here was a break-down--they were training people like mad in the States but not for the tactics needed here, and Adm. Conolly said, "We are not taking any more from the States--I want the men trained here for the job as we decide to do it." I got several people from the army, I mixed them with those from the ships and it turned out to be a pretty good outfit. We did everything there from road work—every morning we were out running a couple of miles—to swimming, kayak canoe work, and we were just getting into rocketry, mortars and that sort of thing. This came on before Sicily. Our basic task was advance recon and to ensure the troops were landed on their designated beach targets. I learned a lesson there from Admiral Conolly, he worked in a very informal way—I could assign and train my own people, and I did—until one day he said, "Tell me. Who are you going to assign where? How are you going to do this? I had chosen a spot, Green Beach; it was kind of a tricky thing with a narrow channel entrance, and he said, "Who's going to handle it?" And I said, "I'm going to take it," and he said, "Now wait a minute, why?" I said, "I think I have the most experience and that's a tricky one to get into." He said, "There are 15,000 troops going over Red Beach and that's where you are going to be." I said, "That's an easy one Admiral, I'd give that to Rip and I'll take the other." He said, "You give Rip Green Beach. Now let's get something straight. You know I ask you a lot of questions but don't ever forget, I still make the decisions here." This is where I began learning a few important things.

Q: What was your mission to be?

Capt. B.: The specific thing—identifying the exits, the roadways—you had to get your troops in and make certain that they are not off 100 yards or whatever, off target, or the army is piled up and very vulnerable. They go charging to take a foxhole or whatever it be, and they do it rather blindly; in the amphibious landings you had to make certain they hit the beach exactly where their little charts said. Their job begins from where we land them and their intelligence targeting is specific in charging known foxholes, gun emplacements, etc.

Q: You had to be the eyes then?

Capt. B.: We had to check it out and be as certain as possible. I repeat, Admiral Conolly gave me quite a lecture that day which I never forgot. He said, "The objective of such a landing is to save as many lives as you can. I concede you are the most experienced person but where the most troops are is where the most experienced person will be." And I said, "Aye, aye, sir." And that's the way it was, although it wasn't the toughest one.

The way we approached this, we would come in in advance of the landing force, I don't recall the time, maybe it was about an hour in advance of the landing craft embarking troops from the ship. We would go in as best we could by identifying shorelines silhouettes, which in this case was difficult because the shoreline was all flat as could be. This recon commences in the middle of the night to around one o'clock in the morning and you usually work under the quarter moon so as to have protection of full darkness as the troops near the beach. You try to center your beach, then you make your passes on it to locate your flanks, and in most cases you have something like a pillbox on one flank and some tangible, identifiable object on the other, after you center, we would normally make a full sweep one flank to the other and it required dropping off a man at each flank. By flashlight signal, whatever code you are giving, he would locate himself at that flank and another scout at the other flank, you the back off your boat until you receive the flank signals and then you can estimate the accurate center of the beach. Then as the landing craft came in, you have to make them come down the alley. That was the very simple procedure. It did get tough at Sicily, however, whatever happened--they turned airfield searchlights on and it looked like Broadway. You have to learn from experience in working from the water or working from a boat and regardless how bright the searchlights are, you are still difficult to be seen. You feel like you are stark naked there in making your runs, but powerful aircraft searchlights over the water provides a glare for the observer also, you may be scared but you are protected on the water. The opposition at Sicily was not the roughest. I feel that some of the Germans there--I was pretty well convinced they were going to surrender; I put my flank men ashore and got my two signals from my flank men, both of them army types, one performed one of the more heroic actions I had seen and he was later awarded a Silver Star for it. He was amazing. From the flank almost the same spot from where I was receiving my flank light signal, the enemy opened fire. I was getting the flank signal with machine gun fire coming right over it and it was steady. I found my sergeant (flank man) on the beach next morning and said, "What in the hell were you doing?" He said, "Well, the pillbox was occupied. I felt the safest thing to do was to get my back right up against it." They were firing over his head.

Q: He was under the pillbox?

Capt. B.: And he was sitting there safe with a shielded light. He was right under their fire.

So we landed the troops. But, as I say, I felt they were going to give up because I had an 88 working over me from the shore--the Germans could do more with those 88s, they handled them like a 38--and they chased me from one end of the beach to the other. They just kept laying it in my wake, I would swing around the other way and come back and he just would make me back off, but I knew he could have hit me if he could control it that well. So, I thought he is playing something here, and not playing for keeps, he is going to quit. As the troops came in, the Germans folded fast.

Q: Was that the sector where Patton landed?

Capt. B.: Yes. Whiskey Knoll.

Q: Did you lose any troops landing on the beach? This would be one of the most dangerous of the operations.

Capt. B.: No, I didn't lose a man. The flanker that did such a tremendous job was later captured, became a prisoner of war and I couldn't find out about him. From there, since I had taken on these army people they had to rejoin their outfits. I got them all back together but they could not continue with me.

So that was a fairly easy one. We went back to Bizerte then and trained for Salerno.

Salerno was a much rougher operation, much more difficult, much heavier casualties.

Interview No. 2 with Captain Phil H. Bucklew

Place: At his home in Fairfax, Virginia

Date: Thursday 3 April 1980

Subject: Biography

By: John T. Mason, Jr.

Q: I think, last time, you had concluded your remarks about the invasion of Sicily and you said you had gone back to Bizerte for training and preparation for the invasion of Salerno, which came up within a matter of weeks. You had only a few weeks to train, did you not?

Capt. B.: I had the same men; I told you about having army personnel and they were dispersed, but I had my basic naval group. As I recall the dates range from Sicily in July and Salerno followed in September. In training we did have considerable change in the tactics to be employed; but basically my group was again an advance group—to make certain of the landings upon specific beaches as we had discussed—to get the landing force in the right location.

Q: I imagine you learned a few things at Sicily that you could utilize?

Capt. B.: Yes, you learn with every experience whether you recognize it or not. I would put confidence as one of the leading factors that you acquire--whether or not it is learned. With a young group, as my boys were, they ranged in age from 17 to 21 with a few older ones mixed in, but you might say, after North Africa and Sicily, we had a cocky outfit by then; Salerno was a joint task-force operation, tactically British command. Our task-force was again under Admiral Conolly. We were separated from the British by several miles on the coast-line there in the Salerno area south of Naples.

Q: In the Salerno area--the landing was divided between the British to the north and the Americans to the south?

Capt. B.: I'm fuzzy on that but I think the British were to the south of us--out of sight though we did join forces as time progressed. That was a very sticky operation, my own experiences were more humorous I suppose--frightening to me, but humorous as you look back on them. Based upon the experience that I have gained with the British, the reconaissance from the work from Malta prior to Sicily, it was decided that we would go in in kayak canoes. My young bo's'un mate and I operated our canoe at the head of the taskforce with the belief that we would be less detected in a canoe than with a powered boat. Now I might go back a step and say that enroute to the operating area the word came by radio that the Italians had capitulated, but did not say what the Germans had done.

Q: The mere fact that this announcement had been made must have had some effect on the morale, did it?

Capt. B.: It left an uncertainty. There was relief on the one hand and doubt on the other. Tragically, I recall seeing many troops do away with part of their ammunition and fill their belts with cigarettes, and that sort of thing--carelessness.

Q: I often wondered why General Eisenhower made this announcement at that point.

Capt. B.: I don't know. It obviously was in error--the same as President Roosevelt had announced in North Africa that at this time the American troops are marching in North Africa when actually we had been delayed by at least 12 hours, and that cost us a lot of casualties. It was a comparable situation at Salerno, but the meaning behind the announcement--I don't think it helped our US forces one particle.

Q: Now, while you are on that particular subject, I would like to interrupt you a little further--had you in any way been affected by the discussion as to whether it would be Salerno or Gaeta or which one, for those who wanted to go north of Naples, or south of Naples?

Capt. B.: I know it was in the higher command--the discussion--but it did not come to our operating level. I have mentioned before the admirable person I have always considered Admiral Conolly to be, and his discussion of detail with those at the operating level, with the junior. We did that much in preparing for Salerno, but we did not have live reconnaissance on the beaches and that was one reason for caution and for the approach being taken by a sneak craft rather than by a power boat--to get a person to the beach in the kayak to see how it looks and to signal our estimate as to the best area for initial landing. There were many things I didn't know were scheduled to occur. One of the more humorous ones--though normally you work with all components and have a pretty good feel (often more than we should have) as to what was to occur in a tactical way, but there was one thing I was completely unaware of and this was the use of a rocket ship--this was the introduction of a rocket ship. To me, this became a very "hot night." The first thing that occurred began with the bombardment **by British ships who at** that time lacked radar and fire control instruments. I was aware of the shore bombardment that would occur over my head as I was in there in advance of the troops, but I had been assured that they would fire long, they would fire long and reduce their fire toward the beach--but it didn't happen that way. They fired short and skipped them in. Ray King, my bo's'un mate, and I had quite a sensation with this naval bombardment by the British destroyers, that was skipping in the water over us in our kayak canoe. A shell coming at you in that salvo looks like a big ball of fire and it looks like its going to hit you right on the nose. It either goes over or it doesn't--they were skipping. We had a bit of a thrill with that you might say.

Q: How many kayaks were involved in this?

Capt. B.: Just the one in this area. We had come in by a landing craft to an area of about three miles offshore and debarked in our kayak and gone on in while our mother craft (the landing craft) laid off dead in the water.

Q: You were to return to her?

Capt. B.: That was the intent. After the first shock of the salvos and as things were expected to quiet down, the next thrill came and we didn't know what, but it developed, it was an amphibious craft, an LCU, that had been converted with about 50 rocket launchers. When they laid their barrage up, actually when you are looking it in the eye, it is more than a battleship salvo.

Q: This was a British ship too?

Capt. B.: This was a British landing craft. They went over our heads, the rockets have a tremendous roar and they went overhead with a swish, swish, swish, and we didn't know what it was. The next experience there, I took a hit. I was hit in the chest--a good thump that took my wind away and I thought, "Well, that's it, it doesn't hurt too much but that's it."

Q: Did it knock you over?

Capt. B.: No, you are seated low in the kayak. So I turned

over my shoulder to my bo's'un mate and said, "I think I took a hit, so you will have to take over." About that time, my life jacket began to smoke and smoulder--I hadn't taken a hit but I had taken a piece of a rocket that was burning the kapok in my jacket. I was kind of embarrassed and my bo's'un mate let me hear about it quite a few times. He would say, "Boss, tell 'em about that hit you took." There was some excitement to it and, as I say, mostly humorous afterward. There was nothing humorous about the landing however.

Q: Continue with your mission--did you get to the beach?

Capt. B.: We got in off the beach and we identified the target landing area from about 50 feet back on the beach--that was another point of the kayak--you could maneuver back out. By light signal we brought in the first landing craft and the waves thereafter, but they took an awful beating.

Q: You had predetermined exactly where they should go?

Capt. B.: We had had photographs reconnaissance and we had to go in and identify those landmarks that provided exits. Roadway exits were the main problem--at Salerno, it being mountainous terrain the troops had to be in the right spot to exit their way up the hills and out.

Q: Your reconnaissance was at night?

Capt. B.: We did not have a physical reconnaissance on this. It was discussed much with Admiral Conolly but it was decided against and we took submarine photographic reconnaissance which gave us a certain silhouette picture, then we ran a few aircraft over the area. The combination was all we had to work with.

Q: When you went in with the kayak, was that at night?

Capt. B.: Approximately two o'clock in the morning.

Q: Did you have any trouble identifying the shoreline?

Capt. B.: When you have a mountainous background, it is very difficult to get much of a silhouette; however in this case the shore fire made it pretty certain.

Q: Was this in answer to the British bombardment?

Capt. B.: Right, they were starting their repeat firing so we knew where their gun emplacements were and you could identify our position as the middle of the beach from where a pillbox was working on us amd from the flanks in the different areas.

Q: You were caught between two fires, weren't you?

Capt. B.: That's right, we were a little frightened perhaps but we weren't hurt and we got the troops in. However, the deepest defenses were far stronger than anticipated and also influenced by the thoughts that the Italians had capitulated. As the situation was later explained and developed for quite some time after that, the Germans had not withdrawn and they were well placed up in the hills. This was our first encounter with the German 88s mounted on flatcars that came in and out of caves and opened fire and withdrew. They actually held off the taskforce for about a week's time.

Q: They seemed to be imbued with a different spirit from what you had found them to have on Sicily?

Capt. B.: Yes, very much so. It seemed obvious at that point that their withdrawl from Sicily was anticipated and they left a rear guard action. The people they left at Salerno were a very capable fighting force and they readily held off both the British and the American forces for at least a week. I think it was about D plus 5 that there was a conference called and it was decided to withdraw our forces.

Q: Marl Clark decided this?

Capt. B.: Well, I understand that he was present and participated in the proposal on it. It was Admiral Conolly who made quite a dramatic speech--I didn't hear it but I knew of it outside--he asked for one more try. He said, "Let us use naval bombardment. If we withdraw we will lose our whole landing force; they are not of the capability and training and experience to evacuate a force. We have never done this. We have landed offensively. Let us utilize all our naval gunfire."

For a three day period--I remember the cruiser PHILADELPHIA burnt out the bore of all of her guns. They peppered those mountains and they really poured it on; everyone fired everything they had. They finally cracked an exit and the troops could move from where they were bogged down on the beaches. As I recall, it was just a horrible mess—we had about a thousand casualties on the beaches. I helped withdraw some casualties in the earlier days until I was pulled back to the flagship and ultimately back to Bizerte.

Q: You intimated that when you and your partner got in the kayak, you had left from an LST and you were to go back to it; did you get back to it?

Capt. B.: No, not immediately. I did a day or so later. A funny circumstance there—there are so many funny things afterwards (after you could laugh at them) I was working on the beach. I had gone ashore and there was my LST high and dry with his bow up on the beach; the skipper was named Sam Tutt and he was a 'hell for leather' operator (a lot of stories on him). He had taken that LST in at flank speed and didn't have the beach gradient information and he put it up there high and dry and it was a situation—walk ashore you won't get your feet wet. They took quite a bombardment until the tide shifted enough that they could pull him back off the beach. I got my boat back on board and then remained ashore a while.

Q: What kind of work were you doing on shore?

Capt. B.: General help; I helped move casualties and did things like that; with my boat and crew I would operate from the BISCAYNE which was the flagship of Admiral Conolly. I believe I mentioned about Admiral Dyer—Captain Dyer then—he was hit during the course of this, on the bridge. I would take orders from there. As I say, there was just one funny incident after another. One at that time, Captain Dyer called down to me--he said, "Buck" (there was a Jewish fellow I think his name was something like Greenberg, a very identifiable name but I don't remember it exactly now), "Greenberg's in trouble over there, (His LST had hit a mine), take a run over and see if you can be of any help." So in my small boat I came alongside; of course we all knew each other well, we worked closely together in our training, and I hailed--he was on the bridge--and said, "Captain Dyer wants to know if we can help you in any way?" He had hit a mine and he had a big gaping hole in the side of his LST but he said, "Yes, you can help me, if you can get me a chart of this area. I thought this damn thing was going to sink and I did like the book says and threw everything over the side."

Q: So he wanted to recover them?

Capt. B.: Well, you can't sink an LST and though he had a gaping hole in it they were all right, and they ultimately got back to Bizerte. There were a couple of amusing points about it. This LST had been rigged not only to carry troops, but they had rigged it with a flat top to use a Piper Cub type plane for reconnaisssance from the LST.

Q: Before the helicopters?

Capt. B.: Oh, yes, before the helicopters, and these little Piper Cubs did quite a job. Once you rigged that so-called 'flight deck' the tank deck wasn't good for troops so they had a load of jackasses--mules--that they were going to use up in the mountains as they progressed.

Q: Where did they corral them?

Capt. B.: I don't know--brought them from Africa; maybe from the states--but here was this LST loaded with jackasses on the tank deck and had a flight deck above it--and hit a mine. Of course, they got their jackasses ashore and that was fine. The little Piper Cubs did a remarkable job: I'll never forget, one of those cubs which I watched from the beach--he was making a reconnaissance and many of the mountain ranges in that area-- they are just like blind alleys--the little cub was making a U circle when he was spotted by two German Messerschmidts. We thought "Aw, hell, they've got the poor devil, he doesn't have a way out!" And he didn't have a way out; he went right to the edge of the mountains, made a U turn and came out and the two Messerschmidts crashed into the side of the mountains at their high speed. We all had our scares; I'm sure he did, but he did a tremendous job. There is an aftermath on the story on Greenberg and his "T". I told you what his cargo was. I happened to beat him back to Bizerte and I was there when he came into the harbor and as you pass your casualty report to Harbor Control, his came in of "One over-age Jewish skipper ready for survey; hole in the side of the ship; tank deck full of manure; flight deck beyond use." That became kind of a classic message. As I say, there was a lot of humor even under rough circumstances.

With Admiral Conolly's taking over and the gun fire--the naval bombardment--it cracked an exit and the troop move was under way. Then I was sent back to Bizerte aboard the same LST that brought us.

Q: You mentioned the fact that Conolly said it would be an impossible thing to evacuate from the beaches. I suppose the power of the LSTs was a forward power, was it? They couldn't back up as readily and as fast, didn't have as much power to back off the beach as to go forward?

Capt. B.: The power isn't there to withdraw. Under normal landing circumstances you can drive a ship in but you are offloading your troops, your cargo, which lightens your ship and you can withdraw. Well, it takes a little doing to ease the ship gradually off, it takes experience. And you don't really practice it except for operational purposes. Of course you take troops back and forth and all that but you don't really care during training--you could have other ships help you and the like--but if we had such a withdrawl--if evacuation had occurred, it would also have been under heavy German fire so your casualties, whether to the ships or the troops, would no doubt have been disasterous.

Q: It had always struck me as rather curious that General Mark Clark, in his book, doesn't mention this fact that there was the thought that they might evacuate from the beach?

Capt. B.: Well, I don't know specifics so I won't say more than that throughout the war, and even as a junior officer, my observation of it was a tremendous rivalry existed--army/navy-- over command and control and the prerogatives of command were very often loudly enough expressed that junior officers were aware of the controversy.

Q: Wasn't there some division of opinion, quite a decided division of opinion between the army and the navy US forces on shore bombardment? The army didn't want the bombardment.

Capt. B.: That is correct. The details of it I don't know. Admiral Conolly convinced them to utilize naval bombardment-- out of desparation--and it worked. That, and Normandy, were the two heavy bombardments--naval bombardments--that I have experienced. It was almost more personal at Salerno because we were so close to it and there was a lot more visible aerial bombardment than occurred at Normandy. Salerno was a very compact area--the exits in the mountains, you could look up from the beach and see where a road was and the troops had to go through mine fields to reach such exits. Most of these areas were mined and we had tremendous casualties from that.

Q: This was another factor. I understand Gaeta Bay didn't have mines, which we knew, and we didn't know Salerno was mined so that was a handicap there. What about the other members of your contingent? They were aboard too in this landing, were they not?

Capt. B.: I had a lesser number there than we did over at the drawn-out beaches at Sicily. Yes, I had them in other areas and in follow-on. In effect with your leading landing craft and until your beachhead is established and active and identifiable, you almost had to herd your waves, run out and jockey them in through just one channel, so to speak. There was no reluctance but with landing craft, even today, there isn't much navigation on them, a compass only and that, as soon as the troops came aboard with their weapons, that little old compass would spin around. It is not as simple as giving a coxswain a course or a boat officer, and saying, "Follow this course, that's where the army wants to go." When a soldier comes ashore he has a specific target in mind; he may have a grenade in hand and head for a pillbox target, but if that pillbox isn't there, he is lost; at that point he doesn't have a mission. The sergeant has a chart and once they regroup they take it from there, get their radio going and say, "Where do we go from here?" Its a little different from naval navigation, or even boat waves or channels.

Q: Did you have any casualties among your men in this particular landing?

Capt. B.: No, my men were dispersed and my own little kayak

was probably the closest, where I took a 'hit' and that was a joke as it turned out. Our British friends had quite a few casualties and we helped evacuate a lot of them on the beach.

Q: How did it happen that these surprises were sprung on you in terms of the British tactics there, and also the use of the missile?

Capt. B.: There are two factors of course, you never want the word to leak out about what tactics you are employing. It is a planned surprise. I remembered afterwards although I hadn't given too much thought at the time, but Admiral Conolly personally briefed me, "There is going to be destroyer fire coming in there but you don't have to worry, it is all going to go in long and then we'll level down to the beaches." So I knew that part was going to occur, I was reassured and, you might say, ignorant enough not to worry about it, because I had never worked under bombardment before and didn't know what those things sounded like when they went over your head. They all looked like they were coming six feet off the water.

Getting back to Bizerte, upon the return of the flagship Admiral Conolly was relieved and sent to the Pacific. Within the next few days I was ordered up to England.

Q: You didn't have any R & R in the interim?

Capt. B.: No. I looked forward to England.

Q: You mean you and your contingent also?

Capt. B.: I took just four men with me. It wasn't really explained in any detail at the time, but it was for reconnaissance on Normandy. I took four of my boys with me and later the entire contingent followed. I picked up another fellow officer that was working out of Oran in the Arzeu area, and he and his four men--Lieutenant Andreason--joined forces. I had another good experience that came out of this but it wasn't the way I planned it. There was a Coast Guard captain, Captain Imlay, he had been a football coach up at the Coast Guard Academy and he knew I had a background of football and we enjoyed "talking football". I was supposed to go in an air flight up to England.

Q: In a British plane or an American one?

Capt. B.: I don't know--didn't get that far. Captain Imlay suggested, "Why don't you come with me on the LCIs?" He had an LCI flotilla all the way around Gibraltar, but he said, "You come aboard with me, we'll get to talk football."

Q: That was a real incentive wasn't it? How did you get your orders changed to do this?

Capt. B.: He took care of that.

Q: And it gave you some rest and relaxation too?

Capt. B.: Well, on top of that when I came on board he said, "Why don't I put you on the four to eight watch every day, its quiet then and we can talk a little more before the ship gets into confusion." So I had the four to eight watch every morning from there to England. But he was a wonderful fellow and I enjoyed him. Those little LCIs went chugging along; they weren't the speediest you know and they are really not luxury liners.

Q: Its kind of rough there off the Bay of Biscay isn't it?

Capt. B.: They bounce around a bit. They are small ships, very friendly and you live close together and we had a lot of fun. We moved slowly and there was only one real incident on the way up. I think we did stop for liberty at Gibraltar and then made the straight run northward for England. There was one incident--these things do happen--there had been a convoy of smaller craft ahead of us, some LCTs and LSTs, and instead of turning to the port for England, one had turned to the starboard and went into France; we never did know what happened to him. He was not a part of our LCI contingent but the word was passed--"Be sure your outfit is all there!" But that was the only real incident.

We came in then to Falmouth. I am struggling for the admiral's name there...

Q: Admiral of the port?

Capt. B.: Yes, he was the initial admiral there, we had a naval base at Falmouth, right on the tip. Andreason and I, and this was a very foolish thing on our part but it all worked out. We knew better--the admiral didn't--as soon as we arrived and were detached from the LCIs where I was a passenger, I reported to the admiral. He said, "You boys, I understand, are about the most experienced we have in reconnaissance. You will be joining the British for reconnaissance on the French coast."

Q: What month was this--it was still in the fall?

Capt. B.: This was early December of '43--I know we were there for Christmas but we had a lot of minor escapades before that. The admiral said, "Now I don't know much about reconnaissance but I imagine the first thing that you should do--we have a command room here--you ought to spend a day there going through the plans we have." Well, we knew better than that.

Q: These were the plans for the landing?

Capt. B.: These were the plans for Normandy--OVERLORD--as they existed at that point. Reconnaissance people very seldom get complete information on anything; if they are captured the less they know the better. So there are certain specifics that you are looking for in certain areas, and normally the charts that you use on reconnaissance of a naval type wouldn't even have markings of longitude and latitude. Others would guide you in part to where you are going and you work it from there-- in order not to reveal, if you are under pressure, any unnecessary information. Andreason and I knew that but through interest and boredom we spent, fortunately, only one day, but we did go through the OVERLORD plans and got the general drift and retained quite a bit of it. This was fine. Next, the admiral said, "Well, you need a little leave, why don't you take a few days off, go to London." We did that. Soon after, higher command planned the preparation of a landing zone for the training of American troops--I think Colonel Thompson, an army training type was to be in charge--and they wanted an area similar to the northern French coast and there, as you may recall, Thompson trained his troops under live fire. He had some trouble with it because in pulling a lot of people up from North Africa, from Sicily and Salerno, who had been living under live fire, they didn't think that was the way to train. You do that on game day only.

Q: They had already been trained?

Capt. B.: Andreason and I were sent to do beach reconnaissance for this training area to determine it was suitable for landing craft, etc.

Q: Where was it to be?

Capt. B.: Slapton Sands was the name of it--on the British east coast north of Falmouth and we again enjoyed ourselves. We stayed in a little British hotel and got ourselves a boat and went out and checked gradients, talked with fishermen regarding tides, currents, obstacles, and developed a basic report without much hardship.

Q: Meanwhile talking football?

Capt. B.: One day we got an urgent call--get back to Falmouth. It seems the area we were working in was all mined and they had just found that out. Communications would often come a little late on such things but since we didn't know of it, we didn't have any escapades.

Q: It had been mined by the British to prevent invasion?

Capt. B.: Yes. I guess it was near Salcombe; we traveled around to different bases and we did different jobs there.

Q: Under whose command were you?

Capt. B.: It was pretty loose really, we were still working out of Falmouth, and I might say we played this to the hilt, we were separate, we were different, we were reconnaissance types and we didn't do routine duties, when they needed us we were on call. We weren't overworked but they kept us fairly busy with things they were setting up. Then we were called up to London and by that time Admiral Kirk had set up the London command, the naval component of it, General Eisenhower and the various joint commands were already settled there. There I came under the captain we were under following our original volunteering for "special duty".

Q: You mean in Norfolk?

Capt. B.: Captain Ted Wellings, he was the operations officer at that time to Admiral Kirk. Andreason and I were to be assigned for reconnaissance of Normandy, operating with the

British from the Isle of Wight. We reported there, an entirely British little island and that was quite a pleasant thing. Prince Philip was there with us, he was under the name of Lieutenant Phillips--a good naval officer. Louis Mountbatten's daughter was a third-class signalman in the same outfit. I never really knew her but knew who she was. Lieutenant Phillips was one of the boys.

Q: Was he engaged in the same sort of thing--coastal reconnaissance?

Capt. B.: Not in the type we were. I don't really know what activity he had. We had a lot of fun in the mess and in the wardroom, he is really a good fellow--as long as somebody didn't slip up and call him Prince or something--he would leave the room immediately--but if he was just Phillips or Lieutenant he was one of the boys. That was another nice experience, same as I had had down in Malta with the British. They do a lot of singing and they have a pretty good bar in their mess. Meanwhile we were learning their type of reconnaissance which, for the coast of Normandy, they had outfitted small landing craft, a closed bow type, with electronic instruments, really, the first of miniature equipments on direction finding. They had rigged them on the boats. The way they accomplished reconnaissance--I have skipped an important link here but will come back to it on what we did at Falmouth--there would be no identification where you went. You were brought in on poles electronically, a miniature or small

Bucklew #2 - 83

boat SHORAN. They towed you in your boat to a reasonable distance, ten miles or twenty miles from the Normandy coast, then released you from the British type PT which is called an MTB and you were "on your own", without knowledge and with a chart without any markings on it. They had rigged that.

Now, I will go back to what happened after the British learned that we had seen OVERLORD Normandy plan. They said we can't use the men, we can't consider people who have been exposed to such knowledge.

Q: How did they learn this?

Capt. B.: I believe through the admiral who casually and innocently commented. Andreason and I were probably the only ones from the U.S. naval staff who knew reconnaissance enough to know you don't do that, but we did it. So, we were the only U.S. navy people with experience that were available, and a compromise was made with the British to include us, but first we would have to go to their Escape and Evasion schools. We did, which was another very enjoyable experience.

Q: What did that consist of?

Capt. B.: They put us in a school which was conducted in a castle near London and we were isolated throughout our time there. The students, some of whom--there were also some girls involved, Polish, mostly spoke different languages. Since most people were being infiltrated into France, though there were some Polish there, were going to be air-dropped into different places in France. We were required to speak French, or not talk, and particularly during meals we were required to eat with knife and fork, European style (eating was considered the most exposing of American customs). Every instructor in that school was an escapee from the mainland. They had actually done it. Some of their tricks and gimmicks were unique: one fellow took six months to get from Dieppe back to England via Gibraltar, stayed in Paris for a while, harassing German occupation troops in any possible manner. One fellow I recall, lived in Paris with a school teacher and learned French that way, and every night he went down to the railway station to talk to Germans who came off the trains and just gave them bad information. They would ask him which way was this and he would give them the other way.

Q: You had to be pretty smart to do that.

Capt. B.: Another fellow, a sergeant from Dunkerque, I will always remember, by the time he got back to England he had promoted himself to captain so they let him keep it. He deserved it really, he was an intelligent person. These were the instructors. All of our meals had to be in European style and we could speak only French at a meal or be silent. That was part of the training. Our classes were conducted in English. In the bar they served drinks freely but you never spoke English. They worked us over well because American pilots had a bad reputation for some of the things that they had inadverdently done by speaking too freely; coming into an area in France and asking "how do I get in touch with the underground" and that sort of thing. In any event, we completed the school and they accepted us.

Q: How long a period did you spend there?

Capt. B.: We were only there about two weeks I guess, we took a lot of briefings and de-briefings.

Q: How did your French improve in that time?

Capt. B.: Well, I had had a little bit in high school and college but we found the smartest thing was not to talk too much. You pick things like your drink and that sort of thing but not as conversational as they hoped. They were very strict about it. For example, the knife in the left hand and the fork in the right, different ways that you complete your meal.

Q: This was to disguise your identity?

Capt. B.: If you were captured, you could mix with the countryside more. You were a Frenchman at least in disguise.

Q: What role were the women to play?

Capt. B.: We never discussed the missions where each or any of us were going, but they were to be parachuted into Poland--they were Polish. We also had several Polish submariners in the group. We were the only two Americans at that time, the rest were European types, refugees one way or another but with a military background. In any event, after that reorientation, so to speak, we went to the Isle of Wight.

Q: They didn't attempt in any way to erase from your mind any knowledge of the plans, did they?

Capt. B.: Not openly. As an afterthought, I feel that they overloaded us with a lot of inconsequential things to confuse us. If so, it was done very tactfully, though later as my part of Normandy developed, I knew a lot more. I think they very discreetly brainwashed us, knowing that in the limited time we had had with the plans. We didn't know very much.

Q: That's very logical--they were adamant at the beginning that you couldn't participate and then they finally agreed to let you participate after you had been to this school. It is very logical to think they did something to try to erase the initial impression on your mind.

Capt. B.: Well, they never tested us for what we didn't know, but I imagine we made the point.

Q: You say you completed the course. How do you complete a course like that? What kind of a grade do you have?

Capt. B.: No grades. As the school was run, I don't know that there was anything compulsory. It was all such an interesting situation you didn't miss a trick. You wanted to know everyone, their experiences, and the lessons learned.

Q: How many students were there?

Capt. B.: About 30 or 40; we were all billeted there, we lived in that big, stone, cold castle. I forget whose castle it was, the Duke of somebody, and I am not real sure how we got there. They used a lot of those larger buildings out in the countryside. We worked.

I'll go back to the Isle of Wight. We made our runs there, some very routine, some practice runs. The procedure we used was that a British MTB would tow the boat and then we would go in from a release point.

Q: At night?

Capt. B.: Oh yes. Taking off from the Isle of Wight there is not too long a gap to France, I suppose 30 to 40 miles. We had one exciting escapade which later was subject of a Navy Log movie, though I didn't want my name involved with it--I told you that some Hollywood fellow named Sam Gallou was doing this...

Q: For the navy?

Capt. B.: And he over-dramatized it. The purpose of our reconnaissance was to obtain sand samples from the Normandy beaches, which were (as it later developed, but I didn't know it at the time and wondered about it) passed to the laboratory and the texture of the sand told them what kind of matting to put down to take the weight of tanks and heavy equipments. It was like racks of test tubes really. We took soundings of different depths coming on in.

Q: How deep down did you have to go to get these samples?

Capt. B.: The tide is rather extreme there and we were at the point of low tide so we didn't need so much. The way you do it on depth is to use a sounding lead with the bottom hollowed out and filled with tallow, so that when it hits the bottom (and you have to have the lead to get it down there) it picks up the sand. I imagine the greatest depth must have been 15 feet at low level tide. This was accomplished, how successfully and what they got out of it you don't know. They had other boats at different times doing the same thing.

Q: Were there two of you in a boat?

Capt. B.: Two British and myself in the MTB, the engine being operated by an enlisted man. We were doing very well on that. All of a sudden everything cut loose, flares--coming from the beach.

Q: You were discovered then?

Capt. B.: Of course you never know what has been discovered, whether they discovered you or something out to seaward, or what. The rocket flares in this case told us it was time to get out.

Q: Again you felt you were naked--revealed in the light.

Capt. B.: Yes, we pulled out and fortunately there was some off-shore fog--its very foggy there--and the next thing we were in a pretty good fog but didn't have the faintest idea where our MTB was. We were working our way out slowly. We were out of the coastal range and the flares but we were in a dense fog and we ran right into a German coastal convoy.

Q: How far out were you from the beach?

Capt. B.: We were retracting, we were taking off and the convoy was coming along parallel to the coastline. It was about a six-ship coastal convoy. We ran right into them.

Q: Escorted by E-boats?

Capt. B.: We couldn't tell what they were, what their escorts were or anything else. The only thing to do, and we did it, was cut our engines and lay dead in the water and they passed right alongside us and passed on. That was kind of scary. In another half an hour we ran into our MTB and were towed back to the Isle of Wight; as the Britishers put it--a jolly good evening!

Q: How heavy was your equipment in the sand that you were transporting?

Capt. B.: It looked like a rack of test tubes--an especially built rack, some with the sounding leads, about all of them were that way with tallow; they were set up in pre-arranged fashion to use at one depth and the next at another, working your way in to and from the beach. On the beach itself we had to come back with a bucket of sand. That bucket of sand is what was made into a Navy Log later though I've never seen it. I think they played it up for me--that's why I didn't want my name involved with it--as if it were a one-man show. The purpose of it originally was to explain how, with reconnaissance, it sometimes is as simple as bringing back sand to a laboratory. That was the entire thing but, as I heard, when Sam Gallou got through with it, it was like a TV western.

The build-ups were occuring then.

Q: How far in advance of the Normandy landings was this sand operation?

Capt. B.: About six months. I don't recall whether it was January or February; I do know we had Christmas at Falmouth and left there for the Isle of Wight. It must have been around the first of February.

Q: The channel was pretty rough at that period of the year, wasn't it?

Capt. B.: Could be--hot and cold--that you never knew; of course that was the same thing for the Normandy landing itself. It got pretty rough and caused some limited delays.

Q: To follow through on the operation of getting the sand samples, did you know how effective they proved to be in the future operation?

Capt. B.: No, not really. I do know where we were because I was there again on D-day.

Q: On OMAHA Beach?

Capt. B.: The Vierville Church steeple was in the background and we were targeted on that steeple. It was a visual target through we didn't know what it was, but on D-day it happened that it was my beach again, an American beach completely, OMAHA RED Beach, and I remembered that steeple before the dawn and knew where it was.

Q: You must have been happy. Did our vehicle operate well on the beach?

Capt. B.: During the intervening time they had added many beach obstacles.

Q: Does that imply that the Germans had some knowledge of these forays?

Capt. B.: I'm sure they did. It was a question of just 'where'. As I have understood, they did expect the attack closer to the Brest Harbor area. The beach defense preparation was a very interesting thing and very thorough--we got many stories from it--the obstacles and the rows of pillboxes. Frankly, had the Germans had their full manpower strength that we bumped into elsewhere, though meanwhile they had lost a lot on the Russian front, but had they had their top-grade personnel I think it is very questionable whether we would have made it in spite of our back-up strength. The troops that manned those defenses on D-day were old men and young boys--the prisoners that we took were also. The beach obstacles were topped with Teller mines and we had a very difficult time getting in; we had to blow the gaps--even on D-day UDTs took a full day to clear a single gap and we lost a lot of personnel, nearly 40 percent of UDT were casualties.

Q: Let's go back to the sand operation, six months before. There must have been other operations in the intervening period before D-day arrived. What were they?

Capt. B.: When we pulled out of the Isle of Wight we rejoined the navy, so to speak, in training army troops. An awful lot of the training for the landing was done in England as opposed to in the US.

Q: These were US troops? When were you pulled out of the Isle of Wight?

Capt. B.: Around March.

Q: Just the two of you--Americans?

Capt. B.: Yes, the British continued as an operating base from there. We would bump into each other and we would have joint training exercises, landings, fire support. Meanwhile my boys had come up from North Africa and more of them had come from the States.

Q: So what kind of a number did you have?

Capt. B.: I think I had 24 crews, 24 officers with 4-man crews each. As to the boats, we had a problem. Actually we operated 12 boats and I made relief crews out of the other 12, but there was quite a priority--not so much on the boats, but for the davits on the ships to carry the boats--the space there to carry the boats. Everybody had a priority. In spite of our cockiness and ego, we began to worry that they didn't need us. We had to be with the lead ships and the army often wanted special and different equipments on them. I don't think the problem was really resolved until about a week before D-day. We were all in the plan but how wewere going to be lifted was a problem. I would get the drift every now and then in a planning conference that there was conflict.

Q: How did you contribute to the training of these troops?

Capt. B.: We had to know the problems and objectives of the outfits we worked with. We spent several weeks with the first UDTs that came over.

Q: Were they identified as UDTs when they first came over?

Capt. B.: This was the only time in the Atlantic that they operated as such.

Q: Had they been trained in North Carolina?

Capt. B.: Well, they came from all over I think, but Fort Pearce was operating then and a good number were from there. They had a large contingent, about a couple hundred men. It was anticipated that they would be with the lead group. We would be the lead group but we had to get them to the right objective area. So we had to............

Q: You had the same role that you played in Salerno and Sicily?

Capt. B.: Comparable, but with more weaponry, more rocketry actually. We added that to our boats. We lived with the UDTs. It was our first demolition experience and we put men all through indoctrination demolition training, which we had not been into before. I think the camp we went to was a place called Willicombe; this was a Ranger base, a Ranger camp, and the UDTs and ourselves worked from there. We did demolition firing every day. I don't recall just where the base was but it was near Plymouth. It was on the south coast, a sand dune area and we worked with beach obstacles. Different from training today, I have since had UDT teams under my command. Training of course in the States here is a very sensitive thing--the size of charges you can use--a half pound charge is typical. A pound is very unusual on an amphibious training exercise here. There we fired regularly 20 pounds and more for training. Of course it was a wide open sand dune area and wartime, but heavy charges and you would blow that steel for half a mile. These were the heavy charges that we were going to use.

Q: How did you maintain any degree of secrecy using such big charges?

Capt. B.: There was no one living near. I think, as troops were being assembled in Britain, there was not much attempt at secrecy. I think the Germans knew how many troops we had. They made attacks on us. One training exercise three German E-boats came right down the alley on some LSTs and sank three of them. We lost a thousand men in training exercises off Slapton Sands.

Q: This was in the daytime?

Capt. B.: No, it happened at night but the E-boats would come and go--that was their channel. I remember at Salcombe (you may recall that Salcombe is where Tennyson lived and wrote his "Crossing of the Bar") an E-boat came right up to the bar, up in this narrow river channel. They were coast watching--that was for keeps--there was always this threat in Britain and the people had an acute awareness of invasion against them. You had sensitivities wherever you had night operations--things like code words, call signs--and you learned that's no joke. In the more urban areas the bombing attacks were going on, back and forth. As for our planes, we were massing huge numbers at that stage and our attacks going one way. On our first trip to London we had three air raids that night. In places down around Plymouth, the industrial sectors, the Germans hadn't given up on their attacks against Britain although they were much on the defensive and running short on supplies and aircraft themselves. On the D-day landing itself even the personnel were less by far in quality than they had been in the past. That was attributed to their German losses on the Russian front.

Q: And in North Africa too?

Capt; B.: I don't think they were hurt too badly in North Africa. They withdrew. Rommel's withdrawal there seemed to be without major losses. We found things at Normandy--I was sent ashore one time to accompany a German sergeant, a prisoner of war, who had offered to take us through the mine fields and identify the live and dummy fields. He explained to us that General Rommel had planned the defense and personally inspected. Dummies were laid to satisfy his demands though live charges were not available. The sergeant was brought out to the flagship and he was interrogated and I accompanied him back--it was a delicate day for me because I felt, what does this German have to lose. He took us right through the mine fields.

Q: This was what D-day plus?

Capt. B.: I would say D-day plus 7 or 8. The flagship was that of Admiral Jimmy Hall, the ANCON. Admiral Kirk was on the AUGUSTA with his staff people over there. The ANCON had the troop level commands, Jimmy Hall had the actual assault command. Anyway, I was sent ashore with this man and he explained--he spoke some English but we had an interpreter. Rommel had made complete personal inspections of these mine fields and he would threaten to withdraw if certain areas weren't mined. If it wasn't done his way he wouldn't play. So they laid mines even if they didn't have the charges to put in them. There were innumerable dummy mine fields but they were all with barbed wire and big signs Skull and Cross Bones 'Auf dem minen'. My job was going ashore with this German sergeant who had told this story, and he would go 'STOMP, STOMP, STOMP,' right through all these mine fields and believe me I was going behind him trying to step in every footstep that he made.

Q: He was quite sure of himself?

Capt. B.: He often said, "Dud field', but how did I know it was a dud field. As I say, I felt, what does he have to lose.

Q: What was your purpose in following him through?

Capt. B.: So we could mark them on the charts, then you could clear and expedite an awful lot of things. The troops had to move through these areas. Of course they were bogged down in the beginning until you got exits cleared. It took the first full day of D-day before you could get exits blown in beach obstacles, get landing ships in, and then, when they started to move you had mines everywhere which didn't mean that you had free wheeling through them. The army procedure of course, once they start they have tape going behind them like gauze and that's the path to follow. If they get through or its blown they zigzag, but where the tapes go troops have moved. In that way you move an exit and open it until you can get a foothold or you get through these areas.

Q: And you had to follow a German?

Capt. B.: Of course we were pretty well established with our exits and channels before this little reconnaissance survey. I have said before, on the pillboxes and the trenches and the concrete defenses--if they had been manned at full strength, they could have held us off for another long period, and it is questionable if we could have cracked it.

Q: And with the weather shaping up as it did?

Capt. B.: That and all the various obstacles, but the Germans were depleted before Normandy, no question of that. As to the weather, that was quite a factor on many things including our own air bombardment. We weren't as successful as we might have been; there was some reluctance; there were political conflicts over high-level bombing and low-level bombing. This ultimately brought the break between the Army Air Force and the Airforce--this came out of those control arguments.

Q: As to what you say about the depletion of the German forces--their not being up to snuff--certainly underscores the arguments of the British much earlier when our high command was trying to get them to join in planning an earlier invasion. They were adamant in not wanting to do it and they were right.

Do you want to go back to the training period of our

troops? What else did you do in that interim period before D-day?

Capt. B.: We seemed to move from one place to another where training was being peaked or to the point of our contribution. We never stayed with them. One of the niceties, if you could call it that in the type of work we had--my boys and myself-- was that we didn't have the boredom the troops had. We would move from one place to another and we were called here and there and maybe spend a week in this spot and a week in another.

Q: Under whose command were you at this point? Who gave the orders for you to move here and there?

Capt. B.: Some of the things, like the reconnaissance, was controlled from Admiral Kirk's staff in London. But once I was assigned to Admiral Hall, we went wherever he wanted us to go. I think we mentioned, this was about D-plus 3 or 4 and that's the way things would happen. Andreason and I were together on the ANCON, I don't know if Andy was with me at the moment but they called me to the admiral's cabin and I thought, "What did I do now?" and there was Commodore Sullivan. They said, "We've got a problem, we'd like to send you in to see what you could find. We need safe havens for this flat bottom craft. We are going to be hit by weather, we're pretty certain of it and we want to find out if there are any rivers or streams that are large enough so that we could pull in landing craft LST size to protect them against the weather."

Q: Wasn't that fairly common knowledge from charts, etc.?

Capt. B.: Well, you don't know how much water is in there. Can you turn the ship around? Would you get them stranded up there? So we had to go and look for these things in the area. We had a very interesting experience during that one--a German pillbox holding twelve Germans and they surrendered to us. We were on foot and going out on a dike-like thing and we thought it had been cleared; our troops had moved on, but they had obviously by-passed this pillbox and these Germans came pouring out with their hands up. There were two of us--what were we going to do? But, there was no problem we just steered them down and turned them over to some M.P.s.

Q: Did they seem anxious to surrender?

Capt. B.: They were half drunk really. They had stayed in their pillbox, they had wine in there and they had drunk the last of the wine and said "This is it boys", and just surrendered without a shot being fired.

I had one disappointment that day. I should never have given up such a treasure, but we went into the pillbox and we were cautious about it as it could have been booby-trapped, but here was a huge silk Nazi flag. It must have been 10 feet by 10 feet, beautiful silk, red with black swastika. We had work to do and we stuffed it (I wanted to give it to Admiral Hall) away and when we came back that night it was gone, Somebody else had come across it.

Q: In this period before D-day when you were being moved around, did you do special reconnaissance for the several different beaches--UTAH, OMAHA and the RED beach.

Capt. B.: No, we never went back to it. From the time I left the Isle of Wight we never did.

Q: Were the British then doing that type of work?

Capt. B.: The major amphibious type of intelligence was taken over by Airforce--American or British or a combined operation. They developed a technique which was the first time it had been employed and it is used to the present day in determining gradients and the like. The procedure is they will make a run on the beach on the hour and then the overlay of the photography will tell you as much about the beach, and a lot more, than you can discover by physical reconnaissance. That was another phase of it.

Secondly, at that time, in the ninety days prior to D-day there was a complete lay-off of the target areas--they were avoided entirely. There were some deception operations, passes made elsewhere. I might say, on deception operations, at the time we made our passes the procedure normally was to run a commando attack, say ten miles on your left flank and they might have some type of disturbance such as a shore bombardment ten miles on your right. We had those cover operations and it was our job to go down the middle to do the actual physical target area. The sophistication and the tactics, as they developed, fairly well concealed our actions in that area. Now it is a far different thing in the Pacific. The Pacific remains today as a far less sophisticated target area on the islands and coastal areas than you would find on European coastlines where there are century old defences and coast watcher fortresses.

So that change occurred and it was a quiet spell for the coast as the main build-up occurred and the troop levels were increased.

Q: What about the Cherbourg area? Was there any reconnaissance there or any attempt to find out anything by landing?

Capt. B.: Not to my knowledge by physical reconnaissance. There was a lot of information gained there from various shipping sources since Cherbourg was a harbor, and infiltrations--the British have a tremendous agent system and they had their people emplaced. To illustrate that, I might go back to the Escape School. I was so much impressed when they took us through British Intelligence and showed us much of their gagetry. They had daily communications from prisoner of war camps. They briefed you on the different commanding officers of the different areas, but they knew him from the tennis games--they used to play international tennis against one another--they knew his temperament, what he likes; the kind of wine he drank and whatever. The British were so thorough compared to our approach. They take in the personal. They are better in languages, so they can place people, infiltrate them.

Q: Of course they have lived side by side for many centuries.

Capt. B.: Yes, across the channel and back and forth. Their experience level I don't think is fully appreciated by American military. I was much impressed, have always been.

Q: What did the Americans think of some of their gagetry--the MULBERRYS and things of that sort?

Capt. B.: Much of it we have adopted, not overnight, some of it over the years. We are still getting a lot of things in the diving and underwater gagetry. They had the two-man submarines while I worked with them at Malta back in 1943, pretty flimsy and they used gasoline cans for ballast but they operated. They always wanted us to assist and to improve the development of them with U.S. production.

Q: I know some of our top people spoke very disparagingly of the MULBERRYS, they didn't think they were of any value.

Capt. B.: Now, when you are referring to MULBERRY...

Q: Those artificial harbors.

Capt. B.: That's what I thought you meant. Of course we participated 100% and towed many of the craft that were sunk for breakwater installation from the United States. In fact, they towed the oldest scow that I first went from Norfolk up to Solomon's Island, Maryland on--it was like an old river boat full of cockroaches, and I was amazed to see that in MULBERRY at Normandy but it had been intact across the Atlantic.

Q: That was the specific operation that my friend from New York, Admiral Moran, the tugboat man was involved in.

Capt. B.: It was a tremendous engineering and navigational feat to bring them in there. It was of course greatly frustrated by the weather but it was regrouped and it was successfully operative. I was impressed, I think it was a very key thing in establishing the supply route. I left there before it was in full swing and I understand it continued for years afterward, so I couldn't play it down in any sense. It was certainly not of a sophisticated US nature.

Q: Did you have anything to do at all with the RED beach, the British beach?

Capt. B.: No, I had detachments down at UTAH, which was under Admiral Moon. We got together afterwards and sent the same people down when Admiral Moon went to southern France.

Q: For a landing down there.

Capt. B.: Yes. He committed suicide down there. He was a tremendous detail man, just knocked himself out. I didn't have thw exposure to him that I had with Admiral Hall. He was the senior one; Moon was a very liked and respected person, his death was very tragic.

Q: He was a war casualty wasn't he?

Capt. B.: That's right.

But then I came back and they pulled me out to go to the Phillipines.

Q: What was your last operation on the Normandy beach?

Capt. B.: A very dramatic one, I thought so at the time certainly. I was being used then--after that Sullivan instance when the storm hit, Admiral Hall would send me ashore to the various forward command posts for direct liaison and possible back-up support from the ships. So I would just go ashore in a boat and start hitch-hiking on whatever was moving forward and go to the command post and report to the General. If there was any service where liaison was necessary I was ready.

Q: They made you into a trouble shooter?

Capt. B.: I was a courier, that's what it amounted to. We worked various little rackets; whenever I went ashore I used to grab all these one page newspapers they put our on ships every day, a little summary; I would get a fistful of them and they could get me a ride anyplace. Pass them out to a Colonel here and there and he'd say, "My jeep's going this way", and I would get to where I had to go on that. We never really had any calls that required real naval support, so come the night I would usually go back and report to the Admiral and tell him what I had for the day--which was another sea story probably.

    I started to tell you, one of the most dramatic experiences I thought, was during Patton's march. His big move. I had been exposed to Patton from North Africa to Bizerte to Sicily but in this case I just sat there with the earphones and listened and of all things that have been said of Patton, a strict disciplinarian, his language, his neckties and uniforms and the like, this incident particualrly impressed me. He was making his swing with his tanks and Patton himself was on the horn, he was on the phone--I knew that from listening--but as these sergeants with their tanks would report in, with pride, and would report, "This is unit umpty-ump, at such a position, five miles accomplished, or whatever," Patton's voice would come back, "Congratulations, take five more 2XY," and the sergeant would say, "That S.O.B." and they would be swearing back and forth with never a thing from Patton. "Go get 'em son." He egged them on from each one and he was cursed out by more sergeants that day I bet than in his whole career but he always encouraged them--"Take more, take this. Great. Go." It certainly exposed me to a driving leader that wasn't just pomp or all that the press had tried to make him. He moved them.

Q: You wanted to tell me about your recollections of Admiral Hall.

Capt. B.: I think he was the most kindly and gentlemanly naval officer--admiral--that I knew in those times.

Q: He was a Virginia gentleman.

Capt. B.: All the way. His treatment of all his people--junior officers as well as seniors--was so humane. In my experience when you were going to be tasked to do something, he like Admiral Conolly that I have also mentioned, personally laid it on. I know there were many controversies, particularly with Admiral Kirk's staff, and of course I have been with both but the way we looked at it at that time we were the operators and they were the planners. You joked about the AUGUSTA--it was loaded with press and everything else. The AUGUSTA fired one salvo at Normandy and broke all their dishes. The troops were talking about that on the beach. The AUGUSTA was not in combat shape, it was an old cruiser, but they called it the show boat, but that sort of heckling between them was usual. Two of my buddies were on Kirk's staff, and we always heckled back and forth. I had been with them before. Captain Ted Wellings was chief of staff until Admiral Struble took over; we knew them pretty well but they wore blues all the time, we wore fatigues--it was that kind of thing. However, there was no question, I can see a fight happening twelve times a day over support services; the biggest fights I have ever seen were over air support; but on supplies and ammo--no one ever has enough. Patton never had enough gasoline to keep his march going and how would you get it to him.

Q: And there is always that great concern--what do you do when you run out? Did you have anything to do with Admiral

Deyo and his bombardment ships?

Capt. B.: No, I observed them and worked under them and knew his name--that he had the bombardment force, but they were never with the amphibious and the shore side of operations. They did their job ten miles out. That's where they had the five old ladies--the battleships that they expected to lose. They fired away, man did they lay it in there but they didn't sink. I forget what all they had--the ARKANSAS, the NEW YORK, the TEXAS--they were a very impressive sight. Our contacts were not very often with them, sometimes there would be conferences--we juniors didn't attend, but we might be someplace in the background.

Q: Now with the number of teams you have involved in this operation and it being such a hazardous one, you must have had some casualties?

Capt. B.: Well, I won't give you names--they weren't all good, I had to beach some.

Q: You mean personnel.

Capt. B.: We had many problems. One, and this later affected me personally, some of these people were not being trained in the states in accord with what we were doing in the field.

Q: This was Conolly's contention wasn't it?

Capt. B.: Admiral Conolly said, "I want them trained here, I want to know just exactly what they are doing." This happened again at Normandy--people that were trained in different types of operation stateside and came in---for example we were using a lot of rocketry, more weaponry than we had before. We had gone in to the demolition side, we worked with them. They had none of that and some of the boys were, in my opinion, not experienced enough and that's why I put them into a reserve--a relieving capacity so that theoretically after twelve hours they would come on and either take over the boats or relieve the boats--the people that were manning the boats. Some were very much offended at this, others were greatly relieved.

Q: Were they all very useful people?

Capt. B.: Yes, I would say so. It is hard to judge ages today but everyone of the officers would have been in their early twenties, between twenty and twenty-five. I had before Normandy one experience for which I was called on the carpet and asked what happened. I was giving a pre-battle briefing to my people--to all hands, all the officers--and it took me two days to do. I repeated it and it was kind of you might say a blackboard and sand table type thing illustrating where your boat should be and how you should do it. I went through it a second day and this boy--an attorney from New York-- at the end of my talk, which I thought was pretty light and making the tasks easy, came up to me and said, "I admire your courage," and I said, "What do you mean?" and he said, "You don't seem to be worried." I told him, "You don't have a thing to worry about, I've been through a few of these, you are not coming on for twelve hours and if this goes as most landings have, by twelve hours things will be quieted down. You'll come in there and you will serve wherever people need you—move around—but the heavy operation will have been completed." And I dismissed it. That officer went back to his ship, took a .45 calibre revolver and beat himself over the head until he fractured his skull.

Q: What he said to you was an indication of his mental concern?

Capt. B.: He apparently was very much perturbed and I got called up and they said, "What are you telling those people?" I said, "I made as light of it as I could, what gives?" They told me what happened; I said, "Well, my guess would be he wants to go back to the States." He had just gotten there and that was pretty apparent. Now that was one psychological problem. I would have had no indication of this beforehand. I had made light of each problem, but you bumped into that sort of thing. I had a couple of other people crack up in different places around the world, but not there at Normandy. We took some hits and some of our people were hurt, though I didn't have a death casualty in Normandy.

Q: You did not—in spite of all the hazards?

Capt. B.: Meanwhile, three of our people were killed down in

Anzio, boys that I had left behind. That troubled me greatly because they were doing kayak work, two of them, which I wouldn't let them do in Salerno. So I felt very concerned over that.

Q: You had concern because you felt they hadn't the experience?

Capt. B.: That, and there are certain physical qualifications you have for each job. They were all athletes, one of the fellows had been an outstanding athlete here at Catholic University in football and basketball, but he wasn't worth a damn in the water. The other fellow was a basketball player who was my number two man but he never became at home in water. You know there is something about it, particularly with water, it worries some people. Its not lack of strength or courage, but an inability to kind of relax and let it protect you.

Q: Terra firma is better for some people.

Capt. B.: Another one of my close friends--you remember the incident of Mark Clark where he was on a PT boat at Anzio that took a shell hit from the shore--my friend was killed, the shell went right through him, Jerry Donnell--he used to play football for me, then we started out together in the Navy, the Tunney Fish program.

You took your casualties in that sense. You took others--I think I told you about "Poss" Johnson--that's a different type of casualty. We had several surveyed and I had several people that took fragmentary hits but fortunately, we didn't have any deaths. Throughout I have always prided myself on that. Even in Vietnam. Our special warfare outfits ultimately had the heaviest naval casualties in the Vietnam War, but they were doing that kind of hazardous work--the SEAL teams and so on-- but we just didn't lose them.

Q: You did say, I think, at Normandy among the UDTs there were very heavy casualties?

Capt. B.: About 40% actually.

Q: Why was that in contrast to your men?

Capt. B.: They were trying to get set up with their demolition for clearing obstacles and there was heavy strafing going on; there were still the pillboxes covering the beaches with fire, and that's where they took their hits--quick--very early in the operation. I know we knocked out one with a rocket--my gunner got it on RED beach, but that one, from a second floor window, was just spewing .50 cal. fire as we were just going down the line of the beach, took a crack at it, and got it. But how many UDT people that machine gunner had hit that were trying to work, before we got him we don't know. Contradictory to many beliefs, UDT was not the first outfit to land over the beaches. I had this discussion with Admiral Morrison. I had luncheon with him and he quizzed me years ago. He took some issue really on that point, understanding the UDTs were the first in." This was not true. Actually the first to land was a very unique outfit that I had never seen before, though I knew they were coming. This was a tank outfit--submerged tanks. They had air bag coverage for tanks (which I might say was not adequate for flotation). They finally got the damn tanks out of there but most of them sank. We pulled many of their crewmen from the water and moved them ashore.

Q: Where were the tanks launched?

Capt. B.: They brought them in with 'mike' boats (LCMs) and from the boats launched them in the water. Of course it was to be at a shallow gradient point of beach but most of them bogged down. They were the first. They were going to move in, sort of a deception and an advance guard, and set up their heavier artillery that would protect the UDTs.

Q: Were those US?

Capt. B.: Yes, but those water wings didn't quite do the job.

Q: How big were the tanks?

Capt. B.: Regular army tanks, monsters, they weren't specially designed. You thought MULBERRY might be unique, I thought that was a pretty unique idea.

Q: I should think the air bags could be readily deflated with a shot.

Capt. B.: Well, they were coming in under darkness. Nearly every landing will be initiated at 2 or 3 o'clock in the morning so that theoretically they are situated on the beach at the first crack of dawn and set up for clearing house.

Q: Perhaps Morrison hadn't had prior knowledge of these, of this fantastic arrangement?

Capt. B.: I think he changed and took my word for it. He couldn't very well dispute it because I said we were first, they were second and UDTs were third, at least on OMAHA RED. He just said, "I didn't know that, probably because it was an army outfit."

Q: Give me your over'all, your general impressions of that D-day at Normandy.

Capt. B.: Again I was riding on a lead ship, an LST that had launched my boat which was souped up for speed.

Q: Capable of what kind of speed?

Capt. B.: Fifteen knots, which was good for a landing craft then. It was gasoline powered--I had stripped most of the metal armament off it. In moving in we had a longer run for Normandy than we had had for any previous operation, I would say it was 12 to 15 miles, probably 15 since I was launched early and while the ship was still under way I could beat the ship in to its anchorage so we had a longer run. I was nervous about this. I knew what was coming and our responsibility to guide them right, but with or without confidence, you always think of the room for error and you are very conscious of what's coming behind you. With Admiral Conolly's lesson and the concern for the troops behind you, I never forgot. I must have been 10 miles offshore when all hell cut loose! On my right hand, it must have been 10 miles down the beach, there were explosions, various types, flares going. I knew I was to be at the heart of the beach but I thought "what in the world--have I missed it?--could I have missed something? I couldn't have missed it by 10 miles when I have only gone 15!" I knew of the Ranger operation on the cliffs but I didn't know the timing was that much in advance of us. They had their problems. You know the Rangers had had to do a cliff-scaling job to come in and they had a flank movement supporting our assault force.

Q: It was kind of diversionary too wasn't it?

Capt. B.: Yes, purely. But, they took an awful beating, they had about 40% casualties. The flares in the black of night and the confusion worried the daylights out of me as to whether I was on the beam headed for RED beach--or could this fighting possibly from my target beach?

Q: You were actually the spearhead to the main operation, were you not?

Capt. B.: As I say, I was never more relieved than to see that Vierville Church steeple that I had seen during the recon, and it was pinpointed as part of the intelligence chart. When I saw that steeple I was probably the most relieved person in the world even though that was just the beginning of the fight.

Then, the next most impressive thing was Admiral Deyo's fire support; they started hammering the salvos in. As I later saw when I went ashore--I have never seen anything before nor since to equal the devastation that a naval salvo from a battleship can do. Some of it was pretty horrible and unpleasant and cause for part of the problem we had later with the French countryside, with the civilians. The furrows those salvos made would run a good 7 or 8 feet deep and 10 feet wide, and the cattle were all killed from concussion--not from hit, just the concussion of those shells going over them. But the salvos themselves would come out there three at a time, big balls of fire, roaring, almost deafening as they passed over us.

Then as we came in on the beach, of course you are pretty damn busy then and don't get much time to think, but I am very allergic to noise somehow, still am, just like in hearing a dog's sharp barking--I jump! Our machine gunning was deafening. I had wadded cotton in my ears but I hate those guns close-up. We were busy. These tanks came in and got in trouble, the UDTs came wallowing in their old LCMs--nothing glamourous about the way they came in--and they got in trouble right away. They went right into the beach obstacles and detonated some of the teller mines, took casualties but went to work. It was a scurrying proposition. We found where obstacles and mines were exploded and a gap cleared with troops landed. The next craft would follow, like LCUs troop loaded. We spent much time with one ship because their troops panicked. They hit the

the water when mines exploded--of course they had packs and the like--it wasn't a matter of drowning but they didn't know; the troops would be hanging on, they would grab these obstacles with a teller mine over their head and they would just cling. We would try to ease the boat in to get them off. I had a scare there. I was on my belly on the bow of my boat, pulling people up and getting them off the obstacles. I took some flack---it was the closest I ever came to really being hurt, I took a fragment cut on my bald head! I had taken my helmet off because I was hanging over the side. Learned a good lesson there. I just skinned my head. Just like a scratch.

Q: Did it break the scalp?

Capt. B.: Just put a red line down there, that's all it amounted to, but I didn't do that again. In pulling people out we were quite busy and I guess we kept that up most of the day.

Q: It must have been pretty exhausting and yet I suppose you were so keyed up you didn't feel exhaustion?

Capt. B.: I bumped into one of my old LST friends I had been with on previous operations and went aboard there, got a meal from the boys, then went back at it again. But in the meanwhile I lost my shoes. The seas were pretty rough really for the small craft and the type of thing we were doing and its the only time I ever did it, I decided I would wear a low shoe and avoid the awkward wet weight of combat boots. I lost my boots somehow—the doctor there said, "Here, take this guy's shoes, he doesn't need them." So I took a dead man's boots and wore them then and later all through China. I didn't get back to the flagship that day. The next day I went back, came on board, Admiral Hall wanted to talk with me, a how are things on the beach sort of talk. I think that's the only time the navy ever offered me a bottle of brandy and, foolishly, I didn't take it. We got a few hours sleep, went back out then and it developed into odd man jobs, wherever you were hailed by someone needing help.

Q: Tell me something about the training as it was connected with Normandy.

Capt. B.: There were some failures and it was apparent there was a breach in training between the stateside training and what was happening year by year and operation by operation in the field.

Q: The stateside training I suppose was more static?

Capt. B.: Yes, understandably so because there just weren't enough operational reports coming back that would give the training commands an update on the changes as they occurred.

Q: In my experience of reports coming back they didn't necessarily reach the proper place when they did come.

Capt. B.: Well, not in a year's time. In any event, Captain Ted Wellings, who was on Admiral Kirk's staff, called me in after Normandy and said I know there are discrepancies on training and you don't have to go into it but I want you to write a letter and describe as best you can what additional things have occurred and what additional types of training have been added since you were back there with these people at Fort Pierce or wherever.

Q: In other words the lessons of war.

Capt. B.: Yes, the lessons we had learned and that sort of thing. So I wrote a rather detailed letter assuming it would go out under the command signature, under Captain Wellings at least, but the damn thing went out under my name.

Q: Where did it go?

Capt. B.: It went back to the Bureau of Personnel. I never saw the actual letter that went out. I say under my signature, under my name or with reference to it. In any event, a few months later, in about October when I was being returned from Admiral Hall's staff and I was being sent, via the states, presumably to go on to the Phillipines where they were planning the amphibious landing. However, by the time that I got back to Washington they had stepped up the time and the Phillipines landing had occurred.

Q: You mean Leyte Gulf? and all that followed?

Capt. B.: Right. They had expected it would be a month or so later and that was where I was being directed, but in reporting to BuPers here, the landing had already occurred and the detailer... I might add a funny story there--here was a crowd of people around this detailer's desk and two or three of them were boys I had had at Normandy--among those that I had put into reserve. I was in the background of this group waiting to talk to the commander detailer and was waiting my turn. He singled me out--I didn't know what he was talking about as I wasn't paying much attention, but I heard him asking some of the boys, "Can you swim five miles with a knife in your teeth?" and the boy said, "No, sir, I don't think so." Then the detailer singled me out in the back row, with my bald head and the like, and he said, "Could you swim five miles with a knife in your teeth?" And I said, "Hell no." And he said, "Well, maybe you are in the wrong place." And I said back to him, "I was told to report to you, I really don't know what you are talking about." And he said, "This is the Scout and Raider desk." That made me a little mad and I said, "Somebody has made a hell of a mistake for the last three years." He said, "What's your name?" I told him and he said, "Would you mind stepping aside and I'll talk to you later." He broke up the crowd and he said, "Would you mind going out and having a drink with me." I was still kind of teed off at his attitude and said, "Look, I don't understand what this is about." And he said you wrote a letter back here regarding training and I said, "I prepared a letter as directed by the staff," and he said, "Well, that doesn't matter, you are now to be the officer in charge of training of the Scout and Raiders at Fort Pierce.

This was kind of a shock to be sent to Fort Pierce instead of the Phillipines.

Q: Why did he use the knife in the mouth as a criterion?

Capt. B.: He didn't know any more about what the Scout and Raiders were doing than they did in the training command. As he talked to the volunteers, he was obviously giving them scare talk before taking them into training. And that's part of the problem, it happens quite a bit when you don't know what people are doing.

Q: So your report did get in to BuPers where it did belong? And it was like all sorts of other things, when you initiate something you get the job.

Capt. B.: It certainly did get there. I both got the job and got out of it, as it turned out. I got some leave after Normandy and went back to Ohio in October. I went back to Columbus and that's where I met Helen. Although we didn't get married until after the war that influenced a lot of things I guess. So I used up my leave gloriously and wildly, though most of my old friends were deployed with one service or another.

Q: How much leave did you get, a month?

Capt. B.: I had a month's leave but had to use part of it for other things. They gave me the leave but then they sent me up to the Henry Hudson Intelligence School to give a talk up there, which I didn't do too well, I'm sure. Then I had to stop off at another spot but in the course of the thirty days I was ready to come back anyway. I went back to Fort Pierce to my old outfit, the Scouts and Raiders, not enthusiastic of becoming the O in C however.

Q: I would imagine you were much in demand with the various agencies because you were unique.

Capt. B.: Well, you might say I could write a letter and criticize the training but I wasn't really as enthused about doing anything about it beyond that. In any event, when I got down to Fort Pierce, a good number of my old outfit were there and there had been some changes. They were training people for the Far East--jungle training. It was quite interesting and I wasn't really reluctant to move into the job. I was there about 30 days; I pulled in all my old boys that had started with me and that I had had through Africa and Great Britain and Normandy, my enlisted boys I mean. In the course of that 30 days, coming from field operations and interesting living to training camp routine half of my people were soon in trouble for one reason or another.

Q: The life was too dull?

Capt. B.: It was, and there were necessary rules and disciplines that they did not agree with at that time, I wasn't too pleased with the whole situation. I talked to the commanding officer and I told him that I was better suited to field operations training fellows. He said, "I would like to go out too," so, I didn't get much sympathy from him. I wrote a letter to Admiral Conolly--he was then in the Pacific. I told him that I knew this was not the navy way of doing things but I was sure he understood how ignorant certain reserve officers were on the book (if you will recall he asked that I read that book the year before) and I said I think you need me in the Pacific. I got a letter back from Admiral Conolly very soon and he said, "I'm sorry but the type of operations we are on now, I don't really see the application of the work as you have been doing it."

Q: Where was he?

Capt. B.: He had a task force under Admiral Halsey, I believe. I know he had a force at the Phillipines with that group. "But," he said, "I have passed your letter to a close friend and I am sure you will hear from him. His name is Miles, sometimes known as 'Mary Miles'." Well, I heard in a few weeks. Meanwhile I was smug thinking somebody is going to pull me out of this training command when one of the old chiefs gave me a trip. He came up to me one day and he said, "I understand you are not really enthusiastic about taking over this school."

Q: Somebody had it at that moment?

Capt. B.: Yes, a fellow had it and I knew he didn't care about leaving really either. So the chief said, "If you want to stall for time why don't you ask for an inventory of what equipment they have in the school. They won't find out in six months what they've got in here." So I said before I take over I'd like an inventory of weapons, equipment, etc. Meanwhile a group came down from BuPers and asked if I would volunteer for an assignment if the Pacific; they couldn't tell me what it was, but I was to select ten officers and a certain number of enlisted men and would be so assigned of it were agreeable. So off we went. Same outfit.

Q: Let me ask you a question apropos the men who served in the Raiders group. They were all on the young side and they were seeking excitement and they found it, they were exhilarated to the nth degree and life otherwise wasn't that exciting. When they did reach the point where they stopped being that exhilarated and came doen to earth again?

Capt. B.: Of the officers, they were all college athletes, not any single category but they were backgrounded in pretty good competitive and physical status; being typical of athletes they could bitch about everything; they hated everything they did and did it very well. Some place in the process however, I think they mature and single down to 'this is not for me forever'.

Q: This is what I mean. When does this happen in a general sense?

Capt. B.: For example, Rocky Ruggieri who was a footballer and a wrestler, and is a big, strong, about 210 pounds, stockily built man, a football center and heavyweight intercollegiate wrestling champion. He and I teamed in China the following few months, but doing 20 miles a day through the mountains I think pretty well convinced Rocky that he had had enough of physical routine. He could do it and did do it very well but when he left the navy he had had enough of that sort of thing. Although he is pushing his sons for the same thing--the patriotic feeling is there but the recognition that this is not the field for everyone comes to them. Others, Bill Noel, played guard for Tennessee's Rose Bowl football teams, is in the construction business. Joe Keenan, who was an all Big 10 center with Wisconsin is in the electrical business. So on down the line. I am the only one from that group either through survival, being alive or whatever, that continued in the military and even in my case it was kind of on and off. The maturing comes. They are not all that enthusiastic for the military, whether it is being attached to home or marriage or profession or comfort.

Interview No. 3 with Captain Phil H. Bucklew

Place: At his residence, Fairfax, Virginia

Date: Wednesday 8 April 1980

Subject: Biography

By: John T. Mason, Jr.

Q: Today we are about to go to China--that was the destination you were not aware of when the BuPers representative presented you with the possibility, which you accepted with alacrity. Do you want to take up your story at that point?

Capt. B.: We assembled my little group back here in Washington for briefings.

Q: Did you have any difficulty getting these men freed from whatever they had been doing?

Capt. B.: No, all of the "volunteers" had been in the European operations as part of Scout and Raider and were all returning to the same school--Fort Pierce, Florida--at least those I chose all came from the same school source, having had the Mediterranean and/or Normandy experience. When I say "volunteers" they were that although there is a tendency among volunteers to say, "Don't tell my wife", if there happens to be a wife. Most of my boys were single but there were a few who were not. No one admits to having asked for it. So, we came to Washington and went through some briefings with returning personnel from Admiral Miles' group in China, and we at least knew where we were going. Fortunately this came to pass during the holiday season and we all got some leave back home for Christmas.

Q: This was in 1944?

Capt. B.: Yes, that's right. I welcomed that and went back to Ohio. I had met Helen, now my wife.

Q: She wasn't your wife yet?

Capt. B.: No, not until after the war. I had met her during the October leave that I had had and it was real nice going back again for another week.

Then back to China. We went to China under not the most confortable circumstances.

Q: By a circuitous route, wasn't it?

Capt. B.: We left from Washington National Airport after sitting around for several days before we got the whole group off. We would go on army transports up to the Nova Scotia, then through the Azores. It was kind of an installment situation flying with army-air force planes--our priorities were not always as assured as they might have been.

Q: What kind of gear were you permitted to take with you?

Capt. B.: Routine sea bag; we had no special equipments. It wasn't very clear on how we were going to be used when we got there, of course. Those officers of us that flew with the army transports—the coldest flights I have ever experienced, bucket seats—but we were designated as couriers. This was a gimmick used by the Navy to assure us not being stranded someplace and in the hands of the Army.

Q: You had a destination and you had to get there?

Capt. B.: Which backfired on me as I will explain. Anyway we stopped first at Casablanca, we got out of there in a couple days time. I was alone at my next stop—our people had to be broken up, one man here, two on another flight—it was a space available sort of thing, but I arrived in Cairo for the first and only time I had been there and I felt this was a rare and unusual experience. I checked in and told the sergeant in charge that as it was no emergency I would appreciate at least twenty-four hours before moving on. He said, "I'm sorry, Sir, but you are a courier and you will be leaving in about an hour on the next flight out." That didn't sound too good to me but I had a stroke of brilliance after I thought it over; I came back and asked him where the nearest infirmary was, that I was not feeling very well and thought maybe I should turn myself in, or at least get some medical attention. He said, "Do you think you will feel better in twenty-four hours, Sir?" And I thought I might; and he said, "I'll see you then." So, I had twenty-four hours in Cairo.

I hired myself a taxicab and driver and we spent twenty-four hours together. He took me to the British Museum, to the Sphinx, the Pyramids, Shepard's Hotel and Bar, shopping for a few items to send home, and we literally spent the twenty-four hours together. I enjoyed the experience very much and had a lot of laughs about it later also. The next stop was Calcutta, with fueling stops in between. This was the rear-guard headquarters of Admiral Miles Naval Group-China operating from Calcutta. There were several different bases of a supply nature--all the materiels had to be moved over the hump--from Calcutta through Burma and the first supply station was Kunming, China just across the Border. The main headquarters for Admiral Miles was at Chungking.

Q: That's where Chiang kai-Chek was?

Capt. B.: Yes. That was the rear guard move and the capital of the moment. Upon arrival in Calcutta our first assignment was developed there, with a little bit of controversy, but there were plans being developed for an amphibious landing from the Philippines to the China Coast. Reconnaissance of the shore line landing areas was needed; there was limited information available of a hydrographic nature because the area had been shut down for a hundred years to American and British knowledge.

Q: The Philippines for the most part had been secured?

Cpat. B.: They had been secured. The question was "Which way next?" "To the mainland or on north toward Japan?" As I say, it was in the planning stages in any event.

Q: Was it intended that MacArthur would go on or what?

Capt. B.: I knew nothing of the command structure, excepting that I, and all of my group, had been doing this type of recon work in Europe and we were the naturals for it immediately.

Q: Had you group been able to assemble in Calcutta by this time?

Capt. B.: Yes, struggling in, we got the whole group together and a good portion of Admiral Miles' intelligence planning staff from Chungking had come down to Calcutta and plans were being developed from that point. The man in charge was the Admiral's chief of staff, Captain Bierley. I believe he was an aerologist who had come out originally on weather problems and coast watching; they were providing weather support to the carrier groups in the Pacific. A lot of that was being done from the outposts that had been set up throughout China in various camps. Captain Bierley was a specialist in that area and though he was very practical in his thinking, my first encounter with him was very controversial. He took one look at me and said, "How can we masquerade you as a coolie and take you behind lines for a reconnaissance?"

Q: You were a little big for a Chinese, weren't you?

Capt. B.: We talked it out and decided they would take a chance on it, but I thought I was going to be benched before I got started (on account of my size). There was another interesting point--the basis for this reconnaissance. It was necessary to do a beach reconnaissance by going overland because of the lack of information, and the decision not to risk a submarine in uncharted waters to bring a recon party to the beach or inshore to do it as we normally had done it in previous operations.

Q: Why was that, because of the lack of knowledge of the depths and so forth?

Capt. B.: We used to joke about it quite a bit--they would risk our necks but they won't risk losing a submarine. In any event, it developed into one of the most interesting and difficult assignments in my experience. I had had a good time at home and was not exactly in the same day by day physical shape. When we took on these reconnaissances I learned a lot about going up and down mountains and carrying my weight. I regretted every drink I had had on leave and I came to respect coolies--their capabilities, strength and endurance. They say a little coolie can carry twice his own weight and I felt fortunate to carry my own weight.

Q: They do a lot of running too, don't they, up in the mountains?

Capt. B.: They can jog along carrying twice their own weight on their shoulders and "yo-yo" poles—it is amazing. On this reconnaissance, we flew from Calcutta over the 'hump' to Kunming. We moved by air in as far as there were established emergency landing fields; they dropped us off and we went a little further by jeep and the rest of the way on foot.

Q: What about the flight into China—over the hump and into Burma? Was that not a difficult flight?

Capt. B.: It is quite an experience. The pilots on the China Airline, CAT, were all civilians. Initially they had been a part of the Flying Tigers and they had flown those areas for several years—by the seat of their pants. They had very limited navigational equipment and it made you a little bit nervous but we certainly came to respect those pilots and their capabilities. They would fly not over the peaks but winding their way in and through them—they knew the route, so to speak.

Q: They also knew the air currents?

Capt. B.: They certainly did. You did bounce around quite a bit on those planes. But, in any event we next assembled at Kunming and then branched off. We went by pairs; my partner was Lieutenant Rocky Ruggieri—he was the heavyweight wrestling champion from Purdue and a football player—he was stockily built.

Q: He wouldn't look much like a Chinaman either?

Capt. B.: No, I don't think either of us did. We did a lot of this mountain work and we get together and talk about it to this day. Some of the tow-paths that we went up on these mountains would be a mile up and a mile down--that is a long way and a lot of lift for 200-pound types. We griped our way along.

Q: Is this just a part of the route to the coast?

Capt. B.: Yes, moving to the eastward toward the coast. We had done part of this by jeep after the last landing field. I can't think of the name of the village that was our stepping off point but here the Chinese liaison from Admiral Miles' staff, provided us with ten guerillas. They appeared one morning and I was formally introduced by the liaison officer, if you can call it an introduction when you don't speak Chinese and they don't speak English. The leader of the guerillas was wearing a black coolie suit and a derby hat, a Luger revolver on each hip. I left with them, alone and in a coolie suit.

Q: What was their purpose?

Capt. B.: They were to take me into the Amoy area and they did quite a job. They were natives of the area and knew it well, but I knew little about them. We didn't chat.

Q: You didn't get to meet Admiral Miles at this time?

Capt. B.: No, not at this point, not until after this.

Q: Did you get to meet the Chinese general who was head of their Intelligence Division?

Capt. B.: General Tai Lee; I did not meet him at this time. Upon completion of this exercise we ended up in Chungking and that is where we met. This recon was known as the Gantz expedition. Lieutenant Commander Saxe Gantz (still active I believe) airbourne type naval commander, was the senior person and officer in charge, though we didn't see much of one another. He had come in at Calcutta, but having been paired off we actually had limited communications. I got to know Saxe when it was all over and we were assembling our report. During the actual junket we no contact; no more did I see my other people--they were paired off going in different sectors along the coast.

Q: Did they also have a contingent of guerrillas with them?

Capt. B.: They didn't get in, they were stopped for one reason or another and it so happened, through no one's fault, but I was the only one who got to the coast. For one reason or another they were stopped and they gathered their intelligence by different means--interrogation and whatever. A good portion of the report here was assembled from existing intelligence documents and coordinated with any available Chinese input.

Q: You had some specifics that you were supposed to achieve?

Capt. B.: Yes--getting to the coast and evaluating the suitability for an amphibious landing in these areas, gaining hydrographic information--depth gradients and various things. As it developed, and I can put the end of the story first, I happened to be the only one who made it to the coastline and I recommended strongly against an amphibious landing for the simple reason that there were no exits. The mountains came up to the shoreline (it was a lot like Salerno in that sense); within three to five miles of the hoped for landing beaches was very rugged mountainous terrain with no roadways whatsoever. It would have been a case of landing and being bogged down on a limited sand strip. With that and several other reasons that we picked up--the gradients being not too suitable and the like--we recommended against a landing. How much that influenced the ultimate picture I don't know. I am sure there were 101 other reasons but our forces moved northward and avoided the China coast.

Q: At least that was a contribution. You must have had facilities for making notes, or did you hold it all in your mind?

Capt. B.: I had a note pad but a good portion of it had to be retained in mind and that coordinated with existing Chinese charts, when we returned to Calcutta. I had a few problems with my guerrilla chief and he was somewhat a nuisance to me; as I said they had come up with a very sack'like coolie suit for me and a huge straw hat on the morning that I departed with my guerrillas, and I was also provided with two grenades which flopped around in my two pockets. That was not very comfortable; I also had a .45 calibre revolver but that didn't work well with my coolie suit and belt and I had to keep everything covered.

I had unique experiences, we would be walking along and would pass coolies coming headon, with their minds 100 miles away as they carried their shoulder burdens; as we would pass one another I would be looking back at them from under my big straw hat to see if they had detected me, and they would be looking back at me saying "What was that?" because I was so out of proportion in size with them.

Q: Were the guerrillas much smaller in size?

Capt. B.: Yes, they were all typical Chinese of that area and I would say the average height was no more than 5 feet 6 inches.

Q: Did you stay close together as a group?

Capt. B.: We plodded along, single file. The tow paths through the mountains would permit only a single file operation; for passing it was very narrow, and in that rugged terrain we were very often looking downhill for a thousand feet. The tactic used by the Japanese, who did not guard this area very closely, where there had been narrow roads, they made "tank cuts"--just exploded gaps on the paths at different intervals so that vehicles couldn't utilize them. It was only foot traffic getting through the mountains.

Q And even that precarious. Ostensibly what were you supposed to be carrying on your back, as a coolie?

Capt. B.: We didn't carry the packs but we passed many coolies who were burdened--this probably gave us an affluent appearance as we were not carrying a burden. As is typical where there are coolies; there may be 20 of them or 50 of them, they may be carrying anything from loads of dirt to foodstuffs; but there are usually the arrangers, the bosses, the employers, who carry nothing and we obviously appeared more affluent than those common coolies.

Q: What did you wear on your feet?

Capt. B.: Sandals, which was one of my problems. I wasn't accustomed to them and I wore them out very rapidly and my arranger from a village got me a pair of tennis shoes, low shoes and that helped quite a bit. I didn't weather it too well. We had several experiences along the line and I lost a lot of face with my guerrilla chief. He knew I had the two grenades and in one instance a Japanese patrol knew that an American was in the area and sent out a search patrol. My guerrillas moved me from one little mud hut to another in a village until we backtracked and got rid of the Japanese patrol; I lost face with my guerilla chief who wanted me to give him one of the grenades so that he could wipe out the Japanese. Of course, he was a pretty aggressive fellow and I admired him for that, but any reconnaissance would have been blown right away with such a fight. The basic law of your recon is to get out without being detected.

Q: He had nothing then to do with the allocation of the grenades to you?

Capt. B.: No, but he did want to wipe out a few Japanese. That would no doubt have been a prestigious thing for him, he was hired by the Chinese Army to guide me through and he was not a part of the army operations, he was an entrepreneur. We had a second escapade when the guerrillas hid me in a haystack when a Japanese patrol came by and stopped; it was rather foolish--they hid me in the haystack and then all my guerrillas, each one sat down completely encircling the haystick with weapons in hand; it seemed very apparent to me that anyone would know there was something in the haystack, and any firing would be into the haystack.

Q: What size was the haystack?

Capt. B.: It was about 12 to 15 feet in diameter and about 10 feet high and I was inside, but I could look out. There were the two forces, the Japanese squadron considering what to do about it and my guerrillas saying, "I hope they do." So I had to sweat that out. Nothing happened but again that's when my guerrilla chief had wanted me to give him a grenade. I was certainly glad to get rid of those grenades when it was over. We never used any.

Q: How far inland were the Japanese in control?

Capt. B.: About 200 miles maximun I would say. As they came inland and the situation was quieter, they had their weapons and spent part of the day on military duty but mainly they farmed, lived off the land and raised their rice; they probably had been there for several years. In some areas we touched upon during this venture and in later operations, even down in the Amoy area, it was very casual living on the part of the Japanese, with the exception of occasional air attacks, apparently intended to keep the Chinese "on edge."

Q: How did the Chinese react to them?

Capt. B.: One of our difficulties with the Chinese throughout our stay in China, not just at this stage of the game, was to stimulate them into some action. They really didn't care about the Japanese--that was our problem; their fight was for the future, against the Communist forces. We had problems throughout but when we would issue weapons or ammunition to them they would stash it away for the future. They were always needing more and what they had hadn't been expended.

I had an interesting experience right at the end of the war and will tell you about it a little later. But, from this we went back to Calcutta, we worked up our recon report.

Q: How long did you spend on this trip to the coast?

Capt. B.: I would say about three weeks over all.

Q: Did you fall victim to any kind of disease--diarrhea or anything of that sort?

Capt. B.: Not at that point; I didn't have much trouble, I had some during the overall time, but I had a couple of bad cases in my outfits of amoebic dysentery and a couple of malaria cases. We were very strict on using mosquito netting and making them live under it and could control the malaria fairly well but the dysentery problem was individual discipline and susceptibilities. I imagine not the most violent forms but probably every China hand had difficulties at one time or another with dysentery. The amoebic type of course is difficult to clear.

Q: Tell me about your excursion along the coast. Did you have any problems with the Japanese there?

Capt. B.: You asked earlier about special equipment. I had a camera--I made a mistake with the camera and did not accomplish any photography. As we got to the coast and it is somewhat like the Louisiana bayous, my "arranger" confiscated a sampan and worked our way on down to the fishing areas. They wanted to put me under the floor boards of the sampan but I objected there. I thought about smothering--also, with a few sacks of rice over me I wouldn't have much of a chance of talking my way back up, but I convinced them that I had to see--that that was the purpose for which I was there.

Q: Was danger so immediate that you had to be hidden at this point?

Capt. B.: I suppose it could have been but as I have said, it was rather casual, they did not inspect each and every boat and there were so many sampans and fishermen tending their own business and the Japanese doing the same. We made our run down to the coast in that manner; at least I got my sights of the coastline, the mountainous terrain and the lack of roadways and exits, much of which I had to derive and confirm later from maps and charts. I couldn't see it all but we made our coastline run and returned; I lost my camera by entrusting it to my guerrilla chief.

Q: He sounds like your nemesis.

Capt. B.: He convinced me that he could go into the villages and bring back pictures. I am sure he sold the camera but he gave me a whopping story when I finally got an interpreter--that he had been captured and they had made him be a coolie for a day and had taken the camera away from him. I'm rather certain however that he found a deal. We did the best we could but it was not the most military and a little bit farcical in some instances. I had some difficulty on the way back to rejoin Rocky Ruggieri; I got what you might say was shin splints but I wasn't convinced myself that I hadn't broken something because as we would very often trot along these pathways and most of our movements were at night and you had to follow right along in the footsteps of the man in front of you--theoretically he knew where he was going. I fell on a pathway and they thought I had cracked a bone in my leg and by the time I got back the doctors worked it over but I really think it was a bad case of shin splints which you develop--this you come to learn--the worst thing in mountain work is going down hill. It works a different set of muscles in your legs completely and being of large size and heavy--we had done a quick 100 miles on foot-the fall embarassed me and I felt I had lost a lot of face, but I was slowing down and limping pretty well and my guerrilla chieftain came up with a carrier chair; they put me in it and away we went. The last miles I rode like an emperor! We were going back inland and I was a little embarassed, but I can't say that I was unhappy with the assist.

Q: If you had become immobile that would have been a great difficulty, would it not?

Capt. B.: Well, I felt I was 1000 miles from nowhere. There is another amusing story about transportation: Rocky Ruggieri and myself (I might say it was the last time I have ridden a bicycle_, when we were traveling together our Chinese arranger at one stage provided us with two bicycles; it was his suggestion and thought that we could move better amd more rapidly on the bicycles. Ruggieri and I, being pretty much the same size and tired, thought this was a great idea. We would push the bikes uphill and going downhill was fast and kind of fun. We did move right along but that was climaxed when we came to a right angle turn on a three foot wide pathway. It happened to both of us at the same turn, one following the other. We didn't make the turn, we went spread-eagled into a rice paddy and the rice paddy is not filled with roses. As far as I know there are two bicycles still off the edge of that path because we didn't bother to go back to them. We found a river and tried to clean and I haven't ridden a bicycle since.

Q: Now tell me about the arranger, you have mentioned him several times.

Capt. B.: He was no doubt hired by the Chinese army by SACO, the Sino American Cooperative Organization. The organization here--the American and the Chinese--Admiral Miles headed the American component and General Tai Lee headed the Chinese component.

Q: This was known as the Sino-American Cooperative Organization?

Capt. B.: Right. Down the line, in that organization, they arranged facilities and provided and worked hand-in-hand with whatever General Tai Lee and Commodore (then) Miles had agreed upon. In the case of my arranger, he had been contacted, set up by someone on Tai Lee's staff and briefed in Chinese (remember he didn't speak English and I didn't speak Chinese) but he knew where we were to go and that he was to get me there. He would arrange for food along the way in little villages, cooking on the ground or in a little mud hut someplace; we ate very well--rice always, and sometimes chickem or even shrimp (large prawns).

Q: Where did you sleep?

Capt. B.: On the ground or, temples are usually your best spot. There are Buddhist temples throughout the mountains, and that at least puts a shelter over your head. It was cold but we were dressed warmly underneath, always with long johns underwear, but in this operation we didn't carry things like bedrolls. On later operations normally my outfit would each have his own bedroll and with pack on back when we moved the outfit. It is catch as catch can where you might sleep. This was in the early spring and it is cold, but your big protection would hopefully be against rain. The temples, which are open, gave a roof over your head. I found in later months this could be hazardous, there were rats everywhere. We had quite a little escapade of that type—one of my boys got hit by a "flying" rat while asleep; he had a mosquito net over him and he woke up firing; we had no choice we had to count the shots and bounce on him after his gun was emptied, but it was like a nightmare to us and to the boy who had been startled awake and didn't know where he was. A temple, with a mud floor, is an eerie thing at best but he was firing at he didn't know what. We didn't trust him with a .45 for several days afterward. You never know what your dreams will be in that environment.

Q: On this particular mission, the others didn't reach the coast; but did they get back in safety; did you lose anybody?

Capt. B.: We had a common meeting place and the entire group returned to Kunming and then back over the hump and the coordination of the report was done in Calcutta.

Q: Why in Calcutta? Why wasn't it just as convenient to do it in Chungking?

Capt. B.: Chungking was off in another direction, a little more distant; communications were better in Calcutta and general facilities for reproduction of the report. I didn't actually see the printing of it, but administrative facilities were obviously better. Calcutta was the clearing house for all Americans coming into China so administrative facilities included a headquarters unit there for office and paper work and the like.

Upon completion of our report, my outfit was split up to go to different camps--a portion of it--but we first went into, the next stop was Chungking, and we went in to headquarters.

Q: Since your report was a negative one, did you get any repercussions to it?

Capt. B.: Not to my knowledge, whatever communications existed went from command level out to sea, Washington, or wherever, and there undoubtedly were many other influences toward, "Let's go on North, let's head for Japan." These negative recommendations may have been the final nail that clinched it, or something of that nature. But, we would hear so very little--in going to Chungking, we had very little information as to what was going on in the United States or the rest of the war. There was an occurrence, which was rather dramatic: While we were in Calcutta my whole group was staying, about 8 to 10 to a room, in what had been a British hotel. We slept there with bedrolls and mosquito netting and it was just like a bunk room. One morning during the report writing period, I walked out on the balcony the first thing on awakening, and I noticed the flag at half-mast. I called Willie Noel who was with us and said, "What do you suppose that is?" President Roosevelt had died. We didn't know, until later in the day about the reason but that one American flag over on the headquarters building indicated it. Then the sequence of things shifted somewhat. We went on into China and then we were even more void of information about what was going on elsewhere. We had limited concern about it, it was more what's the next assignment? Where do we go from here? This was the troops attitude. Avoiding boredom--is one of the greatest problems that you have in that type of field living. There was quite a camp at Chungking, they had movies at night--this was a luxury-- and we were kept pretty busy by day; I was tasked that I would give my outfit at least five miles roadwork every day (that was due to a little escapade we had with some Chinese wine and knocked a door down or something of that nature) and the chief of staff said, "I think you had better work them harder." So I did.

Q: Wear them out? But you had no actual mission at that time?

Capt. B.: We were awaiting a mission. That came soon enough.

Q: Was it at this time that you talked with Admiral Miles?

Capt. B.: Yes. Admiral Miles was a remarkable person in his physical activities--he was just everywhere around China on foot. He was known to do 40 miles a day and I understand had malaria from the day he came there. He was a sick man but he had the guts and the determination and kept going without revealing weakness. He was a most pleasant person. He would go from camp to camp; he liked to see things personally and know every man that worked with him. A typical incident, which was a great morale factor to the troops, one night in this camp that had a walkie-talkie type radio equipment, the admiral was not talking but listening as different camps would be calling their reports in, say nine o'clock one would come in, then nine'fifteen another one, and the camps would communicate with their so-called official communications, but, in this instance, and we were all listening through all of China of course, there was no knowledge to the talkers that the Admiral was on the horn as well; we were always clamoring for most any kind of supplies and the communication was between the certain camp and Kunming, the supply center--they asked for materiels, I forget what, but the answer from the Kunming end was "Sorry, there is hardly enough for ourselves." That was enough for Admiral Miles, he transferred every man from Kunming into the field and put field men into Kunming to take over the supply situation. That was a tremendous morale factor throughout the field.

Q: Tell me a little about the camps that were spread obviously all over the place; what were they engaged in doing?

Capt. B.: It was anticipated that we were training, that ultimately we would be taking these Chinese into combat against the Japanese. I think every American believed that. We had assigned to us maybe 1000 Chinese troops and we supervised their training--you might say in advisory group manner. Outfitting the troops was a big problem, everything had to be flown over the hump--weapons, ammunition, supplies, uniforms and equipment, and that was quite a logistic problem as well as seeing that it got to the right destination and wasn't confiscated. As I have said, much of it was stashed away for future use. The Chinese generals never got enough of anything and getting them aroused-- there were always reasons why they couldn't--they weren't quite ready to go into any battle situation. I would say, in that sense, the overall picture was not at all successful. Now, the primary purpose of the camps had been as weather stations and observation points, coast watchers in the various areas. In the northern areas the weather was most important in that it was coming down the Pacific way and it could influence air operations, carrier operations, and many such problems of intelligence importance. There was the continuing watch of the Japanese activity, there were some rescue missions for downed American pilots, if they were downed in a camp area it was 'go get them'. In fact, the gratitude of one American pilot--caused me a lot of trouble, probably to this day.

Q: You must tell me the story.

Capt. B.: He crashed in China, I don't recall that it was reconnaissance but in any event he was pulled out through one of the camps and later, from the Philippines he flew over once a week and dropped a case (not a carton) of cigarettes. My boys would have been more grateful for some Hershey bars but we smoked cigarettes like mad because we had so many of them. We would be out in the boonies some place (at that time we were down at Changchou on the coast where I had set up a camp for my own group) and here would come a plane and once a week we would get this large case that he dropped. He felt that we didn't have supplies and he made a point of it, probably out of his own pocket. Of course, cigarettes were 5¢ a pack at that stage and were to be had in abundance. The people at home were the ones who suffered. That was his token of appreciation to those who had helped him, however.

Q: And the gasoline he used was on the cuff.

Capt. B.: Then from Chungking some of my people were detached to various camps, as part of the training staffs at the various camps. Mostly this was their preference, rather than doing the leg work and being mobile. They had a preference for that kind of living—the camps were quite comfortable in comparison to field living. They have wooden barracks, you set up your own galleys and maybe hire a Chinese cook with Shanghai experience and the like. Some of them had been from Hong Kong or Shanghai. "Luxury" depended on what foodstuffs could be rounded up from anyplace in the countryside or even by cooking "C" rations. A good cook was a pretty handy thing to have and some of the camps were quite comfortable. The remainder of my group was known as Unit Buck (after me) for communication purposes and we were sent back to the coast for what ultimately was to have been a raid on the Island of Amoy which, thank God, never happened. We took over an abandoned village and set up a camp, outside of Changchou on the coastline. I think we spent a couple hundred dollars but we really refurbished that village for comfort! Through some Chinese contacts we got whitewash and we put in bamboo piped showers; we expected to be there several months and my enlisted boys did quite a job. We found a Chinese cook and we tried to put into effect all the luxuries that we had observed in the different camps we had been in. We were developing quite a comfortable little spot. By a camp I mean we had taken over from six to ten huts that had been a village prior to abandonment when the Japanese came in.

Q: Didn't the Japanese learn about it?

Capt. B.: The Japanese were on the island. This area was pretty much cleared. But the Island of Amoy was a deep sea port, and important. Japanese destroyers came in there and my first tasks were making recons--I could get to places on the shoreline with binoculars and spend hours on end studying what the situation was, by sight.

I must go back a step to Chungking when this assignment developed. An officer came out from Washington, from COMINCH, with verbal instructions and I was not permitted to put anything in writing on this requirement. The purpose of the raid on Amoy was the hope of gaining one of the few missing code books that were used by the Japanese. As I recall there were 12 or 13 in a series, some of which had been captured in earlier operations, and these were keys that the carrier forces were using. Since there had been an airfield at Amoy--it wasn't really operative though they did have a landing strip there--Washington had reason to believe that a final book might be held at the operations shack on Amoy and was worth a raid. As I say, I am grateful to this day that we never got that far.

Q: The raid to be conducted by what, the Seventh Fleet?

Capt. B.: By my outfit in sampans! With Chinese assistance; all sampans! We were to have and did manage to round up a few outboard motors to assist the sampans, but we had no air support and would have no air drop; it was to have been a sampan landing.

I spent some time in studying the channel between the island and the shore, the feasible spots for it, and I observed how they fished and got clams half the day. By watching I could see them till their rice fields and almost the changing of the guard. Like I say they spent about half the day on military duties and the other half on logistics.

Q: How heavily were they entrenched?

Capt. B.: They had a 16-inch gun and that's a lot of fire power against sampans.

Q: What distance from the mainland to the island?

Capt. B.: In some places about a mile and it was increased from that. They were not altogether peaceful. On one day in particular I was crossing to my observation point—it was a good high spot and looking down I could see quite a bit—they worked me over with the gun that day pretty well. They would do that occasionally, not very seriously but they would lay a few shots out to let you know that they knew you were there.

This buildup was occurring, I wasn't pleased about it.

Q: This was in 1945 when--towards summer?

Capt. B.: Yes, coming on for summer. Suddenly there were ships appearing and remaining in Amoy harbor and I said, "This is too much, I don't think this operation is feasible."

Q: You reported that to Chungking?

Capt. B.: We had an Eastern Field Command there--at Kienyang. Major Bruggeman, the Marine officer in charge; another camp so to speak. In any event, it was decided that we should have a preliminary rehearsal to the Amoy action at another area. The locale was changed--it was a comparable situation but lesser defended at Shark Island off Foochow. I took one man with me to make a recon visual of this offshore island which was small and not so defended from Foochow, about 50 miles to the north. I thought it was feasible, it was not a pushover by any means! It still had to be the sampan operation and Ray Fuller and I did line up sampans and decided we were as ready as we'd ever be. I was ready to go back to pull the whole outfit up. It was intended that we do this Shark Island raid successfully and then return a month or so later, to resume the Amoy thing. I went by foot to the Kienyang headquarters to make my report and opinions, and I intended to say we can give it a whirl, "we can go." But, I found all types of confusion in headquarters. The Chinese were covering the whole hillside; there were explosions going off; and what appeared to be aerological balloons hydrogen filled, would go up and boom--explosions. There wasn't a single American in headquarters. Finally from a Chinese I learned, "They are all out there celebrating." Sure enough they were and they were feeling kind of good too. The first American I met I told him I wasn't very happy about my operation and asked, "What in the hell is going on?" He said, "Forget operations, the war is over." I said, "It can't be," and he said, "Yeah, they've some peculiar bomb or something happened." And sure enough they had had the word about that.

Q: So the bomb saved you actually.

Capt. B.: It really did. So, then I got another unique assignment. I was very much relieved, I truly was, as much as any time in the war because I really couldn't see that operation.

Well, I was told you can start down river and head for Shanghai. So I went back, got my outfit, we got some river sampans and were heading down toward Ch'uanchou when I got orders that I was to meet, bodyguard, and escort General Tai Lee to Hengchow and on to Shanghai.

Q: You had never met him?

Capt. B.: Hadn't met him up to this point. I was to take him in to Shanghai. Just prior to receiving these orders, and this was rather typical; we were moving (I was told I was going to go to Shanghai) I was to take the outfit downstream, turn over all my ammunition to the Chinese (which I didn't turn it all over to them, just the surplus so to speak, the bulk of it) and an hour later when I get orders to take Tai Lee. I had to go back to the Chinese to get some ammo. Not a bit would they give back! I couldn't draw any ammo back that I had just given them an hour before. It was fortunate I hadn't turned it all over to them.

Q: Kept a little in reserve--you had learned Chinese ways? Had they actually removed it from the premises?

Capt. B.: Believe me, I could tell some stories on Shanghai thievery and disposal. If you thought you were guarding an item ten feet away from you, give them two minutes, an opportunity to distract, and I'll bet you couldn't find it in five miles. It just evaporates; when they want to disperse something it disperses. I had that experience in Shanghai with a case of cigarettes!

Q: Is this because they are so numerous, so many willing hands?

Capt. B.: Systematic, clever, sly, and they move rapidly. In any event, we escorted General Tai Lee to Shanghai.

Q: What was his mission there?

Capt. B.: He was the right hand of Chiang and the forerunner in return to Shanghai. You might say the mission was recouping as much as they could of anything they could! They were the victors.

On the way into Ch'uanchou I think we had four victory

marches. We came down by river to Hangchou, we went on foot and by jeep from there. We took the first train into Shanghai, with some uncertainties that the tracks may be mined. Wherever we went there was a victory march. The Japanese were still there and they ignored us completely. Their patrols were there. They outnumbered us at least five to one. This same situation occurred after we got to Shanghai, but it was a very nerve-racking thing to have a victory parade with the Chinese--they rode with open jeeps and it was quite a celebration, the firecrackers would go off and those long strings--uh-uh-uh-uh--sounded just like machine gun fire to us and we cringed. We had no difficulties really, but they celebrated their way all the way into Shanghai. We went by railroad from Ch'uanchou to Shanghai which was the first friendly trip taken; we didn't know if it was mined or whatever. It was really a brutal experience there because so many Chinese would try to board the train--it was overloaded in the first place--but they would kick them off literally, and it was a very unpleasant experience, but we moved into Shanghai.

Q: The Japanese had laid down their arms?

Capt. B.: No, they didn't lay down their arms. A typical thing--while I was coming downstream toward Ch'uanchou in a sampan I was stopped by a Japanese patrol and I went ashore; the Japanese lieutenant had two interpreters because with the many dialects it sometimes takes two to go through it; I told him there had been an armistice. This went through the two interpreters and after a period of time the Japanese lieutenant said, "I am a Stanford graduate, I speak very good English, I have heard that there has been an unusual bombing occurrence but," he said, "I have not heard of an armistice. Now," he said, "for your safety, as long as you remain where you are we will not harm you, but don't try to move down the river." Well, I was so damned annoyed to find we had gone through all of this palaver and it ended up that he spoke very good English and over the whole Stanford bit. I waited until dark, then swung around the other side of the river and went on through. We had no fight but that was typical. Once we came into Shanghai, the patrols literally patrolling back and forth--they ignored us. We happened to be the first group in, Admiral Miles got there probably the next day and we were set up at the Shanghai-American School, still sleeping in our bed rolls. The conquering heroes were sleeping on the floor and the Japanese occupying the hotels and comforts! Of course we had a handful of men---maybe a hundred and they had their full occupying force there. They literally paid no attention, it was just as if we weren't there, although we had the freedom of the streets and activities. They had been ordered to do nothing, I guess. For several days we milled around not really accomplishing anything. Chinese were coming in, so were our Americans gradually filtering in from the interior camps. Another experience: One morning Admiral Miles called me in at the Shanghai-American School and said, "Buck, we need a headquarters; I want you to find us a suitable building along the waterfront for a headquarters." "Aye, aye, Sir." I didn't have the faintest idea how to go about this. I got into the heart of Shanghai and noted a British bank there--I went in to see this banker; I guess someone had told me he had been interned throughout the war. I stated my problem to him and asked his advice. He suggested, "There is a building down here, the Glen Line Building. That could be available and I think we could help you with whatever paper work is necessary, but you won't need it, the Chinese will take over. You might go look that one over." I did and it seemed like a suitable building so I passed it to the Admiral and he said, "Fine, I remember the Glen Line Building, that will be ideal. Get it cleared." Well, the Japanese were living in it, they had their habichis, their women, their families, I went through that mess and I didn't have the faintest idea how to get those Japanese out of there. I was standing in front of the building, just looking at it, and a man came up to me--a very unusual person. I had first seen this man on the beaches of North Africa at Casablanca; he was very unusual in that he had maybe 20 Sikhs (Indians), very tall, long swords, all their colorful dress and pantaloons and the like. I remembered him just by the uniqueness of appearance from Casablanca, with those Sikhs, and that he spoke French. I next saw him in Calcutta. And here he walked up to me and said, "What's your problem, Lieutenant?" which I felt I had one. I said, "I'm supposed to get that building cleared of the Japanese; it is fully occupied." He said, "Well, maybe I can help." He said a few words, in Indian I suppose, and those Sikhs went into that building and you have never seen people come out of a building like a pack of rats and flies. It was cleared in half an hour's time.

Q: Was this man an East Indian?

Capt. B.: No, he was an American. I told him, I had seen him around the world although I had never met him and asked, "What is your job?" And he said, "Well, I'll meet you at the Palace Hotel tonight and we'll have a drink." We did. He told me that he had been for a long while in Cairo as a civilian, a businessman, but also as a deep cover intelligence officer for the navy (U.S.). When the war came along, fluent in several different languages, he received several "advance guard" assignments. We talked about Casablanca and about clearing areas, and about being on the beach at Normandy and Calcutta. He looked exactly like W.C. Fields, he had a bulbous red nose, he was a big man.

Q: Did he keep his bodyguard all the time, in all these places?

Capt. B.: Oh, yes, he had about 20 of them. How he moved them I don't know. He didn't tell me much about the Sikhs, they just disappeared too. I remember them in the Italian mountain fighting, they did a tremendous job but they worried the troops working alongside them. You know they pay by the ear, and they took ears. I think we saw them in their less violent mood--they were just silent, but colorful operators. I will never forget them clearing that building; and that became the U.S. Naval headquarters.

The next big problem was billeting. Our troops were coming

in from the camps and Admiral Miles, much as I liked him, he didn't do me any favors those days. One morning he said, "Buck, we need a billeting officer; you're it." Then I had to go around to hotels and take over space for all of our people coming in. I didn't think billeting officer was a very prestigious job.

Q: Though it was for the man who wanted a billet.

Capt. B.: In later years it served me very well. People that I did not remember did favors for me due to my billeting job. Once I got a trip from Pearl Harbor to Japan--when I walked in the fellow said, "I haven't seen you since Shanghai when you got me a room." I didn't know him from Adam but he got me off right away and on Pan Am.

It wasn't a bad situation but I did feel a little bit demeaned, though I guess I shouldn't have. We moved people as they came in from the field and to aboard ship; for a lot of them it was going home time. I was a bachelor and I didn't care really-- was having a good time--kind of exciting. Then, at one stage, I had four different jobs, because as people went home I would come to work and get another new job. I got into one of the stickiest ones--I was made senior shore patrol officer, and head of investigations. I still had the billeting, and I had one other trivial job. But the shore patrol and investigations got into quite a few details.

Inflation really hit Shanghai at this time, it hit all China, about 40,000 to 1 rate in some areas--you would find from one province to another 40,000 down to 20,000--that sort of thing. If you got paid in one place and would come into the next, it was amazing. I wasn't on the money making side, but became much involved. They were reorganizing to have a Shanghai Base Command headquarters also in the Glen Line Building and on the next floor would be Naval Forces-China, under Admiral Miles and the Chungking staff but the Base Command was to handle the local Shanghai problems. Meanwhile Seventh Fleet was coming in and Admiral Miles had one major personal ambition: When the Seventh Fleet arrived he wanted to have a dinner--a banquet for every officer in the Seventh Fleet. It was a personal thing-- he had been there through the entire war.

Q: And he was going to be the host!

Capt. B.: He was going to host them and say "Glad to see you" when the fleet came in. He had not drawn any pay throughout the war, I guess. He planned to draw it off the books and have an elaborate party. The Admiral had appointed some girl correspondent to handle this banquet. The war correspondents were cropping up from everywhere, the Chinese were having victory celebrations still; then the tragedy occurred. We were in the Cathay Hotel--the finest hotel in the Far East. As billeting officer I had taken over a Navy portion of the Cathay Hotel and when this incident occurred I was serving as assistant aide to the admiral. The Chinese were having a large banquet and the admiral was sick really--malaria--and it was catching up with him and the drinks were flowing. He was in the back room when they called him to the banquet and the Chinese wanted to ask him one question: "What was your reaction when you looked out from your balcony in the Cathay and saw the Seventh Fleet coming up the Whangpo?" The Admiral beamed and answered, "Now General Wedemeyer can stuff his entire army....." The U.S. Army Chief of Staff was present and ordered, "Arrest that man."

Q: What, arrest the Admiral?

Capt. B.: They packed the Admiral off, we got him down the hall, on to his plane back to Chungking and our doctor there declared, "He is sick; you cannot arrest a sick man." Then they got in touch with Admiral King who sent out orders to send him home. Now, the interesting part of this story--the Admiral had drawn his money off the books for this banquet, it was in my closet. We put the suitcases on the plane and he went back to Chungking. The admiral knew he was in difficulties so he told Cy Morris, his aide, "You had better cash back in the money, turn it back to U.S., looks like we are going home." Cy did, in Chungking. The difference in inflation was a $40 thousand dollar profit; Captain Bierley who had been going along with him, and I think he cleared about $20,000. I skip ahead, some months later, my closest relative, who was my sister-in-law received 20 yards of beautiful Chinese silk, as did the wives of every officer serving under Admiral Miles!

Q: You started to tell me when we went off tape--that your

sister-in-law got a gift of 20 yards of beautiful silk.

Capt. B.: That exchange on the Admiral's departure and the profit—he spent every penny of it in sending gifts to the dependents of every officer who had served under him in China.

Q: Well, what a gesture! When he was threatened with arrest, why was it not possible to appeal to Chiang? He worked with Chiang didn't he?

Capt. B.: It was a U.S. problem, I would say, and the rivalry, you can call it that, between the army command and the navy; the Admiral had been there so long; he was accepted and loved by the Chinese. In fact they wanted him to become Commander in Chief of their Navy at that time. He decided against it naturally, due to his U.S. Navy career, but they had that respect and liking for him personally. It wasn't the same with the army. They never trusted them. I'll go back to the beginning. On the Sino'American agreement between President Roosevelt and Kai-shek when the Americans were to come into China, I forget the exact wording of course, in effect Chiang said, "We welcome the Americans, we would like their assistance, but we don't know the U.S. Army, they have never been here but the Navy had been here over the years and have been visiting our ports and our coastal areas so we would like Naval personnel to be assigned here." And the ridiculous part is (we always laughed about it) they assigned naval personnel to train army troops, put us in army uniforms and most of the work that we did there was army or marine type activity. There had been that feeling over the years that the U.S. Navy and the Chinese people were close. The army had just never been known. When the senior army people did arrive, there were sensitivities. I was probably the only Lieutenant that was ever relieved personally by a four-star general in my own office on one little job I had—price control—and that by General Wedemeyer.

Q: Tell me that story.

Capt. B.: I told you inflation had set in and the commander of the Shanghai Base Command was Captain Jack Andrews. As part of one of my jobs, he called me in one morning and said, "Look, we've got to do something about these prices." I didn't have the faintest idea what you do about price control but he said, "You know how it is," and I said, "Yes, I know, I was out the other night and it cost 100 dollars for dinner." I was with a medical commodore at the time and he didn't want me to pay his bill. It was kind of embarassing and he sent me around to make a settlement on it, but—very unusual for them I think drinks were around 2 dollars apiece which back in 1945-'46 that was unheard of. All prices were skyrocketing that way and there was a concerted effort to take advantage of the troops, navy, army, or whatever. The Chinese residents weren't suffering this as much—it was "Get the Americans!" Andrews said, "See what you can do to stop it." I took one of my boys—Jackson Wills, now an attorney out in Coronado, whom I have seen in later years; I sent Jackson around to make a list of prices in all of the restaurants, all the bars, get whatever info we could. He came back in 2 or 3 days with all lists and we sat down with them--this may be ridiculous but it is the way it was--and we said, "That's too much, they ought to charge 25 cents for that." We made up our own price list of what we thought to be reasonable, which I know wasn't fair, but we weren't then knowledgeable enough to know it wasn't.

Q: You were going to do it by fiat?

Capt. B.: We just plain told them, we'll put you out-of-bounds or you can comply with what we consider fair prices. Well, just about all restaurants and bars went along with it, or compromised within reason. The Cathay Hotel, the finest in the Far East, with the General in a suite up in their penthouse, had been providing a bottle of liquor every day and gifts every night, and for the naval admirals we had five suites on one floor for the admirals that would come in from the fleet, but the Cathay manager told me that he was not about to change prices. I went back to Captain Andrews for authorization, "Do you want me to take action and I'll put them out-of-bounds." At the Cathay this was unheard of, but the General's Adjutant was giving back presents all over Shanghai and the Cathay came around, and by more luck than sense, price control was set in Shanghai. Bucklew became quite a hero to the Stars and Stripes--"<u>Naval Lieutenant goes where Generals Fear to Tread</u>". I was headlines for a few days, looking out for the G.I. One morning a Colonel and the General came into my office and said, "You have done a fine job Lieutenant but I think the Army can take it over from here."

Q: This was General Wedemeyer? Then what happened? Did it revert?

Capt. B.: No, it didn't revert, it held for a while but after the General departed, actually he put the Colonel in charge (I don't remember his name), when I say a four-star relieved me but he did it personally, he came in and the Colonel said, "Look, I've been provost marshall in twenty some countries but I've never been chewed out like I have been today. Would you mind giving me your books." I gave him all the books and price control became an army matter. That was a ridiculous one.

Q: I hope you are going to tell me the story that Admiral Miles carries in his book, about the hotel room—the V.I.P. who demanded great quarters and who had all sorts of medals, so you were commanded to wear your medals. That is a very sketchy outline but I would like the story from you.

Capt. B.: There was a naval captain who got a little bit out of line. There was a shortage of rooms, of course, and though we tried to do as much as we could for the shipboard people, there was this cross-action of people who were coming out of the boonies on their way to ships to go home, and there was just so much space. If we had it we were glad to take care of anybody we could overnight; but this captain got a little bit arrogant; he had been out fighting the war and you people here are living it up and he sort of boasted about his decorations and the Admiral told me to put mine on. That's about all there was to it.

Q: Yes, but they were more than equal to the Captain's werent' they?

Capt. V.: Yes, they were.

Q: Tell me something about the Chinese general--the Secret Service man. He is now dead but is quite a character in history.

Capt. B.: That is Tai Li. Unfortunately he died in a plane crash right after the war. Tai Li was the son of a wealthy family, in one of the interior provinces. At the time that Chiang Kai-shek was building up his stature as a war-lord and fighting one province commander until they could take over and he would build up his empire. Tai Li, I understand was a rival faction and used a different technique. Tai Li didn't fight anybody, he undermined them, he went underground, moved into a province until he was in a position to take over, and he was building up a comparable stature to Chiang. Instead of fighting one another they got together, and Tai Li became Chiang's (I don't think the title was Chief of Staff) head of Secret Police as we knew it. He had a remarkable underground intelligence system through which he received in China daily what was going on in Tokoyo. This was while war was going on. He was an agent operator and, from my limited observation--though I did see quite a few things that he accomplished--he was an expert in the field. A fore-runner in many ways to what we would have liked to have had our CIA operations develop. His intelligence chain was far reaching and effective, with tactics restricted only by himself. (I am told he could be a brutal authoritarian as required.) But he was more of a pleasant social type as we saw him. I learned (probably for good reason) at the time I had to body-guard him through to Shanghai however, that the man was afraid of his own shadow. He wouldn't go to the so-called bathroom alone; he had other people go with him and sit beside him (they were four and five-holers) and such things as that.

Q: Was he afraid of being shot down?

Capt. B.: Probably he lived so long in that environment that he trusted no one, though as Americans we would never have known that; to us he was a jovial, social type. When we came into Shanghai he had several big celebration parties, the drinks flowed, the food was good, through his friends and contacts he used wealthy homes where he had these parties and he included all the American officers as they came out of the field. He was developing something not only for that time but for the future. Probably the person he most respected was Admiral Miles; he was very devoted to him; they were counterparts and whatever Admiral Miles suggested Tai Li believed and followed through. Their cooperation was tremendous. Then approximately six months or so after the war, ironically, his plane crashed and he died.

Q: Was it entirely an accident?

Capt. B.: I had just departed China but I understand there have been uncertainties on it. Whether it was due to the style of life the man followed is uncertain, but nothing was ever proven. They have a statue of him in Taiwan. I found in later years that much of my SACO work was very helpful when we worked in Taiwan, on amphibious operations and the like.

Q: If he had survived, do you suppose the picture on China would have been different? Would Chiang have survived in the China mainland?

Capt. B.: I think they would have lasted longer. The overall problem, as I saw it, with Chiang's forces in the interior, the whole system of living off the land, of taking hostage the eldest son from each family, conscripting him and bringing him into service; it was anything but a voluntary service, Chiang's armies were huge but their desertion rate was so high that seemingly they had as many men on sentry duty to prevent desertions as they had under arms. It was a top-heavy situation numerically but it wasn't strong and with the size of China and trying to control such a broad expanse of territory, it seemed to me inevitable that they would collapse or be undermined. We found when we worked in the interior that though the peasant folk had no political interest they were more inclined toward the Communists than they were toward the Nationalists. The Nationalists would come in and take three quarters of their food supply as well as often conscripting a son to keep them quiet; and that type of abuse.

Q: It wasn't a philosophical adherence then?

Capt. B.: Not at all. I found in the interior that there would be posters for example, with Chiang's picture and I would ask, "Who is he?" They didn't know and didn't care. It was a different world. In China, what's on the other side of the mountain they will never know or care, only concern for their own little rice paddy that for several generations they had worked. The political side and the big city side, whether it be Peking or Shanghai; it wasn't really known, it is a different world, far different people from the farming class. How Tai Li might have handled such a situation I don't know, but I do think, with better judgement. I think there was too much impulse of the Chinese to get even; in Shanghai, following the war, they looted their own people. The motivation was regain, recoup all their losses during war, whether the people that they hurt had had any responsibility or not you never knew. I guess its a natural thing--all their favorite people were placed in the big jobs--mayors and the like, not unlike our political spoils system. We as Americans were treated wonderfully well by these same people, but we couldn't help but observe the harm that was being done although it was kept from us as much as possible.

A second factor I always attribute as the underlying cause of collapse to this day. If we had just gone on for six months more without pulling the troops out and sending the boys home,

I think without another shot being fired, a stability could have been accomplished with the Nationalists on the mainland, this in spite of the long-term threat between Communists and Nationalists that had been suspended temporarily for WW2. That build-up was long and thorough but we just needed a little more time on the spot to assure stability. But once the bell rang, the goal was to get everyone home.

Q: That was universal?

Capt. B.: Yes. We received many criticisms from the British in particular. Of course they are more experienced, they serve for 7 or 8 years and think not nearly as badly of it as we do for 2 years.

Q: Yes, but that whole thing was aided and abetted by our government, the Congress and everybody.

Capt. B.: Oh yes, it was apparent they wanted these boys home, that was evident with neutral pressures from parents, wives, and families.

Q: And it was largely sentimental, wasn't it?

Capt. B.: I thought so. Now on the opposite side of it, MacArthur created a pretty good organization in Japan, and a solidity. But the troops either were not withdrawn or they were replaced until he completed the job. But in China, it was not long until they moved to the Island, pushed off.

Q: And in the Fleet.

Capt. B.: It was precipitous.

Q: When you look at the SACO operation in retrospect, how do you summarize its accomplishments?

Capt. B.: A tremendous potential never fully realized. I don't refer to it as SACO alone, but the American presence was needed through the political settlement period--a continuance of it; but SACO would have to be considered in close parallel, whether it might have been the dominating role in such presence, their accomplishments in good relationships, in cooperation. I think from both top level and down the line with the Chinese, there was not the Ugly American feeling that has existed in many countries, at least that I could see. There was bound to be resentment in some areas, but I think SACO and Admiral Miles' efforts accomplished more in that regard than I have seen in any other country. Of course, as the Nationalists evacuated--withdrew to Taiwan--it was a wiped out thing.

Q: You mean the effect was dissipated immediately?

Capt. B.: Yes, and the feeling today on Taiwan, is of the greatest admiration and respect for Admiral Miles. In my return visits there, navywise, I was hosted many times by people I didn't know. They looked me up as a former SACOite though I was just a commander in the navy.

Q: Aren't the mainland Chinese the dominant factor in Taiwan, the ruling group?

Capt. B.: Oh yes, although they are getting old and are being replaced. A number of them that I have known--four-star admirals and generals--have since been, not retired, but deactivated. With Chiang's army, I think it had changed in the last few years with his son in command, but they didn't retire anyone, age was no factor, there was nothing for them to do if they pulled them from it. They did have a top-heavy military on Taiwan but efficient in the way they handled the offshore islands and the like; they were of the better trained forces.

Q: That is the testimony I receive from a number of people. May I ask you about what appeared to us very often as a myth-- their stated determination to go back to the mainland and take over again. Was this ever a possibility? Did they really think it was?

Capt. B.: I think they forced themselves to believe that. I've heard many of the younger people say we must go and we must go soon. This goes back ten years; but even at that point they would feel 'its getting late, our children don't know the traditions, they are losing the background'. Of course Chinese tradition, respect for their elders, for their ancestors, burial in the ancestral grounds or areas had always been very important to them, but they are modernizing in the sense of losing the close family ties that related to the continent. Home will always be where it originated by their traditions.

I have always considered China the most impressive, though less combatant, of my personal experiences of WW2. I was so imbued with it that I went back to graduate school and studied Chinese for a year. I thought of Foreign Service on a career basis, but unfortunately the language study was too much. I had to unlearn most of the Chinese I had picked up--too much G.I. talk I guess.

Q: You say it was different and not so much combatant but as you describe some of these things it was certainly equally dangerous. Equally with Normandy, wasn't it? The Japanese sentries around the haystack would have been just as relentless and just as ruthless as the Germans on the cliffs in Normandy.

Capt. B.: Perhaps. We recognized the hazards but we were a pretty cocky lot at that stage, I guess. And we were young, which makes a difference.

Q: I just want this as an addendum to this interview: While you were in China you had a nickname, Big Stoop?

Capt. B.: That goes back to Terry and the Pirates, the cartoon strip and my coolie suit thing. They had a rather giant Chinese in the comic strip and, as I recall, he was a mute. But he was featured in the strip about the time we were in China and that combined with my travel in a coolie suit made it logical to relate me to Big Stoop. I saw the humor in it but I was never really flattered.

Q: Now if you had had malaria and gotten the yellow color you would have been a more authentic Chinaman.

Capt. B.: We lived so much without shirts and unnecessary clothes—-as far as color went I became pretty well camouflaged.

Interview No. 4 with Captain Phil H. Bucklew

Place: At his residence, Fairfax, Virginia

Date: Thursday 17 April 1980

Subject: Biography

By: John T. Mason, Jr.

Q: We continue today with some added thoughts on your sojourn in China when you were working for Admiral Miles. Last time you told me about your tour down to the coast, your survey, and all the vicissitudes in life as a Chinese coolie.

Capt. B.: I believe we touched upon VJ day--the end of the war and my first task there moving toward Shanghai downriver by sampan to Hangchow then on to Shanghai. I was tasked to bodyguard General Tai Li who was the right hand (sometimes called the hatchet man) for Chiang Kai-shek. Tai Li was quite a character.

Q: How old was he?

Capt. B.: I couldn't answer that. As an Oriental he was rather young appearing; I would guess approximately fifty years old, but as you know they are a beardless type, full head of hair, young appearing. He was short, a little on the chubby side; he ate well and looked like a very affluent person, which he was, as he had a wealthy background. I think we discussed his system—undermining. I was surprised to find, this being the first time I had a close association with him, that he was quite cautious and frightened—in a personal sense. Probably, he had enough threats against his life that he literally took no chances. Even unto insisting that someone go to the bathroom with him. It was a little on the ridiculous side but we had no problems. There was one incident which was rather typical of the times. When this assignment first came I was ordered to turn my ammunition over to the Chinese, which I did, and within a couple of hours received the order to escort Tai Li. I wanted some ammunition back and they refused to turn any of it back to me. Fortunately I had retained enough.

Q: You had been there long enough to learn the ways of the land?

Capt. B.: Yes—don't give it all back.

Upon coming to Shanghai, we discussed some of the initial problems and the setting up of headquarters for Admiral Miles; the fleet coming in, with the problems of billeting so many people; of getting transportation for them back to the States. Everyone was anxious to get back home. I was a bachelor at the time and in not so much of a hurry, and I thought it a very interesting experience. It was a time in which you might start the day having one job and finish the day having had two or three additional tasks added because of someone departing.

Command might say, "You better take over this." Whether you knew anything about it or not that's the way it was. It was a very trying time for the Seventh Fleet ships, particularly those of the LST category, the smaller ships. As they could come up the Whangpo and be tied up at Shanghai, their personnel would have the points permitting them to come home; as a result there soon was not enough manpower to move the ships.

Q: They got to Shanghai and that was it?

Capt. B.: That was it, the crew went home--legitimately and as authorized by our law and regulations or whatever decided it.

Q: Didn't some of the men have some qualms about leaving their ship stranded?

Capt. B.: I don't think commanding officers took that attitude; no more did most of the officers, but this became a problem in retaining an operating crew, such as your firemen, your engine-men, electricians and the like. It wasn't a lack of patriotism necessarily, there were pressures from home, parents and wives. It is understandable that they felt their boys had been out there for four years; now why can't they come home. So there is a two-way street on that circumstance, but in any event it became quite a mess. We had to organize mobile crews to go from one ship to another just to oversee daily the routine maintenance and perhaps to move the ship in order to get another ship into position--such as a supply ship. This was quite a problem, in some instances there were revolts aboard ship, I recall. One commanding officer had--at this time I had shore patrol, though that didn't necessarily mean going from bar to bar as we see it more in the United States, but under that category of responsibility, we would get riot calls. There were only about 15 crew members aboard this particular LST but they had on board several Chinese girls; the commanding officer didn't approve of that but it was out of control and it fell into the category of mutiny. Another typical incident, we had a riot call at one time when Chinese troops being embarked upon some of the LST's-- the purpose was to transport them to Tsintao, but we thought the war had recommenced; you could hear explosions back clear to our headquarters. It developed that as the Chinese embarked loaded with ammunition turned over to them, someone decided it best not to bring grenades aboard and as each man came over the gangway he would pull the pin and throw his grenade over his shoulder to get rid of it. It wasn't quite the riot that we anticipated but the sound effects made it seem that way. There was one incident after another of that type.

Q: How did you handle the mutiny incident, for instance?

Capt. B.: We always kept our mobile ready outfit to answer such calls. We were limited on communications. Some came by telephone and we did have a few short-wave radios; sometimes a running Chinese would come in--as rickshaw coolies they are pretty good runners--bringing up a message. In our shore patrol headquarters we had to have several interpreters--they were far more versatile in their language capabilities than our American types, as they would speak several languages. (I had a driver who was a White Russian and he spoke many dialects in the Chinese as well as his Russian.) Shanghai being a cosmopolitan city and I assume it still is, there were French, Germans, Russians in all sectors of the city, as well as various Chinese. It is a very unique city, the most colorful city that I have ever experienced. But while the Americans were coming out of the hills, so to speak, from our naval group in China, the Seventh Fleet had come in, there were troops embarked and we had a conglomeration of American personnel that were quite anxious to go home and not at all happy at delays--there were blacks and whites, and we were just coming into the racial problems. This was a new experience to all of us but many problems occurred in rioting, street fights, and the like. Meanwhile the Chinese on the streets of Shanghai were selling razors, knives, brass knuckles, blackjacks--two or three stands on any street corner.

Q: Where were they manufactured?

Capt. B.: By the Chinese. The Americans were I think, first intrigued by the novelty of it and then with so many men, for the futility and the problems of control. I was completely inexperienced with this type of police operation so probably learned something every day--or every night and made my share of mistakes. Meanwhile, the prices--I touched upon our price control system that we worked up, but the Shanghai merchants were trying to make all the money back that they had lost during the war during the time of Japanese occupation. There were many very valuable souvenir type things--fine linens and silks, ivory trinkets and that sort of thing. But, whatever it might be, whether a bar room and the price of drinks or items for taking home, the prices were escalating and this was quite an irritation to American personnel. They had quite a bit of money from having been at sea for a long while, but no one likes to be clipped. That didn't help the situation. Also there were taxi-dance halls that sprang up from nowhere. I had one experience that I'll never forget related to a taxi-dance hall that had, I would say, 500 taxi-dance girls available. It was on the ten cents a dance order--I forget what the actual price per dance was--but the gimmickry there was selling drinks on the side, and girls. Trouble soon developed. We bumped into the black and white issue. On one night the black soldiers might be given liberty and on the alternate night the white sailors. This worked fairly well for a while.

Q: Was it a coordinated thing?

Capt. B.: It developed into that, of alternating the nights, but it all back-fired. I wasn't really aware of it until trouble hit. I knew there were a lot of dance-halls and I looked in on a few of them and thought fun is fun and saw no harm in it until perhaps the schedule got switched and a white sailor would come ashore and find his girl friend of the night before with a black soldier tonight--and as I described before with all the weaponry on the streets--brass knuckles and what-not--fights broke out. On first exposure to this, I took one look and closed this large dance-hall down--put it out-of-bounds and kept it out-of-bounds for five days. I got many complaints from Chinese officials but stood my ground and sincerely felt I was right in so doing. But, about the sixth morning, in my office when I came in was an American. It developed that he was the man behind the dance-halls, and whether true or not, his name was associated with Al Capone. He had been a refugee from the United States living in Shanghai for many years--a Mafia type--and I let him sit for a while. Finally I agreed to talk with him. He walked into my office (meanwhile he tried to send gifts--whiskey and all types of things that we rejected; there was a whole stack of it in our lobby, untouchables and they better damn well remain untouchables--but it was that type of trying to pay off which was the old Oriental custom) and said, "Commander, you have good intentions but you know you are absolutely wrong. You know it won't work." That irritated me somewhat but I did hear him out. He explained saying, "You are having fights break out all over Shanghai and you do not have, and you will never have enough personnel to cover all of Shanghai. The only way that you are going to control things is by opening up my dance-halls again and placing a few more personnel around them and with my cooperation we will quiet fights as they occur." I ran him out of the office, but was humbled a few days later in recognizing that he was absolutely right. There were more fights breaking out, more brutal fights throughout other areas of Shanghai; I talked it over with my Captain who had been an old China hand in the pre-war days, and he said, "We'll have to go their way." And we did.

Q: Did you call this man back in again?

Capt. B.: No, I never faced him again. I did lift the out-of-bounds and let them simmer back into the taxi-dance play, though it only took a couple of nights. But I was quite repulsed by this former American.

That's another typical experience that occurred. I had many of them and must say that perhaps I was not always too fair. I might have a bar tender come in or the owner of a bar and he would want several thousand dollars in damages that had occurred by military personnel in his bar. It wouldn't take many questions to find not only what his prices were but he created an environment that any one would have fought over, and I would brush them off, I would refuse to acknowledge any American responsibility for such things—for which I was criticized. I once put a Merchant Marine officer in the brig. He had somehow managed a room in the Cathay Hotel that wasn't assigned to him and was later caught running down the hall without his clothing, and then he complained to us that he lost his billfold. I didn't sympathize. He complained to the Maritime Union of the harsh treatment that I has given him. Of course nothing ever came of it and I did learn that in such a position you need not and do not always regard the letter of the courts as we know them today. But we did our damndest to level off things. We had problems—one very tragic one occurred when an American sailor driving a six by six truck; he wasn't intoxicated but he was a reckless driver and the truck got out of control and I think there were approximately a dozen people killed as he ran through them--queued up in large groups waiting for something. This was tragic and it took some soothing and resolution of problems with the Chinese.

I recall an incident that troubled me very much. The army provost marshall contacted me one day and he said, "I have a problem involving a couple of American sailors, would you witness my arrest?" He picked me up and took me to some little office building where, on a time basis, we stepped in and I witnessed two sailors aceept 3 or 4 thousand dollars in exchange for their sale of a U.S. military vehicle. They had approached the Chinese on it, the Chinese had reported it to the Provost Marshall and these two sailors who had been at sea for four years were caught red-handed in the transaction that I had to witness. I gave my testimony later and I have always felt badly about it just thinking about a couple of boys four years away from home that probably wouldn't get back for another two or more years. It was that type of thing--trying to quiet them--many incidents occurring, not all of which we could be proud.

Meanwhile there were slashings on the streets, Americans against Americans. I recall one night they brought a young boy in to our headquarters that through his heavy pea coat he had been slashed by a razor, by an American, a black in another racial incident. It required over 200 stitches in that man's back; he survived, but you can well imagine what it takes to go through a navy pea coat and to do that much damage.

Q: What would provoke a fracas like that?

Capt. B.: It was a color issue and that "I want to go home" feeling--it was nothing personal. At that time I called on help from the army Provost Marshall and we brought in every black sailor we could take off the street. Had an amusing incident with it. I had them lined up in the patrol headquarters and I wasn't doing a lick of good, I just didn't get a response, I was mad and ranting and was as sincerely menacing as I could be without laying a hand on anyone. One of my roommates, along with Rocky Ruggieri, was a boy named Frank McLean who had been a personnel officer with SACO. He was a very small fellow from Georgia, rooming with us and awaiting ship to go home. Mac watched me in my frustration, eased up to me and said, "Would you mind my taking a crack at that Buck?" I was rather annoyed but said, "Sure if you think you can do some good," and he said, "Let me have a night stick." He beat on the deck two or three times with that night stick and he said, "You all betta shake down anythin' you've got on you." And you know we had knives, blackjacks, everything dumped on the floor immediately. Little old Frankie just laughed at me and he said, "Takes a Southerner to know how," and he walked out. But that type of incident-- they weren't all funny.

We had other things. It was a revelation to me; although we weren't in investigative type of responsibility I would have to go some times with the Provost Marshall whenever they felt that American navy personnel might be involved. As such, I went with him on a couple of raids of opium dens and had no previous idea of what they might be other than what I had perhaps seen in an unauthentic movie, but they weren't too far different. Smoke filled rooms and girls and pipes--it was clear them out and take them away. You develop a very harsh and cynical attitude. It was not a pleasant experience.

I have touched on this before--the black market was thriving, American cigarettes were going at great prices. We were doing our best to stop this but it was a futile effort with cigarettes abundantly available aboard the ships, and sailors wanting money to afford the prices ashore. There was an incident in which I drew a full case of cigarettes to back one of my men in a pre-arranged sale in which--we were trying to get to the black market source--who was behind this. My representative had been approached, asked for a case, and a price offered him; I got him the cigarettes and said, "Go ahead" and we'll grab them. I was with an "arrest party" of about twelve men hidden in doorways and we weren't a hundred feet away from that transaction--the man took a case of cigarettes and went into a building and we have yet to find hide nor hair of him. We followed him on the run not thirty seconds behind him and we routed everyone out of that building but we never found a thing.

Q: Did you find the cigarettes?

Capt. B.: Not a cigarette, not a paper. As Captain Andrews, my boss, used to say, "Tell me the story about how you stopped the black market." He kidded me quite a bit on that one.

Q: What was your theory on that; how did the man disappear so readily? Was it secret passageways?

Capt. B.: They all worked together. Every one in that building, and there were probably 100 people. I think the cigarettes must have parted a hundred different ways. They are very talented.

Q: What was the attitude of the Chinese officials or were they concerned at all about any of this?

Capt. B.: Not really, I think they were very tolerant; they were very cooperative on the face of things, but could care less about such things as blackmarketing. This had gone on for years if not centuries and that was just a trivial matter. As I have said, there was a much greater interest on the part of the new administration coming in to re-establish themselves, both financially and into the best positions.

We had another interesting experience when Chiang Kai-shek came into Shanghai for the first time in I forget how many years—long before WW2 when he was first driven out—we "body guarded" him into the Cathay Hotel, with army and navy guards combined and stationed every six feet wherever he moved in the hotel, including the elevators, passageways and at all times. He didn't stay long, to our relief, following little pomp and ceremony, he moved on to Peking.

I mentioned General Wedemeyer and the price control which he took over for the army, but Admiral Cook, Commander of the Seventh Fleet, sent for me and was well aware of the problems that were occurring. For each of these incidents we were building a multitude of shore patrol reports, and discipline aboard ship had to be administered there by the commands. Shore patrol does not discipline; we didn't have enough brig space to take care of these people as we brought them in from serious incidents. Admiral Cook called me on the carpet to explain my version of the problem. I had never met him before and I had heard that he was rough and tough, a hard man but he heard my story and asked for my recommendations. My first, "If the Navy is to maintain control, we need a company of Marines to bolster our patrols and assist maintaining order. As they are coming out of Tsingtao they could be assigned to patrol duty here in Shanghai. The city is too large, the problem areas are scattered from the French quarter, German quarter, International Sector, waterfront; it is impossible on vehicles to do it otherwise." Admiral Cook replied, "You are not going to get a company of Marines. What is your second recommendation?" My second recommendation, "For every man that we arrest, the Commanding Officer should come and get him. I hope that will bring a stronger discipline from the ship's side so that they are not smiling at escapades that are happening ashore." So he ordered that, and it did help.

Q: You mean the skipper of the ship had to come and get his man?

Capt. B.: He had to get every man that we arrested and notified the ship. It happened in the early stages that the commanding officer might be coming in to get a dozen men that had been arrested in that period. But it did have effect.

I tell these stories only to indicate that it was not all just "Let's catch the next ship home." Sure we had a lot of funny incidents. A naval officer friend of mine stole Admiral Kinkaid's piano; they put it on a rickshaw got it aboard a LIBERTY ship and its been one of the classic stories of Admiral Miles' group since. Incidentally the man who stole the piano, Commander Archie Brown, is a federal judge today. When I had the Intelligence School later he was also commanding officer of a reserve unit and would send his people to Coronado for the two week intelligence course. He attended a course himself and we renewed some of these old tales, but out of orneriness I enjoyed telling his reserve officers about the time Archie stole the piano. He was put in hack for three days, missed his ship going home but was put on the next one. That too was kind of a joke from the higher level.

Q: And the end of that story, did Kinkaid get his piano back?

Capt. B.: No, he raised a little hell about it, was mad at his aide more than anything else that it was taken from his suite. He liked to play the piano, it was a relaxing situation to him. A piano was dug up from some place in the depths of the hotel just for his amusement; but I think the boys who put it in that cargo hold probably got better use out of it going home than he did. I had several complaints, from Archie Brown, down in Texas, saying, "look can't you knock off that story to my people?" So

I told it more often.

These are some of the unpleasant things! I had one suicide case, a young man that I knew, he had been in one of the China camps. It was rough times, he was a very religious boy, a Chief Yoeman at the age of 21, a very capable lad and very well liked. In the evils of Shanghai he became involved with a prostitute and it so shook him up with his religious beliefs and background that he committed suicide for which I got into almost serious trouble. I got the call personally, not knowing what it was, and found a letter to his parents and I withheld the letter. I didn't think it was a fitting thing to pass to the parents, it was more of a confession of the problem.

Q: He was outlining his problem?

Capt. B.: He outlined exactly why and apologized to his parents and I just didn't think it was a fitting thing. However, I didn't destroy the letter, I put it in my safe but I got a pretty good reading on regulations and the violations of it by the Chief of Staff before I produced the letter.

Q: They knew it existed?

Capt. B.: Someone observed and said that I had taken it and I thought it just as well that they thought I had destroyed it. I don't think they ever delivered the letter but Chief of Staff was making it clear to me that there were regulation ways of handling such things.

There were many unpleasant things and meanwhile a hell of

a lot of fun. There was a lot of activity.

Q: How long a period was this?

Capt. B.: From September until, I think I came home in April, it was about six months of intense activity. It was slowing down then.

Q: What sort of living quarters did you have? Under what circumstances did you exist?

Capt. B.: I lived very well. Starting from the time when I handled billeting. Although the purpose was for location, I had a small room in the Cathay Hotel which as I have described, was known as the finest hotel in the East. Later, with my various jobs and in order to be accessible to our Naval Headquarters round the clock, I retained a larger room (I always had roommates--Rocky Ruggieri, Frank McLean) a three bedroom in the Cathay. Our meals--we mostly ate in our room, and I would say today you would term this as a several hundred dollars a day suite--had a bath and we had hot water, it even had a little servant ante room on the side. I once had a coomodore come into my room and he said, "I lived in this room back in the '30s with my wife and my two children and it cost us five dollars a day." Times have changed. I don't know about the settlement but at that time no individual was paying hotel bills, we had just taken over the Cathay, the Palace and the Park Hotels and they were clearing houses both for fleet personnel and for field personnel as they were processed for going home. We were moving them out as fast as we could. Any type of cargo or transport ship would be loaded with troops, personnel going home. The ships I spoke of earlier that were stranded, were turned over to the Chinese. They were more the amphibious, the slow moving types, and they were not used for moving troops back home.

Q: Was it the intention of the Americans to move out entirely at some future date?

Capt. B.: I had no awareness of future plans and policy. At the time I returned, I believe I have told the story about the dispatch from BuPers came in to my commanding officer, which had been initiated by my brother back in Ohio, wanting me to answer whether or not I wanted this coaching job--football coaching job--in Cincinnati. I had not heard from anyone concerning the job, nor had mail service improved. We went for several months without mail, everyone blamed the typhoon in Okinawa that hit the post office--this was a standard gag but it did actually occur--but if you didn't get any mail for two or three months it must have been that typhoon in Okinawa! Well I had heard nothing of this coaching offer and wasn't very interested. My Captain, Jack Andrews said, "We've got to answer BuPers on it. Why don't you go home; I'll give you two weeks leave and after you get there send me a telegram and I'll extend your leave two weeks. You've been out a long while. It will be good for you, but before we do this, I want you to go before the Integration Board for U.S. Navy. You tell me you are coming back so we'll take care of that right now." So I did.

Q: You went back by way of ship?

Capt. B.: No, they flew me back and things looked pretty good back here and I also got together with Helen. This influenced my decision to accept the job at Xavier, so I went on to Washington and saw 'Mary Miles'. I had some courier materials to deliver to the Admiral in Washington. I never heard anything of that Integration Board decision until 1963. I happened to be back on a Selection Board for the Navy; had never seen my own jacket and thought I would look at my own record. I found I had been integrated into the navy back in 1946. But that too never reached me, just like the job offer.

In any event I came to Washington at which time I separated from the service. 'Mary Miles' pulled a little trick on me then; I reported to him...

Q: What was his job in Washington?

Capt. B.: I think compiling a somewhat historical report which was the basis for his first book, SACO, The Rice Paddy Navy, that Roy Stratton developed later. I saw the Admiral alone in his office and he started quizzing me. "Now give me the straight story. Did Archie Brown steal that piano?" (This happened after the Admiral departed Shanghai.) We talked about such matters and he wanted to know of incidents that had occurred after his departure. Then he said, "I have a conference coming up but if you wouldn't mind waiting over in the next room, I'll see you later." So I went into the next room and there were six of my buddies from SACO, all working for him as his staff--which he hadn't told me a word about. We took it from there. It took me about three days to get separated due to their help.

Q: It was a long and tortuous process?

Capt. B.: I was very much intrigued with China and that later influenced my plans to the point of going back to graduate school on Far East studies. I was very serious and hopeful of getting into Foreign Service type work. I have told you about some of my experiences at Columbia, but one that I think influenced my thinking most was the impression I was getting that liberalism, communism and radicalism was the trend of both students and faculty philosophy. I was very cynical about some of the graduate school teaching and their attitudes. In 1948, in the middle of a personnel cut-back I was asked to come back to active service--that due to another former commanding officer of mine who was the professor of Naval Science at Columbia; he asked me to come back on active duty, still as a Reserve Officer. I did, with the conviction that the military had as much, if not more, really political strength and influence at that time than did the Foreign Serice in the State Department. I guess I was also influenced somewhat by the fact that General Eisenhower had come to Columbia. I was coaching football as an assistant to Lou Little during this period.

Q: You had some direct contact with him?

Capt. B.: Ike only worked half a day. His blood pressure was pretty high and he spent several afternoons a week just coming out and watching football practice, and chatting with the boys. I was very much surprised when they recalled him to military duty in NATO, with the knowledge that he wasn't in the best of health. I marvelled that with the pressures he operated under both with NATO and then the presidency, how he survived as long as he did.

Q: By that time they were developing drugs to control the blood pressure, weren't they?

Capt. B.: That is probably the situation; but he would literally come out and sit in the stands, just sitting in the sun and he would say, "Well, I'm just a little tired today." He didn't do the things that he did later, he didn't play much golf, but he did get back into the active swing.

In any event I was back in the military.

Q: Did you have any occasion to talk with Eisenhower about your thinking along the lines of military versus diplomatic service?

Capt. B.: No I didn't, I had some indirect comments, exchange of things. An interesting story on Lou Little--he had been at Columbia for a number of years as football coach...

Q: Thirty, and was nationally known.

Capt. B.: And we had a very good year my first season there. I think I told you how I came there. Lou assigned me to scout Army along with another fellow named Bob Bruce. At that time Army had the record throughout college of continuous winning, I don't think they dropped a game in three years. So Bob Bruce and I scouted them for five weeks and Columbia broke the win streak.

Q: You picked up some points?

Capt. B.: In all honesty it wasn't our scouting as much as it was the boys catching passes and throwing them and the breaks of the game. But that fairly well established me and the rapport with Lou Little, who was a very colorful and unique person. All the other assistants had played under Lou so he was always Mr. Little and treated with the greatest of respect and almost fear, but I had met him as "lou" and you don't back down from a first name introduction, I didn't. I had a very pleasant relationship with Lou and I--we would exchange, he woudl tell me stories of the old days--even had me help with some ghost writing for magazines. He would say, "You know these stories, write 'em." He didn't want to bother with them. One of them occurred and this is the point of my story. At the end of that season Lou was offered the Athletic Directorship and Head Coaching job at Yale, which was higher paying, and with a lot of other niceties included. I don't express a preference between the schools but a lot of desirable things were at Yale and different from the New York environment. Lou had given his verbal acceptance to Yale when he was asked to come down to Washington with General Donovan to meet General Eisenhower, who was then considering coming to Columbia. So Lou had breakfast with the General and the substance of that, as told by Lou, the general said, "Lou, there are only two people I know of at Columbia, one was Nicholas Murray Butler and the other is Lou Little. Butler is dead; you are not going to leave me are you?" Lou cancelled the job at Yale and remained at Columbia until his retirement. There are a hundred and one stories on Lou--but this is factual.

Q: That came from him direct? He was in the category with Bob Zuppke and others--the great coaches of the past.

Capt. B.: Yes. Lou had cancer of the throat. I'll go back another step--part of my rapport with Lou--he had been at the University of Pennsylvania in WW1 and had gone into the service. I believe he came out of the army as a Captain. He went to Europe and got so seasick that upon his return he swore he would never set foot on a ship again. He used to say, "You ride those ships! You don't mind it?" He thought, as a naval officer, that I was part of a super-human group and he was really funny about it. He dreaded ships and he just felt anyone who did that must have a cast-iron stomach. As I started to say, his rapport with the General, and there were a lot of exchanges made in good humor and some were serious as Lou repeated very often, "The general promised me two big tackles if he came to Columbia," but we never did get those tackles.

Q: Where was the general going to get them, from West Point?

Capt. B.: In any event, I continued at Columbia. The Korean War broke out. I still wasn't taking the navy very seriously; I enjoyed every bit of my experience but I was a reserve officer and I hadn't thought of it on a career basis as yet. That's why I went back to the graduate school, but being recalled...

Q: Let me ask--how did Helen look at this whole problem?

Capt. B.: We were newly married, we were married in '46. I had had an unsuccessful and dissatisfying year of football at Xavier and I left there under mutual agreement, then went to Columbia. It was a new experience to both of us. It was not the most affluent living by any means; there was a housing shortage in New York and we lived in the Columbia sponsored community residence, an estate called "Nevis", in Westchester and it was a year and a half before we got an apartment of our own. We both went to school and enjoyed it. We did it together and we commuted together. I did a lot of scouting and Helen would go with me on weekends; meanwhile I also was working for the Professional League, scouting for them. We had good times but I think Helen's feeling was "What are you going to do, are you going to continue on the football route?" But Helen had no navy background until I was recalled and it really is not navy life to be an assistant professor of Naval Science in a university. I wore a uniform and she met a few other navy families in the same category, but with the Korean War I would have felt very wrong in getting out at a time when I was told I was one of the few people on active duty with a WW2 background in the special operations field--that's what they contended the computer kicked out down in Washinton. Also, it was another experience to set up a new outfit, to be a commanding officer. I had a funny one there, when they did send me orders, that I would be commanding officer of Beach Jumper Unit II--what in the world was that? So I called the flag secretary at ComPhibLant at Little Creek (Virginia) and instead of getting the flag secretary, a fellow named Lieutenant Commander Phil Porter, for some reason Admiral Robbie Briscoe answered the phone. I thought I was talking to the flag secretary and said, "What in the hell is a Beach Jumper Unit?" I didn't realize until we had talked for about ten minutes that this was the Admiral and not the secretary, but he said, "I'll tell you, its what we make of it. There has never been a Beach Jumper Unit and there are a lot of ideas we are going to put together here." He gave me some generalities and he said, "We'll sit down and talk this over when you get here." It was about that time I realized I was talking to a three-star admiral.

Q: What did Lou Little think of this turn of events?

Capt. B.: At the time I went back on active duty, I had just taken a full-time job with Lou. It worked out very well. I told the navy I had signed a contract, which you do for football in the spring to carry through the fall. Navy had contacted me in June to start the NROTC fall semester and considered the football to be fine for public relations. They realized that football practice doesn't commence until five in the afternoon at Columbia so you can carry your full schedule on both jobs. The same thing applied with Lou. He had some ulterior motives I am sure; he made it known to me as time went on; he wanted some of his football boys protected from the draft and felt that if I were with the NROTC I could shepherd them. I did, and I defend doing it in that some are still on active duty. Of those that I got into the NROTC program, five of them served with me later, each served longer than was required--at least five years of active duty after being commissioned. I met one not long ago who is now a marine aviator colonel. I believe I told you about him--the navy wouldn't accept him because of mal-occlusion so we got him into the Marine program and he has had a very successful career.

After I went to Little Creek, Admiral Briscoe was relieved by Admiral Spike Fahrion, a very avid football fan. and with my football background I was made football coach in addition (always additional duties) to my Beach Jumper command duties.

Q: You were also 'in' with the Admiral?

Capt. B.: It did help.

Q: When did you move down to Little Creek?

Capt. B.: In June 1951. I was there until 1956.

Q: That was quite a spell.

Capt. B.: Yes it was. Again, due to Spike Fahrion—I left there about a month ahead of him. He would make the statement, "You were the only man here who has been here longer than I have. It won't end up that way." We got along great. Later they dropped football.

I went to Korea from Little Creek and I didn't see Spike for about three years and he retired at La Jolla.

Q: His last assignment was at Philadelphia, wasn't it?

Capt. B.: No, he retired from ComPhibLant. You are thinking possibly about Rear Admiral Bob Speck who went to Philadelphia. He had been Chief of Staff and he went to the Philadelphia yard and then to command of the Home after retirement.

I met Spike about three years after his retirement when I returned from Korea and we visited him up at La Jolla and you know he started giving me hell right away. He said, "You had no business letting them drop football at Little Creek, I was in Korea," and he said, "That has nothing to do with it." He was that way and we had a lot of laughs.

The navy coach came in at Norfolk then, his first coaching job.

Q: Welsh? Now tell me about sitting down with Admiral Briscoe, when you first went down there, tossing around ideas as to what you were going to do?

Capt. B.: Admiral Briscoe was a man with singular ideas and beliefs. He had been in Research and Development and believed there was much that could be done, that the surface had been scratched in this field in WW2 but particularly in electronic warfare, in the use of jamming, in the use of deception tactics, communication monitoring, and that this electronic capability should be combined with the several other specialized small units which included capabilities like the underwater demolition teams, the ranger type operations. That was the actual intent and basic doctrine that the Beach Jumper Unit was set up on, but with the Korean War, it didn't work out that way at that time.

Q: He, himself, was involved in the Korean war, wasn't he?

Capt. B.: Yes, he went from Commander of Amphibious Forces, Atlantic back to the Pentagon as Op 03, Operations, so his part of the Korean War was from the Pentagon as Operations. I think I mentioned, that we got the BJUs going pretty good with Atlantic Fleet operations and he was aware of it. I was called to Washington and asked if my people were ready to go to Korea. I said, "I've got a pretty good outfit; what type of tasks do you anticipate?" He said, "Well, just like it was from the beginning, you will probably be used however the commanders out there can use you, on your general and versatile capabilities." And I said, "I think we are ready for that." He said, "The Pacific Unit is not yet ready but if you are willing and able to go from the Atlantic?" "Yes Sir." Then he was told, "But you can't do that Admiral, you will have to go through the PacFleet commander and we cannot, from our Washington position, send people to the other theatre."

Q: Were you under CincLant?

Capt. B.: Yes, we were under Lant. Our unit then, did not go to the Pacific. They didn't use either of the units there. So our participations were mainly in landing exercises and various fleet training activities. We started from scratch but built up a squadron of ten boats with various electronic warfare capabilities.

Q: Tell me how you built it up. You were the moving force.

Capt. B.: At the first meeting with Admiral Briscoe we talked in general terms. He said, "I want you to go up to Washington and spend a couple of weeks there. In the Plans section there is a Captain Renken, talk to him and spend time with him, read all the background you can, then we will take it from there. I did that.

Q: This was an entirely new concept because it didn't exist in any other navy, did it?

Capt. B.: The British, in part, but none of it with the coordination of these units. I might skip ahead. This is what happened to me in 1963, which is the Special Warfare Group today, so that lapse from 1951 to 1963 occurred before we finally became coordinated. When I was tasked to organize the capabilities in 1963, we were called the Pacific Support Group--that was because Admiral Rivero didn't like the term Special Operations within the Navy.

Q: Why didn't he like that?

Capt. B.: I don't know. Admiral Rivero didn't like a lot of things. In fact, when I reported to Washington in 1967, I'm skipping around the years, (I was the first commanding officer of what was called the Naval Operations Support Group that included the SEALS, the UDTs, Boat Support Group, BJUG, and various things inVietnam) and at the change of command there was a little publicity on it and I had been asked the question by some of the press, "Do your men wear green berets?" I said, "No, but as a matter of fact they are wearing green berets,"-- the boys had adopted them themselves. The press made quite an issue of 'New Outfit Formed, Black Berets' so when I met Admiral Rivero the first time he said, "We call them 'White Hats' in the navy, I don't know any 'black berets' and I want that term wiped out." I hadn't really used it in the sense that the press played it.

Q: What was Admiral Rivero, V-CNO?

Capt. B.: Yes, he was V-CNO, and he was determined, in fact he put it in writing, that the navy would not become involved in any shallow river, muddy warfare. As we know, the picture changed in Vietman and the navy became very much involved. But that was his determination when he was V-CNO.

I don't mean that as a criticism of Admiral Rivero but he was a positive man in his thinking and he was in a powerful position.

Q: Would you go back to what you started to tell me--how you began to build up this unit at Little Creek?

Capt. B.: Well, we jumped quite a bit. I suppose we had maybe 25 or 30 men at the time of commission and within 2 or 3 days following my arrival (a few of the officers were there ahead of me and we actually had about 20 officers being assigned, more officers ratio-wise than enlisted men that were intended for this type of work).

Q: What kind of background did they have?

Capt. B.: Most of these boys at that time were recalls after very brief WW2 service. They were young. It was unfortunate that it was a very difficult time for the boys in that many of them had come into the service in 1945 and they were out in 1946 and they were just getting established in jobs when recalled. One of my boys was with Alcoa; he had spent two years under training programs with them and was called back into the service again just at the time when he reached the first rung of the ladder. Others were teaching school but just getting their feet on the ground financially being recalled they didn't know if it was for another four-year period. As it had been in New York, it was a difficult time in Norfolk, there wasn't sufficient housing. Helen and I lived in a single room with a bath at the end of the hall for 2 or 3 months before we could find any place to live. These people coming in, if you could get a small motel room you were very fortunate, though it was costly. It wasn't a pleasant situation at all.

Q: I wouldn't think these men were very happy then at this assignment?

Capt. B.: Well, the combination of things, being recalled and as you remember, it wasn't the great wave of WW2 patriotism--let me in the service, I want to go and do my part--at that stage. In no way do I imply that I had an embittered group, but they had their problems. Three out of four were newly married and there were young babies--that sort of thing, and the personal hardship of trying to get them situated, and the uncertainty of how long they were going to be in this. Two or three of them had come off ships and they were far better established as they had been in the service longer.

Q: You then had morale problems?

Capt. B.: Well, it was a good outfit and it all worked out very well and we did it together. They had assigned us a headquarters building in what had been a brig. Everything about this Beach Jumper Unit, all the previous WW2 doctrine was top secret--not secret but top secret. We finally got the overall status downgraded to secret which was a major accomplishment. Those who knew this was going to be a classified operation felt that this brig would be an ideal location.

Q: That's a curious association.

Capt. B.: It is still there and operational today. There were a lot of changes made—started by us. Admiral Briscoe commissioned us. They brought down from PhibLant headquarters folding chairs and a big pot of flowers, (the pot of flowers has remained in this story over the years), a coffee urn, and a plate of cookies and we were officially and formally commissioned by Admiral Briscoe. One hour later there wasn't a chair in the place and they even took the pot of flowers. So we were all in the brig.

Q: It was all cosmetic? You were all photographed with the pot of flowers?

Capt. B.: That's right, that pot of flowers goes with every story on how Beach Jumpers were formed. We had not a stick of equipment nor had anything been requisitioned, nor any plans developed to the point of knowledge of what equipments we might need.

Q: The Admiral was perfectly right on the telephone, you had to come down and talk about it.

Capt. B.: I spent a couple of weeks in Washington, picked up some background there and brought a few papers back on WW2 operations, top secret knocked out, not just secret; we didn't have a safe but we did have a brig. We scrounged a little bit of furniture, begged tables and would sit and scheme how to start this.

Q: You didn't have any enlisted men on deck at that point?

Capt. B.: I had about 15 and this bo's'un mate (I saw him a few years ago) made the point, (along with the pot of flowers), he said, "When they left we didn't even have a broom." So it was his job--he begged, borrowed, or stole and I never asked him--he got brooms and the men cleared this place out and we started renovating. In the cells, we knocked down walls and made them into offices, conference rooms and various things of our first building. The first equipment that we received--we started requisitioning everything from brooms to whatnot--and ironically the first load of equipment delivered to us were 50 G.I. cans, so we had G.I. cans stacked all over the place. It wasn't all that bad however; it took some time and some doing and ultimately we ended up taking over a barn next door which we made into a sail loft. They later provided us with one of the Butler Buildings--aluminum ones--where we had shop equipment. Ultimately we had 12 boats on which we had distributed among our 12-boat squadron the electronics equivalent of a cruiser and worked it into a team effort by which we did intercept, monitoring and jamming. We got into some things due to the trend of the times; we had a lot of fun with it perhaps and gained a lot of questionable experience. At the time, the atomic threat was very urgent among all type of operations and particularly the amphibious landings. The concern existed that one nuclear weapon in the heart of an amphibious landing might destroy all. So we were tasked with providing a simulated atomic explosion and with enough deception that the ships could read something on their radars. We got into a by-play of balloon type--kytoon--operations. I never heard of these before but there is a piece of equipment called a kytoon, which would appear to be a miniature zeppelin type balloon, inflated it would be 15 to 20 feet in over all length and maybe 8 or 10 feet in depth. By the use of these balloons towed behind our boats to simulate the speed of a ship, and from them using radar reflectors dangling as you might a kite tail, we could simulate a slow movement of aircraft--we didn't then have the speed movement--and this was how parochial we started; we even experimented with box kites, and various kinds of equipments that we could tow; we used smoke pots to create the visual illusion of explosions and we used as many as 50 of them at a time. Our men were all checked out in demolitions and we simulated gunfire by explosive charges, also beach and land mines. We learned by feel and experiment. Again we were the general handymen, whatever jobs they needed they would throw us in.

Q: How did you generate these ideas?

Capt. B.: A combination of ideas, no single person could plan such activity. I had one very capable fellow, an academic type, an assistant professor at the University of Miami, who was great on researching. Sometimes I would accuse him of getting ideas out of the Weird Story magazine; some worked some didn't, but with round table discussions we could conceive both through experience of what we had done and what might be and give it a whirl. We developed our own shops and we built our own equipment.

Q: How valuable was your own background experience in this?

Capt. B.: I probably enjoyed the boat operations most, I had the best feel for that. I had over all amphibious background and how deceptions could be related, maybe more so than my younger officers who had not been in actual combat landings and didn't always visualize other than what you saw in training films and that sort of thing. I think we each and all contributed in a different way. We were broken up—we had our boat section, an ordnance and demolition section, an air section which included the kites and the other electronics, and a plans section.

Q: How large did you grow in numbers in order to be this way?

Capt. B.: Our complement was about 100 enlisted and 20 officers. However, due to our good friend and sponsor, Admiral Fahrion, any athlete who came into the amphibious force was automatically assigned to my outfit, so I ran to about 30 officers and 220 men before my tour ended. Athletically, we participated after hours, in fact we had one amphibious landing during the football season that we brought half the team in by boat an hour before game time--just made it--left from the locker room back out to the landing area.

Q: How disturbing were you to the community in which you lived?

You spoke of jamming--what did you jam?

Capt. B.: That is definitely a problem to the present day. There are no suitable training areas within the continental United States, east coast or west coast. It is a tremendous problem and you have to stick to certain frequencies or jam all the commercial and civilian television along the coast. We had some problems of that type and you have the same problem with demolitions. A charge of the type I described that we used in Normandy would have blown out every wondow in Norfolk and the Virginia Beach area. We had to train with lighter charges until you would get down to some places like Guantanamo--Guantanamo Bay was, is, the only real firing area that we have on the east coast. The Camp Lejeune area is partially restricted, you still don't use heavy charges and you have to limit your electronics activity. Many schemes were developed. Sometimes it was simply the refuting of them, a task that we would have during the amphibious landings. We would have at least two major amphibious landings a year in which the entire force would participate, on these we would become the aggressor force--the enemy.

Q: This is under the aegis of CincLant?

Capt. B.: Right. We used our boats for sneal attacks to train our ships in alert and the like. We were quite successful in this, as people tend to take a lax attitude until they get blasted at the critique pretty hard. Admiral Fahrion thrived on that and it roused, at times, some antagonism within the force: This little outfit that gives us a hard time! I had one experience that old Spike pulled me out on: We knew that the communicator and the communications staff at PhibLant because of their problems and conflict between commercial and military could, on in-house communications from flagship to the various ships go in the force, through Radio Washington with relay back to the ships. By this method they could read on the hour and get their messages without interference to overall commercial frequencies and the like. We contended from the beginning it could be jammed or intercepted. The landing exercise was scheduled for six or seven days duration and about the third day or third night, we put our own message in to Radio Washington, under guise of being ComPhibLant, and asked that each commanding officer report aboard the flagship at ten o'clock the following day with the purpose of suggestions on terminating the training exercise. Now I was a little cautious, but thought that last part of our message was ridiculous enough that they would read through it but that we would get it on record that we--a deception outfit--could do the same thing they were trying to do fleetwide. However, about 50% of the commanding officers reported to the flagship the following day and confusion prevailed. They were complying with the orders they had received in this accepted communication channel, and it took several days before they found out where it originated.

Q: None of them guessed it immediately?

Capt. B.: No, they missed it, they took it for gospel, which proved my point very well. Captain Bob Speck was chief of staff and when we got back he called me on the carpet and he was chewing me out thoroughly for doing such a thing. I protested that, "We were trying to prove that a deception outfit can do it if you can do it." He was beating the desk when Spike Fahrion came in from his cabin next door and said, "Buck, that was a great maneuver, it proved a point." He pulled me off the hook with Speck who closed our discussion with "Get out." We had many incidents of that type--trial and error. We sometimes proved a point; it sounds like a very small thing but it threw that whole communications concept out. The same deception principles today apply in Europe, Iran, and a lot of places you can do that today, and you can do so much more than I can cite. We have the electronic power and the jammers that could blank out an entire country, radio communications as well as commercial television. This is a relatively simple action. During this same 1950s period, the cruiser NORTHAMPTON was being outfitted with electronic equipments to do this from a large ship level and in compact centralized form, rather than distributing capability among a bunch of small craft. That was one early facet of development.

We had many other things going. We were tasked with various assignments.

Q: Did the Atlantic Fleet give you assignments too?

Capt. B.: Occasionally.

Q: They began to cooperate?

Capt. B.: Yes. Of course we had many and varying (Admiral Claude V. Ricketts was my first operations boss, he was Captain Ricketts then) assignments in several instances when we were developing a plan theory, Captain Ricketts would say "Come on", would reach for his briefcase and we would walk over to CincLant Fleet headquarters. He would go right with you and follow it through on the spot, and with his help, things would get done, things a lieutenant commander could not have done in a month, so we got to moving. Meanwhile we were requisitioning equipments and building up various facilities.

Q: Did you have any problems with your requisitions?

Capt. B.: We got response with some help and I pulled a few ignorant maneuvers I suppose. I became very frustrated at one stage when it was very slow in outfitting, in starting from scratch, and I prepared a report citing the salaries, the costs of officers and personnel and the waste and inactivity that was being incurred. At that time I think Admiral Briscoe was down at Guantanamo on the flagship and his response came back via the Logistics Officer, who was much senior to me. We talked it over and had a little tension for a while, but every requisition went through and the flow of equipments soon began.

The navy didn't have available all new equipments that we requested, but things came in--shop equipments, lathes, tools came from around the countryside, and within the next two or three months we had a going concern. With boats, I would come to Washington and BuShips and we would trace down every suitable boat. I mentioned earlier the Soviets, about this time they were turning back some of the WW2 PTs--they were junk but rather than pay for them, they were giving them back to the U.S.

Q: They also turned back the MILWAUKEE as junk.

Capt. B.: Well, we would have to inspect each of these and decide if it was feasible to bring it to a state of repair so we could use it. Not many of them were, most of our boats were air-sea rescue types. CNO was then appropriating some funds for prototype PTs and trying to keep that program alive and, at one stage, I had operational control temporarily, (because they were 'test and evaluation'), of four aluminum hull PTs, very high speed boats, all above 80 knots. They worked a couple of weeks operations with us on sneak attack work, (in fact we broke the record with them and we kept them operating for 24 hours continuously). They had never continuously operated that long before without breakdowns. Of those same boats, I had two of them assigned to our SEAL teams during Vietnam and they ended up being used as torpedoe targets--worn out, and no spare parts in existence or production.

Q: Those you had down at Little Creek were they under the aegis of the MISSISSIPPI?

Capt. B.: They were under CincLantFlt control and it was the Test and Evaluation Group they came under.

Q: The MISSISSIPPI was stationed down there--the mother ship--for that whole effort, I think.

Capt. B.: They had a lieutenant commander in charge of this project. He and his crews--they were never integrated into our outfit--were assigned to us as a component and worked with us at that time.

Meanwhile, we tested and evaluated several different boats for CIA. I set up a division or department to handle these various projects. CIA was running all types of tests on clandestine type craft, (they might assign one man to the project), and my people would do the testing, make the reports on them, make recommendations on their capabilities.

Q" Was there any problem with the navy as such doing this sort of thing, it wasn't under contract to the CIA?

Capt. B.: Not to my knowledge. We had the same situation on the first hydrofoil boats, HIGH POCKETS they called it. It was a little fellow about 20 feet long, a prototype. We worked with HIGH POCKETS and tested it every way and tried to break it up for six months. We also had the Baker Boat which was a hydrofoil, powered by aircraft engines. While working with us the Philippine attaché visited and we took him for a ride; we had Baker himself with us at the time, on contract to the navy for six months. The attaché, when he got off the boat asked, "How much would they cost?" I think at that time they were about $300 thousand apiece and he said, "I want three immediately for the presidential campaign in the Philippines. They will be ideal to go from island to island." I checked on those boats years later when I was stationed at Subic Bay and was told "you can see them over on the beach." For lack of maintenance and spare parts they had been beached and abandoned.

Q: They had been in use?

Capt. B.: They used them, with no maintenance, when they broke down they ran them up on the beach and they were scuttled there. In test and evaluation we worked with many and all types of boats. We used that little hydrofoil boat on sneak attacks and proved a lot of things against our ships. Our radar rooms wouldn't pick them up. It proved the need of improvement within our own forces. In that sense, though we were not accomplishing anything significant operationally, we were assisting, you might say we were a support unit. We had other assignments, ridiculous things—they were making movies of amphibious landings, big navy projects about that time. One of the movies was "Aweigh All Boats". We had to simulate the gun fire at night, which we could do, and this developed into another little personal incident. Bloodsworth Island was the firing zone so we took the movie people up to Bloodsworth and with our developed simulators, flashers really, which gave the appearance of a naval gun at least for camera effects. The weather turned bad, a little choppy and the boys were bringing the movie people back from Bloodsworth Island down to Norfolk; the camera people huddled down in the engine room to keep warm (these were gasoline fired boats, former air-sea rescue boats and not in too good condition--as good as we could make them, but they were antiques). There were some sparks flying in the engine room; we were accustomed to that, knew our own cautions and not to do foolish things. It developed into quite an incident. These movie people felt they had been in some very dangerous situation and commented about it to Captain Eph Holmes, who was then our OP's officer on PhibLant. He called me in and was quite disturbed about the matter and finally said, "This could jeopardize your and my naval careers if you had an incident of this type. Why haven't I heard this before?" I responded, "Captain, you will find a report in your files for every month, once a month for the past year spelling out the problems and the changes and the repairs that are recommended." He went to his file, found the reports and said, "As of this moment you are grounded, those boats will not operate in that condition." "Aye, aye, Sir."

A couple of weeks later the flagship was out preparing for a hurricane warning; the full force was away from the Norfolk piers and into the Chesapeake Bay area dispersing to safe haven areas. I received a message one morning asking us to bring the morning papers out to the flagship. I came back with a message that said, "Squadron grounded." So I took the papers out personally, also got authorization for repair and maintenance on all the boats.

Q: How long had you been grounded?

Capt. B.: That was only for a couple of weeks, but it had taken about a year in pointing out our problems. It was that kind of a struggle.

I don't mean that was negligence of the navy--there wasn't any money; it was very tight throughout that period.

Q: And you certainly weren't in the main stream of action.

Capt. B.: That's right, we weren't vital to the war effort--if there was one. Of course that was before things popped. It was a Congressional problem; same as exists today on money matters and many things military. I recall, on landing craft, at that time you could buy a new landing craft off the production line for 75 hundred dollars, which Congress would not approve, but it was costing 10 thousand dollars to repair the WW2 ones that were being used. False economy.

Q: On these projects you undertook and the things you proved as the result of your efforts, did the navy take these up and do something about it?

Capt. B.: The concept changed over a period of years--not overnight. The electronic concept was separated from the small boats and moved up; it was developed and it exists today with larger ships. At one stage, for example, each cruiser had a sealed electronic compartment that was not used as a part of their routine operations. Then came the PUEBLO at which time, ironically, I was in the Pentagon and the PUEBLO came under us, although it was under National Security Agency control and not under the navy. But it was the same concept of outfitting a ship electronically for a purpose—in this case the PUEBLO—for monitoring enemy communications. The concept had been developed and the other aspects of it that I mentioned earlier. In 1963, the "special warfare units" were coordinated under Atlantic Pacific Fleet commands by pulling together the smaller commands including the Underwater Demolition Teams, the SEAL teams, and at that time, the Beach Jumpers. Under my old operations officer, Captain Eph Holmes; I was selected by Vice-admiral Eph Holmes, ComPhibPac, to go right back to where we were, 1951-56, and to coordinate these commands which were first called the "Naval Operations Support Group" and today called the "Naval Special Operations Group", Atlantic and Pacific.

Q: Did the NSA people get into the picture with the electronics part of it?

Capt. B.: Not actively at that 1950s stage. I had only one encounter that I personally experienced. I was called to Washington in the mid '50s and asked could we monitor a Soviet Navy maneuver. Nothing ever came of it. They wanted me to rig a fishing boat with electronic equipment and operate it in the Caspian Sea at a time of Soviet maneuvers and asked "Is it feasible?" I replied, "I guess its feasible, its starting from scratch, I don't welcome the opportunity but I believe we would be the most capable source if you decide to do it." I heard nothing more on that. That's the only contact I had directly with them. We had numerous Washington visitors during this overall period. They would come down, some times would ride our boats during these various maneuvers, and would become very enthusiastic about it.

Q: Were you tempted or did you do anything with the Russian fishing trawlers who were following our fleet units around for all the operations in the Caribbean and so forth?

Capt. B.: No, they weren't as active at that period of time and we wouldn't have had the real sea going capacity.

Q: They became more active after the missile crisis, didn't they?

Capt. B.: That's right. Round the world. It was happening in the Pacific, in the Baltic and wherever. There were destroyers that were playing tag with them at that stage. We were getting a lot of reports of that type while we were in Korea.

Q: At that stage of the game what were you doing with the UDT people down in Little Creeek, Virginia?

Capt. B.: We not only put all of our people there, we had a UDT detachment with the BJU. We used explosives on simulators and various deception equipments, so all of our people went through UDT course. It was intended (though I didn't talk about it as I had had my instructions from Admiral Briscoe back in the beginning) to take over the UDT, (as was later done with Naval Operations Support Group), but they were old buddies of mine and we had a good rivalry, athletically, and they worked with us often. They rode our boats in operations and we worked together. I never did discuss with them that—"We're supposed to take you over." In fact, they had their own problems at that time on which Admiral Fahrion pulled them off the hook. They were having their administrative problems in getting pushed back under the training command's control and UDT was fighting for survival. The Korean War revived them. They were assigned to the Beach Group but Admiral Fahrion said, "I don't like that. I want you assigned to my control." We, the commanding officers of the UDTs and myself (BJU) were assigned additional duty on ComPhibLant staff. We went out to the flagship, the UDT and the UDU commanding officer and myself, together, attending two staff meetings a week. BJUs were already established but Admiral Fahrion was the one who pulled UDTs from under the training and kept then in an operational capacity.

Q: They had certainly proved themselves in WW2—this was lost sight of so quickly?

Capt. B.: Yes. That is the most regrettable thing I have seen in my years with specialized warfare units—that in the lessons learned and the importance of keeping alive and active at least small components of these capabilities—it is forgotten every five years. It is the criticism of the specialist that is directed at the Chief of Naval Operations usually. Very bluntly, it occurs, I think, with the exception of Admiral Tom Moorer, we have seen it happen time and time again when an aviator comes in to the Chief of Naval Operations level, he thinks only in terms of aircraft carriers. We small fry feel that small patrol craft, the high speed craft, must be continued or you lose the capability. You can't start up every five years.

Q: You might also include Mine Warfare capabilities.

Capt. B.: By all means, these smaller craft have mine sweeping capabilities as well as mine laying. There are so many things of that type that crop up again, as they are doing today in discussion periods. They can do things the large ship cannot accomplish. The same problems we special operators have been critical of, it was a major criticism on our part during Vietnam. The army felt you could bomb out everything, bomb out bridges, tasks that two UDT men could have accomplished. We bombed away, expended all the duds, WW2 surplus, and left the bridges standing.

Q: Endangered the planes, the very expensive personnel.

Capt. B.: Yes, the multi-million dollar aircraft on a job that the 'sneak and peek operation' could have done. The 'sneak and peek operation' has never been appreciated fully other than by those who do it. The man who has never done it, feels it is impossible.

Q: I wanted to ask one question about the regimen at your outfit in Little Creek; did you put your men through a 'course of sprouts' similar to what I understand they had in the UDT school.

Capt. B.: No, we maintained a continuing physical conditioning program but not of the type that UDT screens prior to accepting trainees in their program.

Q: Is it 'hell week'?

Capt. B.: That's been a controversial matter over the years. I've been on both the pro and con side in my different capacities when UDT came under me. UDT people feel very strongly in favor of continuing the rigorous tests of pre-training. It does screen out a lot of people. On the other hand, in your special operations field there is also the intellectual training, specializations such as electronics and communications that might get screened out physically, and it isn't always a necessity. I am more of a believer in a physical conditioning program being continuous, but not of the extreme nature that is required for the underwater work.

Q: So you never inaugurated anything like that at Little Creek?

Capt. B.: No I did not. It is significant that during my later years at Coronado when I also had these same programs and including UDT, there were continuing objections to that physical training and of the unfairness of it. It is a pro and con issue. Sometimes it has been extreme and they have been forced to cut it back. There is a problem there when training instructors are perhaps on the job too long. They go to extremes.

Q: The Marines discovered that too.

Capt. B.: Yes, very similar problems. A sergeant gets his own ideas and goes a little too far and injuries can occur.

Interview No. 5 with Captain Phil H. Bucklew

Place: His residence in Fairfax, Virginia

Date: Thursday, 8 May 1980

Subject: Biography

By: John T. Mason, Jr.

Q: Last time we were down in Little Creek and you had been there for five years. In a most interesting phase of your activities you were beginning to develop a new idea different from those that had been utilized in invasions in Europe and you were turning your attention in other directions. Would you take up your story at that point?

Capt. B.: My next assignment related very closely to the type of work we had been doing with the Beach Jumper unit in Little Creek, and specifically with the boat operations we had been experiencing and conducting research on. At the time of assignment I didn't fully realize or appreciate the relationship. In any event I had at the time also been coaching the amphibious force football team. BuPers had indicated my next assignment would be London or Paris, CincNelm staff, working with the British on deception. But the football season had to be completed before my orders would be issued!

Q: Naturally, you couldn't get away from football.

Capt. B.: We were fortunate in having a good team and season and we were invited to play the leading army team, Fort Ord, in a post season charity game down at Galveston, Texas. This delayed my orders somewhat. My relief was in at the BJU however and approximately the first of the year a new set of orders came, ordering me to Japan, this is January 1956. I was ordered to the staff, Commander Naval Forces, Far East. Then under Admiral William Callahan, with concurrent travel for Helen. We were fairly pleased with the orders. I was first required to come to Washington for an indoctrination period. I did so, in fact I commuted back and forth part of the time. It was rather a prolonged ordeal of six weeks or so and I was not cognizant of the whys of the delay other than they were awaiting some special security clearance for me. I was a little surprised at this because I had held top secret clearance throughout my last several years, but it finally came to light that I was being assigned to the CIA for clandestine type operations in Korea.

Q: You hadn't been told this?

Capt. B.: I was not told this throughout until the security clearance was completed. That was the first they told me. Meanwhile, Helen had been closing out our house in Norfolk and some of our furniture put in storage. She joined me in Washington before the paper work had actually been completed.

Q: The indoctrination you were undergoing, was that in navy?

Capt. B.: Partly with the navy, and partly with the agency to a limited degree, in what type of clandestine operations they were participating in the Far East. I was mainly being interviewed, interrogated about boat operations and my experience and how much I had worked with foreign people and how to handle them, my patience with them, and various things. It wasn't very revealing as to the actual intent.

Q: In this indoctrination, talking about people did they attempt to give you the differences between the Koreans and the Japanese, so to speak, and that sort of thing?

Capt. B.: In part. As is frequently the case however, the Washington desk officer may be in an introductory position rather than in an experience position. It prepares him to go to the foreign assignment, rather than pulling the man in the foreign assignment in to the Washington desk, where he could do a much better briefing job. I have noted this as a fault, not just of the agency but in military capacities as well. In any event, it turned out to have a good ending but problems were just beginning.

I first protested that I did not want an agency assignment because as a long-time reserve officer it was now my intent to complete my career service and I didn't want to jeopardize it with any separation from the navy. As Admiral Fahrion had always advised me, "Don't worry about these other programs, you just keep operational and you are going to be all right for as long as you want to stay." But, it wasn't that simple. We went through the same ritual--that I was the only qualified person for this specific job, boat experience, and they needed PT operators and I had had former China experience and the like. However, I was not going to Japan as my orders had been written and wives were not allowed to go to Korea. So this brought quite a shock to both Helen and me and I said, "Look, we have rented our house in Norfolk, our furniture is in storage, my wife is here with me and now you say she can't go." So there was a few days of protest--arguments--

Q: You had certain leverage at that point, didn't you?

Capt. B.: Well, it just happened that Helen had decided that she would like to go back to work on our next assignment as she was getting a little restless with the housewife routine. The agency representative asked could my wife type, saying they needed stenographic help. I said, "By all means, she is quite talented," and that resolved the issue. Though I was assigned, in uniform, to ComNavFor FE and had as my immediate superior, as it turned out though I didn't know it at the time, Captain Rufe Taylor, N-2 Intelligence Officer for Admiral Callahan. Things worked out monentarily. The next major controversy--its humourous effect--when we got Helen's situation resolved I said, "Now, how about my dog?" He was a very important member of our family and was about five years old at the time and had come a long way with us. He was a bulldog. This was a shock but it too was gradually resolved and he traveled also, concurrently.

We drove across the country and there at San Francisco I found there were other difficulties; that since Helen was now attached to the agency as a stenographer--I don't recall the title they attached to their work--she traveled first class and as a naval officer I did not. When I turned in our tickets she was immediately given her reservation, but I was set aside for a military plane that would precede--I would go with a draft of navy people, and beside that, I wasn't eligible for first class flight.

Q: How was the third member of the family to go?

Capt. B.: First class, with Helen. However, when I walked in to PanAm to complete arrangements, I was not satisfied but reconciled that that was the way it would be, the fellow behind the desk hailed me, "Buck, I haven't seen you since Shanghai. I never did get to thank you for the help that you gave me when you provided a Jeep and you got me off on the way home." Honestly, I didn't recognize the man, didn't remember having seen him before, but thank God I had. He said, "What's your problem?" And I said, "My wife is leaving on such and such a flight but I'm not eligible and need to go on a draft." He said, "No problem at all, you got any leave on the books? You take one day's leave and I'll get you on the flight you want. I can fill up that plane with others." So, as it turned out, Helen and I went together but everything was a hassle on this. We sat side by side and across the aisle from General and Mrs.

Van Fleet. The general was retired but he was returning to Korea for a visit. Throughout this trip, as I say, Helen had first class accomodation and I, Lieutenant Commander in uniform, did not. When they would serve drinks through the hospitality of PanAm, the stewardess would come out and give Helen her drink and I wasn't eligible. The stewardess recognized this on her first time around, General Van Fleet, across the aisle, when offered a martini said, "Young lady, I have never had a drink in my life, nor have I smoked a cigarette, nor do I intend to." She said, "I am very sorry general, but we shouldn't waste this and, if you don't mind, I'll give it to the Lieutenant Commander." After the first twenty-four hours of flight the general was getting pretty annoyed because the stewardess offered him a drink every time and then gave it to me.

Q: Incidentally, General Van Fleet was going on a mission was he not? An inspection of some sort for the president?

Capt. B.: He no doubt had a high-level task. General Van Fleet, in addition to his military record, was a very highly respected and loved American. He did a tremendous lot of good fot the Koreans in retirement. He was stocking the Island of Cheju-do in Korea with Texas cattle and they had never before had cattle on that island. He was doing a lot of benevolent things, how it was sponsored, whether it was group work, I don't know, but later on we met the general and his wife during our time there and during their different visits to Korea. His relationship was very close with President Syngman Rhee and with all the top-level Koreans. He was a greatly loved person and did a lot of good for the Koreans. So we arrived in Japan. Helen of course, could not go to Korea at this time, she did a year later, but she was employed in a CIA compound located on the U.S. naval base at Yokosuka. She was provided housing on the economy as arranged by the CIA group. I was technically attached to ComNavFe headquarters on the base. However after three or four days I was hurriedly being sent to Korea. I had briefings at ComNavFe with Captain Rufus Taylor and got my naval instructions. In effect, Navy would not interfere with any operations conducted by the agency and would coordinate efforts there on the base. I would not have to give Navy formal reports because they would ask for them if we wanted but they would see the reports asked of me to be sent back to the agency. I was to be attached to the Naval Advisory Group in Korea and you would have additional duties, liaison and whatever activities the agency expected me to carry out as a collateral or additional duty. My counterpart would be the Director of Naval Intelligence for the Korean Navy, Captain Kim Se Won. (During this period they changed it around and Westernized it to the point that it would be Se Won Kim--putting Kim as the family name last.)

So I went to Korea, reported in to the Naval Advisory Group, met my counterpart and I lived at what was called the Navy-Marine House with all the naval and marine advisory group. It was a large Japanese built house, a very interesting one and very appropriate to house two groups of comparable ranks and rates in that the Japanese who had built the house had two families, his wife's and his mistress's, and the house was divided in the middle into two identical parts. You might say it was a mansion but there was no arguing which was the better side, they were identical, and it was utilized for both our navy and our marine corps advisers.

Q: Was this located in Seoul?

Capt. B.: Yes, in Seoul. I was billeted there and had all meals there, we all did. My office was in a building away from the Naval headquarters, about a quarter of a mile away which was entirely for Korean Intelligence. It all worked out very well; it could have been a difficult situation perhaps, but it so happened that Captain Kim Se Won and I got to be very good personal friends and we remain so today. Out of that personal relationship we had many interesting experiences, and a year later when Helen came to Korea, we were two friendly families--Kim and his wife and Helen and I had several travels around Korea, enhanced with their explanations of history and traditions. It turned out to be a very unusual and pleasant experience for us in what was considered a hardship tour by the State Department and other U.S. government representatives.

Q: In a general sense what was your mission in Seoul?

Capt. B.: The agency had a compound there with approximately a hundred U.S. personnel attached. They sponsored the North Korean intelligence collection activity, as their part of the Korean mission. Advisory groups, by regulation, are not supposed to engage in any intelligence collection activity against the people whom they are advising. The agency had procured three WW2 PT boats and these were operated by Captain Kim's Korean Intelligence personnel and being used for many purposes against North Korea. The primary responsibility that I had with the agency was to oversee the operation of these craft. There were many problems of maintenance and in coordinating and "selling" some of the plans proposed by the CIA operators for Captain Kim's execution.

Q: That is why the emphasis on your experience and background.

Capt. B.: The type of operations they were conducting were quite interesting and they were all keyed on Captain Kim Se Won. There was a language barrier of course, for agency personnel as well as advisers, and in collecting intelligence on the North Koreans that language capability and understanding was quite pertinent.

There were several other secret operations that were handled by various security agencies that I became a part of. It was sensitive, in some ways. I was assigned to groups due to my US Navy affiliation and, in other instances I was assigned due to agency interests. The type of operations that were being conducted through the Korean intelligence--included monitoring posts on the northern islands of Pi Y Do, three islands at the border between North Korea and South Korea, though they were under possession of the United Nations and the South Koreans, they were actually north of the line. Monitoring had been

Captain Kim Se Won's career success as he started it on behalf of U.S. Army actions during the Korean War. He was a communications officer at that time on a Korean mine sweeper and in one specific instance while they were in port down in Inchon, Kim Se Won was merely listening to North Korean communications and intercepted what turned out to be a very important message involving a counter attack by the North Koreans. Inchon is only twenty miles south of the border, and Kim Se Won forced his way to the American general, a division commander, related his message, convinced him what his intercept meant. The American general gambled, countered the counter attack successfully, and immediately set Kim Se Won up in communications intercept operations--pulled him off his ship, and awarded him the American silver star, of which he is most proud.

He set up the communications link at Pi Y Do for constant monitoring of North Korean communications. There were two American units there also, one operated by the US Air Force and one by the US Army Security Group, Kim's outfit which was entirely Korean. It so happened as time passed--I was not cleared for this operation by the Security Group who guarded their work very closely--but Kim's group, with their language capability, would normally be one to two days ahead of the Americans due to translation difficulties. Kim, with respect for my being a naval intelligence officer and as his counterpart, would bring his information to me first, and I would take it to the U.N/U.S. 8th Army, and very often beat our American groups, as I said, by one or two days. Frequently the U.S. units would have to relay their communications all the way back to Washington for translation and back out to the field. And this is the beginning of a fault that I think just occurred in Iran.

Q: Very cumbersome.

Capt. B.: And we have followed that pattern for a number of years, through necessity in some ways, and controversy over control for others.

Q: For control and also due to our inadequacy with language isn't it, they were not that fluent?

Capt. B.: That certainly is the major problem, our language inadequacy. Secondly, however, is the command fear of deception being utilized in such communications--the same thing I worked with with the tactical deception program back in Little Creek. So the commanding general might be concerned--"how can I believe this?"--and it needs full analyzation before taking any action, in addition to the translation problem. It is probably a necessary cautiousness, but it is a handicap as well.

Q: Do the British employ that kind of caution?

Capt. B.: No, not in Korea. The British were not in an operational capacity other than as part of the United Nations staff up on the border. The British were quite critical of us at times for our slowness in such action and they felt that we had the solution if we would be more aggressive about such things.

That was one phase of the operation. Now, back to the PT

boats; what were they used for. In some cases, in part, we would land agents in North Korea. This was an interesting experience to me and some of it was rather farcial. Some agents were not only "double", but "redouble". They worked for both sides, they passed information back and forth and we delivered it. We have had incidents in which I went along with Captain Kim Se Won when he needed penicillin and sulfa drugs to negotiate a deal up in P'yongyang through an agent. So I went back to Captain Taylor, outlined it to him; he provided them, and in exchange for these very valuable drugs we got a bunch of Korean socks and ginseng--a sampan full! So we had some bad ones there.

The second phase of the boat operation--it was quite an interesting one. We would launch in meteorlogical balloons that were loaded with propaganda leaflets; by calculation of the high level winds these balloons launched from a seaward position from the PT boats, would hopefully fly over P'yongyang or the intended targets and reach an altitude there where a pressure burst would occur and the leaflets would shower over that objective area. The themes of these leaflets I could never contribute much to as my counterpart would explain, you Americans do not understand the expression and philosophy that a Korean expects--the Oriental way, the love for tradition. It might be a flowery expression of some purpose; the leaflets were all short in their message, normally one paragraph--perhaps a lengthy one; the subject was usually criticism of a high official, or government controls, or indicating that South Korea had a much better situation--"why don't you come south" and that sort of thing.

In all it was a very cleverly run operation. The mechanism of it, and I marvelled at the Korean meteorlogist, his accuracy of predictions--we would receive confirmation reports, when you hit a target by something as simple as setting free a hydrogen filled balloon with only the control of the weight calculations and the drift calculations, the tactic deserves much credit. But for one time--this created a little excitement! We operated from an island offshore of Inchon where the preparation, the rigging of the balloons and the boats were stationed there. It was about 30 miles offshore and was an uninhabited island other than for the navy intelligence unit operators. We had a little base at Wolmi-do, the Korean military was pretty numerous in strength and they had bases at Inchon and other outposts going on south to Pusan and Chinhae and the like. Our failure mission created quite a stir all the way to Washington--but it was beyond control of the U.S. A leaflet launch was made--I don't recall what the exact theme was but it was appropriate enough to cause concern--and the wind shifted. The entire leaflet launch came down on the palace of Syngman Rhee back in Soeul instead of on P'yongyang in North Korea. General Decker was the United Nations commander at the time, I can't recall who his chief of staff was, but they were fully informed of each of these operations. However, within his staff, they were not informed; without consulting the top commander, the Air Force alerted that enemy planes had bombed Soeul with leaflets--that the border defense was ineffective against air attack--the early warning system was not working! This created a stir clear back to

Washington and there were publicity releases that North Korean planes had been flying over Seoul--all it was was the wind shift on our balloons.

Q: Kind of a jittery military?

Capt. B.: And a jittery military staff! It did prove the effectiveness of this program. It took a lot of doing but such an exposure did great damage for continuing future operations. We had another type of operation that was conducted by the U.S. through the Korean Naval Intelligence.

Q: What role did you play with the group up at Panmunjam?

Capt. B.: No direct role. At this specific time Admiral Quiggle was the senior naval officer and he used to come down to Seoul nearly every Saturday afternoon and I would meet with him and we would informally discuss little things but he could not let his job in any way be overlapped with military operations.

Q: No, his patience was stretched to the limit just sitting there, wasn't it?

Capt. B.: Oh yes, the admiral was a sick man, too. I later saw him in Japan and he then knew that he had bone cancer and, as you perhpas know, some time after that he fell overboard from a naval transport returning to the United States. There was controversy over this.

Q: His assignment was only for six months when he was up on the line, was it not?

Capt. B.: Yes, there were some extensions but six months was the normal tour, and quite enough for the nerve-racking procedures and frustrations that they have. There was quite a change that occurred after my first year in Korea, we had many incidents. An interesting one--an American pilot got lost, flew over the border, landed up in P'yongyang; it was an innocent effort, he just plain got lost, I gather, but they had a U.S. aircraft and the problem was they were willing to give it back but they wouldn't permit the U.S. to fly it out or to pick it up by ship! How else do you get it out?

Q: What do you mean?

Capt. B.: Well, I learned a little bit on Korea at the time, I had to do a lot of research. We considered every imaginable way to move that plane, take its wings off, bring it down by flatbed on a rail car (I learned a lot about the tunnels in Korea, you can't do that). They would not permit a U.S. ship to come in to P'yongyang. They wouldn't let the plane be flown out on its own power, so how do you get it out? Do you dismantle? This is what we ultimately had to do, bring it out in parts.

Q: Did they permit United Nations personnel or U.S. personnel to go up there and dismantle it?

Capt. B.: It ultimately came out that way but they merely played a game with us—something like the Iran people—they thought of every deviltry that they could, saying "sure its your plane, come and get it."

Q: Isn't it surprising they didn't want to keep it? or wasn't it prototype they were interested in?

Capt. B.: It was just a training aircraft, but they got all the information they wanted.

Q: What about the pilot?

Capt. B.: They released him and he got back safely.

We had another incident in which they captured, I think, three South Korean fishing craft and took them in to Wonson Harbor. There was a long period of negotiation, very comparable to the PUEBLO incident a few years later. They treated the personnel to great hospitality, but kept them for about thirty days! They outfitted them! They clothed them, they entertained them, took them across country to P'yongyang and ultimately released them after about thirty days after, you might say, a little Communist indoctrination. I always questioned how much they had implanted in these Koreans and how many of their own agents developed from that.

There were continuing incidents of agents being picked up by the Korean police along the shore line, having landed by various types of small craft—fishing boats, sampans. It was almost impossible to patrol and guard that coastline, although there were Korean patrol craft covering the area. With thousands of fishing craft, literally, there was very little political regard on the part of either the North or the South Korean fishermen and people--they go where the fish are. Every spring when the rockfish run you will find a thousand fishing craft all mixed together this day--North Korean and South Korean. There are incidents in which either or both of the North Korean and South Korean patrol craft might open fire and some incident would occur. Very little regard however on the part of fishermen--till they get their load of fish, they could care less.

Q: It is their livelihood.

Capt. B.: Exactly. So there was that type of incident. The agent activity--there were many of these turned over to my counterpart, he would interrogate them. It was done at our intelligence naval headquarters, I never observed or wanted to know too much about their interrogations, I'm sure it was not always a gentle matter. Captain Kim Se Won came to me one time saying, "I need a lie detector." I responded, "You don't need a lie detector." "Yes," he said, "I need something of that type to interrogate these many agents we get." And I said I wouldn't request it because I didn't think he needed it and he argued the point with me until I said, "Make yourself one." "How do I make it?" I advised, "Get yourself an inner tube and an air gage--that's about all it amounts to anyway." I was surprised when one day I walked into his office and he had made one. He had used a small inner tube--its just like a blood pressure machine which is all it amounts to--and from what he told me it

Bucklew #5 -

had successful psychological effects.

One that really amazed me--part of the advisory role is to supervise the budgetary requests that are the basis of the military aid support. It is an advisory group responsibility to screen the requests and this can be a problem in countries due to language; the Koreans would make out their budgetary request forms, including itemized lists of equipments and items that were needed--it is usually far less for an intelligence organization than it would be for a field army unit with weaponry and ammunition and spare parts, etc. But I was given a rather imposing list, then had to get it translated and I had Kim help me on it and the amounts on it. I came across an item, I forget the exact quantity, but it was 20 or 40 tons of birdseed. I thought this was a translation error and quizzed Kim on it. He explained, "Well, I guess I better tell you about that operation. Its been going on for many years. During the Korean War our Koreans in Japan sent us a number of carrier pigeons that we have used since the war to avoid intercept of our communications for security reasons. I will prove to you the effectiveness. If you will get one of your people down in Inchon to send you a message up by courier, I will, at the same time, have my people release a carrier pigeon and I will show you how much more rapid it is without the hazard of a jeep driver." He proved his point. The carrier pigeon came in to the cages I hadn't been aware of in the loft of our building, he gave me my message and an hour or more later in came our jeep driver courier; it is only 20 miles from Seoul to Inchon but it is a long, dusty lumpy road—with heavy military traffic. Kim said, "We've been successful with these pigeons. They can go as far as Chinhae and back." That's about 200 miles south of Seoul. "However," he said, "I have been having some problems. In the spring some of these birds have been diverting off to Pusan, and I blame it on romance."

Q: Nightclubs?

Capt. B.: In the mating season of carrier pigeons discipline goes to hell. So we had our funny little incidents.

Q: In recent months or years, we have been reading about the tunnels the North Koreans have attempted to dig under the line. Was there any indication of that in the '50s?

Capt. B.: Yes, although most of the incidents occurred the following year. In 1957, there was then a reorganization of Naval Forces Far East, and the establishment of Commander Naval Forces, Korea, at which time Admiral Albert E. Jarrell became the first ComNavFor Korea, as well as the Chief of the Naval Advisory Group, and Navy U.N. representative at Panmunjam, he had three hats.

A continuing advisory group problem can be attributed to the many people short-toured (one year tours) in consideration of peace time routine and undesirable hardship areas. One of the major problems with such a system in advisory groups, particularly in countries where there are language barriers, an adviser spends about six months trying to find out what his job is and the next six months he is thinking about going home. We lose a lot in that system. If its a hardship country they are separated from their families at hime, they are not very happy in the first place, and consequently, they may spend as little time as possible in direct contact with their counterparts, particularly when they live in one area and the counterpart in another. There are many problems.

When Admiral Jarrell wanted me to continue as his intelligence officer and I did. He was a fine man but had the usual problems with a new staff and setting up all the organizational paper work, the doctrine, and regulations--that in itself is normally a full-time, several months proposition in getting established. I was the Intelligence officer for Naval Forces Korea, as well as the adviser to the Koreans---my affiliation with Kim Se Won continued. I had two offices, the office of Naval Forces Korea was in the Eighth Army compound and almost across town from my other office with the Korean navy, so my time was no longer in full time association with Kim Se Won, but fortunately we had become very good friends and spent more time socially together. At that time Helen came over to Korea from Japan assigned to the U.S. Embassy in the political section. We rented a house, through the help of Kim Se Won and lived on the economy. This provided some hardships but many pleasures too. We were included in much of the Korean social life which was quite an experience but somewhat of a hardship too. As General Decker used to put it, he was United Nations Commander and Commanding General, Eighth Army as well, but when we would meet at a party he would say, "Oh, yes, Bucklew, you are that fellow that is living with his wife." There were only four wives of the military living in the country. Something was always happening Korean-wise, army, navy, air force, or at the embassy. We had very rugged social routines but it did help me very much in contacts in my job.

Q: Who was the American ambassador then?

Capt. B.: Ambassador Dowling.

Q: Will you tell me about that mining operation? the tunnels?

Capt. B.: The demilitarized zone was approximately a ten-mile strip from coast to coast, dividing the two countries.

Q: Was it a stationary line in your time?

Capt. B.: Yes. There were many armistice violation incidents, sometimes firing across the neutral zone and there had been tunneling attempts on which the intruders might not get all the way across, but they would be getting within firing range where either they or our sentries were killed. It was a case of continuous squabbling in the Armistice Commission at Panmunjam. There were literally hundreds of incidents being reported and it was a very tedious job for those people assigned—they would sit day after day and hear the complaints of the other party, and then would have to register with counter charges. There was very little in resolution to any of the incidents that involved perhaps a sentry being shot or a plane being brought down on the other side of the border. This would take several weeks of discussion in the commission before coming to terms--not unlike the problems today, negotiating except that it was done around the conference table at Panmunjam.

Q: Admiral Burke told me in his time which was earlier, the line would change over night, because they were still battling, so this made for a very grave problem as our side wasn't always informed as to exactly where the line was, what hill they held and what hill the enemy held.

Capt. B.: It seemed that it would narrow in spots and though I had no direct knowledge, I felt both sides were offenders, from the comments and observations I would hear from these conference participants. It had quieted down during the period of 1956 to '58 and there was respect for the line by aircraft. There was really little necessity for them to be flying there, mostly the type of aircraft used was the small Beechcraft in flying those areas, as opposed to combat planes. Where there were requirements of going up to the islands on the border, Pi Y Do--they would fly from their base and over the sea, avoiding the inland or targeting. There was tremendous respect for the marksmanship of the North Korean anti-aircraft units. We did not have any incidents of North Koreans flying south during my stay; it was generally accepted that their air power had been dispersed much of it having been returned to other Chinese operations.

Q: Were the Chinese much in evidence at all during your time there?

Capt. B.: Not really. We had a few intelligence reports that there were Chinese patrol vessels nearing the Korean coast line. Naval patrol and aircraft would be dispatched to investigate and there might be a little chase involved. No real incidents in which they were in any major violation or attack. Continuing suspicion of one another, however.

Q: Suspicion with a bit of fear attached I suppose?

Capt. B.: Yes, that and the challenge of thwarting and such intrusion.

Q: Admiral Burke told me about another incident and I was wondering if anything similar occurred in your time. It had to do with communications when they were in discussion and they seemed to be in daily session up there. It suddenly occurred to Burke and his counterpart that the North Koreans knew what the Americans learned but they knew it in advance of the Americans. There was some way in which they were getting this knowledge through communications and it was something that came out of Washington.

We were talking about something off tape that I hope you would talk about on tape and that is the interflow of North Koreans and South Koreans, the inability to distinguish one from the other. There was a difference in accent, was there not? Or does that necessarily mean anything?

Capt. B.: A difference in accent wouldn't be discernable to those of us who weren't natives or linguists. But so many people, as my counterpart Kim se Won, was born in P'yongyang, North Korea, and he had relatives there; it is significant however, that though his parents are in Seoul he never associated with them--never made contact with them to my knowledge, and to me that he could not due to his position as Director of Intelligence, and with any attachment to them they might be in jeopardy. I knew him for two years before I knew he had a brother in Seoul who was in business there with his wife and family.

The Chief of Naval Operations for the Korean navy was originally from North Korea. Their divisions politically came at the time of the war, before that really; they had broken away, they were refugees. The housemaid that we had in Seoul was from North Korea; she had left her husband who was a Communist serving with the North Korean forces; she was vehemently opposed to their actions and she came south on foot with two small children, as thousands did.

After hostilities had quieted down some of these might well have been North Korean agents--there was no way of discerning that. They were given ID cards and the Korean police force would know those in their community. The police force was the law as they are sectioned around their various villages and cities; the Korean police were very powerful and if a stranger bobbed up he was immediately suspect and was interrogated. He might then be released or he might not; we couldn't really tell or understand much of that and never interfered. They had a very sophisticated system among themselves in policing for agents. It would be a different matter if they picked somebody off a fishing boat that was not immediately identified--he was a stranger who bobbed up in the last three or four days or a week and they probably worked him over pretty well. There was much other police activity.

It is significant at this time, in the '57 to '58 period there were constantly sea mines bobbing up, another naval intelligence responsibility we had -- to get people down there to clear them. They would wash up on the beach. They were dropped so voluminously during the war period and apparently with very limited knowledge of where or how many had been laid that they were apt to come up at any time. There were casualties involved.

Q: Were they Russian mines?

Capt. B.: No, these were our own, U.S. mines. I had another very revealing experience: A man came out from the Chief of Naval Operations, on a very secret mission. He explained the problem, that there was a great inaccuracy in the mapping available to the U.S. military, that the most accurate available would be a North Korean map that dated back 40 or 50 years and he was there seeking a North Korean map of this type, could I help him?

Q: Was this a topography sort of thing?

Capt. B.: I went to Kim se Won and I said, "This is the problem--how in the hell would we get maps of Korea developed out of P'yongyang in years past?"

He said, "I just happen to have some; they are in my old sea chest that I have had from officer's training school in P'yongyang long before the war."

We learned, as pointed out by the Chief of Naval Operations representative, that the shore bombardment as well as air attacks throughout the Korean War had been based on mapping, charting that was sometimes in error as much as 20 miles in our version of the Korean coastline. When Kim brought his maps in we laid them down as an overlay on our present U.S. map and it was amazing to see the variance of the coastline.

Q: How do you explain this discrepancy?

Capt. B.: The same as the China coast in World War 2--there had been years of inactivity, Japanese occupation of Korea for more than 40 years during which time the U.S. was not welcome and the Japanese developed the maps, but they weren't published on a world-wide basis, as they presumably are today in most instances. It was a rather shocking revelation. Of course, all bombardment isn't done by the chart but you can appreciate how many tragic mistakes could occur with that much of a deviation.

Q: When you talk about the population and the flow which has continued back and forth, what does this say about the eventual need for the unification of the country? How can it be two countries; they are engaging in talks supposedly for unification. What does that mean?

Capt. B.: Well, it is a very similar situation in the overall Korea and the overall Vietnam. Industrialization, water power, electricity is in the north, the industrial area is in the north; the agriculture--so-called--is in the south in both countries. It has always been an amazement to me that with our United States political participation that we didn't learn from Korea that it is not feasible to divide such countries into two parts but we followed up on the Korean political division and did the same thing down in Vietnam. Such division may have been expedient at the time but it was not really necessary. There was, of course, the Russian, the Soviet, intervention in Korea at the very tail end of World War II but, as I have commented on China, I have always felt that six months more might have resolved many of the problems that we have created for the next generation.

In Korea, it was an amazing thing to see the power lines come down from the north and be cut off, stopped, at the demilitarized zone. The Japanese had developed that country; they were hated. But in 40 years time they had industrialized and modernized and utilized every available resource for electrical, water power. I knew little, only what I read, of the factory system but it is far more extensive and operational in North Korea than was ever developed in the south. They had little or nothing there; it was a completely dependent country at the time we were there. Today it has developed remarkably and I think in time it will become a unified country again. Whether it goes Communist or Democratic, there is a compromise situation that remains to be seen. I think they are getting closer and closer with their talks and the fact that they need one another.

Q: That is the perplexing part of these talks reported on unification. Both sides are so adamant about their own political situation, one wonders how they can talk about unification.

Capt. B.: During the period of my tenure there, of course, Syngman Rhee was a very controversial person. From my observation, however, so many of the accusations made against the man were absolutely impossible. We knew that intelligence-wise; he was very well monitored. He was a man in his mid-eighties. Among his closest, trusted American contacts was a U.S. army doctor assigned to him. We considered the doctor's the best intelligence reports that came out on Rhee. His working hours of the day were no more than four. As any man of his age, he spent most of the time resting and sleeping. He was accused of many things that I don't question some of his associates were involved in. His vice president, Y Ki Poong, was reputedly involved in most political graft and escapades. Y Ki Poong's wife was also a powerful politician—I can't recall her name.

Q: Rhee's wife was an Austrian, was she not?

Capt. B.: Yes. Y Ki Poong's son ultimately murdered his mother and father and committed suicide himself. But they were the liaison with the corruption. Rhee himself, I think devoted his entire life to just hating communists; well justified in the torture he had been put through in his younger days--pulling out his fingernails, burned, many things--imprisoned; his hatred was intense. He threatened and justified most actions in opposition to desired United States policy by threatening to go north.

The whole system of the advisory groups--army, navy and the like--was to ration fuel, to ration gasoline. This was partially effective but not realistically so. The Koreans, who after 40 years of being subjected to Japanese control and domination, prided themselves on their ability to steal from the Japanese, and they certainly practiced it against us--as we were fully aware. When the Koreans knew you well enough, they would boast of what they could do. They said if you give us a month's fuel and give three months' time, we will have saved one month's, we will steal a third, and we will have three months' ration available--you can't stop us from going north if we have to go north. Syngman Rhee would challenge any policy to which he objected with, "We'll go north," and he would drive on those points.

But of the other corruptions that were occurring--governmental-wise--we believed intelligence-wise that it was physically impossible for the man to be involved in those things. He did too many other things. I have chatted with him for several hours at different military demonstrations and functions; he was an affable but feeble old man, completely exhausted after observing military maneuvers or something like that, and he had to rest. He distrusted most of his own people. He would only ride in the airplane of the U.S. attache who was then Commander Corky Lane--that was the only pilot with whom Rhee would go back and forth to Seoul or Chinhae or wherever. He wouldn't take a chance with a Korean plane that might take him north. They had many problems like that. You couldn't depend on loyalties. There were incidents in which Korean pilots flew their planes and defected to the north same as there were North Koreans defecting to the south, understandably so in many ways, due to family relationships, separations and traditions. These are typical problems in a divided country.

Q: Actually as you have described it, it sounds like one country even then though divided by a line of demarkation.

Capt. B.: I experienced it in China, later in Vietnam, and in Korea. I have never seen what you might describe as an intense hatred between north and south. In three major areas we have been in a position of impelling these people to fight against their own, when you could not identify one from the other. The Vietnamese were the most open, the most vicious toward one another that I observed, but even so their villages in South Vietnam, it might be that one village was Communist and the next one was not, so infiltration was a pretty obvious circumstance.

Q: How did the South Koreans feel about these interminable conversations going on up on the line?

Capt. B.: Perhaps, again I rely on comments of my friend Captain Kin Se Won, they considered it just too detailed. They were more inclined to call a spade a spade, or a liar a liar, rather than bother with diplomatic tact and splitting hairs. They felt that so many of our actions were excessive in talk, paperwork, and all forms of detail. Their understanding of justice and ours is far different. When you see our court systems today I am not so sure they aren't right.

Q: Did they have any solution for this, did they see any end to these discussions?

Capt. B.: I think they believed in action a lot more than we evidenced with caution; perhaps it is a lesser regard for life itself. Throughout the Orient, first with my China experience, I believe their respect for life is far less than ours. Perhaps this is based on their religion where you've got it made by dying honorably.

Q: By dying honorably Nirvana comes your way?

Capt. B.: Similar to the kamikaze for the Japanese.

Q: Then these discussions were something of a charade for them, they being similar in thinking patterns to the North Koreans. Were they not a charade to them too?

Capt. B.: Yes, I believe that was the case. One fault of it was that we always dominated the discussions, the South Koreans had very limited participation. They had a representative but his wasn't a fully respected position. You catered to their rank but throughout their huge military our respect wasn't there that a general was really more experienced or knowledgeable than a U.S. Navy lieutenant commander or an Army major. He hadn't been in the military as long as the major or the lieutenant commander. They were Johnny-come-latelies in that sense. If they had background of wealth, they automatically started off in rank; any political position just moved them in. Their militaries were built so rapidly under the stress of war that certainly very few had the background of experience similar to the American types that had gone through World War II, so there was a lesser respect.

Now I have heard the reactions and criticisms at Panmunjam, "So we had General Chung with us. What good was he? We'll do the talking." It was a little different on the northern side--the Communist pitch was a lot more wordy. They didn't answer the questions but they carried on the debate.

Q: They did indeed. The naval officer I talked with who was

up at Panmunjam and on the line conferred quite frequently with the Chief of the South Korean Intelligence, and he was of great assistance to him, I gathered, in meeting the confrontations up on the line.

Capt. B.: Well, I think you put your finger on it right there. He was of assistance but he wasn't in the controlling position. It's a great problem with advisory groups throughout the world, and I have observed several, that the American can't avoid looking down on his counterpart. He is bound by experience and knowledge in pushing U.S. weaponry, doctrine, and training. He has more experience but this is a very sensitive thing. If your counterpart outranks you and you know more than he does, he remains very sensitive and aware that--one, he knows he is in a false position, but, two, he doesn't like to have you show it.

Q: That's understandable in terms of human nature. How does this translate into your own particular situation there in South Korea? Having had a tremendous amount of experience elsewhere in the world and being there as a representative of the American government and all that that signified, how did that translate in your relationship with the Korean intelligence?

Capt. B.: Fortunately, as I said, my counterpart and I turned out to be pretty good friends. He was a very talented fellow. He turned 40 years old while we were there. We joked quite a bit--he had picked up the expression, "He's over the hill," and I think he meant it. He felt he was quite an old man.

Incidentally, with the death of Syngman Rhee (Kim was very loyal--he was not a political participant in any way, but he was loyal to his president) and with the assassination, with the overthrow of the government, there was no challenge of Kim se Won's loyalty and they made him the Consul General at Hawaii. He was there for several years and then made Ambassador to Finland--but they did not let him return to his own country. His family, that we knew as babies and children, graduated from college without ever getting back to Korea.

Q: That's an old ploy, isn't it?

Capt. B.: So he was trusted but not trusted at home.

Q: Did he ever return?

Capt. B.: He returned. From his Christmas card this year I learned he is now a member of the Korean Olympic Committee. He became--I saw him several times--met him here in Washington on his way to Finland and saw him several times in Hawaii in my transits out to Vietnam--little things they did to him. He made commodore after I departed but they made him a Consul General one month before he would have been eligible for a military retirement.

Q: So they kept him at arm's length?

Capt. B.: Always in a dependent position. How he stands at the present time I have no idea.

Q: Perhaps his status has changed since the death of President Park.

Capt. B.: I just don't know. I have made many inquiries at the Washington embassy and they are very cautious. They say, "Oh, yes, he is in Finland and likes it."

Q: At the time you were there in South Korea, if I recall correctly, our attention was being focused on the Chinese offshore islands of Quemoy and Matsu. Were there any repercussions in South Korea? Did you have any role in connection with this?

Capt. B.: Not really. The Koreans had representation in these various countries and they were expanding their relationship during that period. We had one incident that backfired. The Korean Symphony Orchestra was invited and provided a tour, I believe all the way down to Malaysia. I wasn't aware of it until, on the return and the orchestra was being transported by a Korean ship which stopped in Hong Kong, we received intelligence reports that opium had been procured by some of the orchestra members. We next received the reports from Taiwan. They came through Kim se Won and he cut me in on it immediately.

We obtained support ultimately from Japan, which was needed, and when the ship arrived in--I don't recall whether it came in to Chinhae or Pusan--but Kim had his men there to go aboard, confiscate materials and inspect. They had purchased a lot of talcum powder which mixes very well (due to the light coloring) with opium, and they felt that must be it. I arranged for support from Japan to analyze the talcum powder and Kim confiscated the whole shipment which turned out to be void as can be! It was all souvenir and gifts that the orchestra had procured. We never did find the opium, if and as it was reported. That was a little thing. We joked about it a bit--it was just one of those you lose.

The point, in answer to your question, they had representation in each of these countries and whether diplomatic or an on-board agent circumstance, they had a good network of communications. Of course, in Japan, there is a very large Korean population that had originally been moved into Japan as a labor force, kept in menial positions. There has been much exaggerated pride that a good portion of the Japanese development should be credited to the Koreans--this being spoken by the Koreans. I was told at one time that they, the Koreans, had actually built the great Buddha. I doubt this; I didn't dispute it. But they had and continued to have an intense dislike for the Japanese, although they maintained a continuous communication with their people in Japan. It happened through Captain Rufus Taylor that I escorted Kim Se Won and two of his people as sort of a "reward basis," to Japan. Captain Taylor had suggested it and Kim Se Won thought it was the opportunity of a lifetime--they gave me a lot of headaches but they had a wonderful time.

Q: Were they known to the Japanese for what they were?

Capt. B.: No. It was done through the military command in civilian clothing but with full American privileges. I'll never forget, it made me feel very foolish--they were given PX privilege, so I accompanied them on Yokosuka Naval Base. As soon as they came in the exchange they each bought a trunk. I said, "Now wait, you don't want to carry that around. Let's get that last." They looked at me like I was...

Q: They were going to fill it up?

Capt. B.: Exactly, but I didn't get the point. They pulled the first trunk over to the lingerie counter and they said, "I'll take that shelf." They cleared out the whole lingerie section and put it in one trunk. I cringed but saw the point. We got through it. They did Tokyo on their own, so I'll never know what happened there, but I finally got them back on the plane. They had two or three days or a weekend and I felt like I had gone through a campaign.

Q: Tell me, while you were in Korea, did you have any contact with the Japanese? Were they involved in any way in the Korean business?

Capt. B.: None whatsoever in Korea. I would be making my trips back and forth over to Yokosuka and to Tokyo to report there every six weeks or so.

Q: That was reporting to the U.S. naval people in the CIA.

Capt. B.: And as such I would have some contact with the Japanese, but limited. Now Helen, in the first year there, lived in Japan while I was in Korea and she got around a lot more. She had a very nice housekeeper lady who was a good companion and they traveled a bit and the people she worked with did. She saw much more of Japan and the reactions of the people than I did.

Q: At that time they were somewhat under wraps still, were they not, in terms of military?

Capt. B.: Yes, and to the present to a high degree, they are restricted in their activities. I probably had more association after that tour, when I had the amphibious intelligence school in Coronado and we had Japanese officers among the group--we had them from about 20 countries--for a six-week period. I had a closer communicative relationship with them then than I did in the Far East, with the Japanese.

Then in my later tour with the COMPHIBGRP ONE, we spent quite a bit of time in Japanese ports with the amphibious group and we covered many countries every quarter. In our operations there you got to know them a lot better, but they were very restricted in their expansion, the responsibilities they could take and, as you know, with their abhorrence of nuclear weapons and of ships carrying such coming into their ports. They functioned as a Coast Guard type operation and saved a lot of money on their part.

Q: Now, about the Japanese involvement in Korea in any way in the day of Syngman Rhee, and he was very anti-Japanese because of his past history?

Capt. B.: As an example: Chief of Naval Operations of the Korean Navy at that time, Admiral Jeung Kuk Mo, had been in the Japanese Merchant Marine service in which he received his naval training. Of course Korea had no navy at that time. Jeung had not only lived there but had functioned in their Maritime Service. Then DCNO Operations Officer, Admiral Lee Hi Chong (known as Inchon Lee), who was much decorated by the American army for his service during the Inchon landings, and quite a character. He had gone through school and college in Japan, and was a black belt Judo champion there. People of that background had a closer and warmer feeling toward the Japanese, although they were restricted in their own government from any association.

Q: That borders on the international fraternity of naval people anyway, doesn't it?

Capt. B.: Yes. They talked a harsh game when there would be a Japanese fishing boat sighted in Korean fishing waters and you will recall Syngman Rhee was the first to attempt to extend the fishing zone. Two hundred mile limit, I believe is the Korean one, particularly in those waters between Japan and

Korea. There were many harsh comments and flurries over both Japanese and Chinese intrusion into their waters. But the Japanese influence in Korea, in spite of any great abuses that no doubt did occur with an occupational force, the benefits to Korea were, I think, quite evident, even at that time. The progress since, in the development of South Korea--the automotive industry and various things--it is phenomenal.

Q: Would you say something about the status of the Korean navy during your time there?

Capt. B.: I am loosely speaking of the number of ships but I would say approximately 40 amphibious type ships were included. These were provided by the U.S. from World War II surplus. The Koreans were reasonably progressive in their activities and did a good job with limited background of experience in operating ships, and in maintaining them within the navy. It was always been a problem to convince the Orientals on preventive maintenance and care of their machinery, but I think the Koreans did a fair job, considering the limited number of years that they had operated their own forces. At Chinhae, their naval headquarters, they had a shipyard where they had requested U.S. naval assistance (and funding) toward putting in a drydock; they were turned down and they built their own. They had the only effective drydock facility in the Far East at that time.

They maintained naval bases, their main base being at

Chinhae, and Pusan was their main naval port. Inchon was a problem area in spite of the publicity received in the U.S. amphibious landing at Inchon. The tide there is a problem-- I think it ran up to 27 to 30 feet, so you have to shift boats and ships back and forth with the tide or let them dry out with each tide and that certainly restricted the use of the port -- though much has been done in the way of breakwaters and other facilities since.

One thing in which I was personally involved and impressed me as to the interest and enthusiasm of the Koreans for improving their own efficiency: By coincidence, when I was back in Yokosuka, a large number of technical naval books were being discarded, which included a broad scope of navigation, electronics and engineering training manuals. It was true the books were outdated--they were all in English--but I thought it was a shame to throw them away and said "I'll take the whole batch." They crated them up for me at COMNAUFE and I took them back to Kim Se Won, who took them to Chinhae where they translated those books into Korean, reprinted them as the basis for a library at Chinhae, shared by Navy and the Marine Corps.

Q: How enterprising.

Capt. B.: I thought it was quite an act.

Q: How long did it take them to do that?

Capt. B.: They completed it during my tour so I would say it was around six months, which I thought was a remarkable job in translation alone. I thought nothing of it after the turnover to them until I was later commended by the Chief of Naval Operations for helping them set up this library, which pleased me no little. As I say, I admired what they did, I was just salvaging a bunch of books. I thought this was indicative of the spirit behind their navy and marine people.

We had problems with our own intelligence boats -- a lot more than the Korean navy. At one stage, the Korean intelligence force must have had about 40 boats operating. Kim Se Won was a bit of a scrounger. I was asked by either Captain Packard or Captain Taylor, if I could discreetly arrange the transfer of three boats to the Korean navy, gunboats that had been procured by the United States from Japan during the Korean War with the stipulation that they not go to Korea. With Kim's help we maneuvered the transfer, got them to Korea, and they operated as proud additions to the Navy.

Q: Were there any repercussions on the Japanese part?

Capt. B.: They never knew what happened to them. I took the paperwork and between Kim and myself, we got the ships over and they operated out of Inchon with lost identity. I don't know what developed when Japanese spare parts were ultimately needed!

Q: That was just a residue of feeling that existed I guess.

Capt. B.: That's right. Let bygones be bygones. However, as I started to say, with an intelligence operated fleet, this is not as good as an organized navy operation and maintenance was one of the problems that we had with this hodge-podge of clandestine type craft which included sampans, fishing craft, three gunboats and a couple of PTs.

Q: The personnel were primarily interested in something else?

Capt. B.: Well, it is an inherent fact that maintenance, to the Oriental, doesn't really register. Checking the oil seems like an unnecessary thing unless you are obviously out of oil and, of course, then you will do a lot of damage by letting things go dry.

One thing that impressed me was a justification on the part of Captain Kim--a time when I was criticizing this poor maintenance system. He said, "Well now look, you must realize that our Korean people had never been aboard or operated a sophisticated craft until the war occurred." And he said, "You taught us, when the Americans came on board, if it was a piece of radio equipment--you turn it on here and you turn it off there. I went to different schools and I know that is not the way that you emphasize in your training programs."

"That's the way, however, that most Koreans had been taught --'Don't touch this knob. Turn it on here, we will adjust whatever you need.' When Koreans have been working in company with Americans, they still had had little opportunity to learn the basics. Our problem is to start training today where we should have started ten years ago." I think he had a pretty good analysis of the situation.

Q: It's a shame they sent him on to be Ambassador to Finland. He was needed at home.

Capt. B.: Yes, a very capable man and a good analyst of many problems. Though he didn't take political sides he was quite aware of problem areas and people. I believe that he will be heard of in the future of his country.

Interview No. 6 with Captain Phil H. Bucklew

Place: At his residence in Fairfax, Virginia

Date: Thursday, 15 May 1980

Subject: Biography

By: John T. Mason, Jr.

Q: You talked about your sojourn in Korea and the activities there, as far as you were concerned, came to an end in July of 1958. Will you pick up your story at that point, when you were to return to the United States?

Capt. B.: As I explained, I had a two-hatted assignment, part of the duties with the CIA and their clandestine operations in North Korea, and in 1957 there had been the reorganization of our own forces in the Far East and the establishment of Naval Forces, Korea, under Admiral Al Jarrell. This explained, at least in part, or covered my unusual tour of two and a half years in Korea, in that a new command came into being and the Koreans did not evidence any question of that. By that time Helen and I had formed some strong friendships and enjoyed them very much as well as, I believe, I performed a better service for Admiral Jarrell by my previous experience--which is what he had asked for. I felt this was about the limit though-- two and a half years in-country when everyone else in the

American military was on a one-year tour that the Koreans would have me aligned with the CIA and other long-tour people.

Q: Were they still using your services with the PT boats at that point?

Capt. B.: Yes, I had two offices, one across town from the other. After the formation of Naval Forces Korea, I spent a lesser time with my counterpart Captain Kim Se Won, the director of Korean Naval Intelligence. We saw each other frequently and socially and it all worked out but was becoming more and more involved. We were having less of the North Korean type operations--there was more hope of reconciling things at Panmunjam and more restriction on Korean activity during the 1957-58 period.

I explained my situation to the agency representatives and they were equally understanding that my being on duty in uniform for so long a period was a little unusual, so that tour was terminated and I received my orders.

Q: After all that had been designated as a hardship tour area. Would you tell me about command relationship where you had a Naval Command, Korea--what relationship did this now have with the South Korean Navy and with the United Nations set-up over there?

Capt. B.: Admiral Jarrell had three hats, so to speak--as Commander Naval Forces, Korea he served the capacity that had been Naval Forces Far East, that was broken up to become

Naval Forces Japan and Naval Forces Korea. The United Nations command located in Tokyo was Admiral Jarrell's immediate administrative superior, and in Korea Admiral Jarrell would come under the United Nations Commander militarily. Admiral Jarrell became chief of the advisory group to the Korean navy and also the United Nations naval representative at Panmunjam, so he had a three-hatted responsibility. In a subordinate position I had a comparable relationship with both Koreans and U. S. forces and served on what is known as the Watch Committee with the United Nations Command. The Watch Committee controls all clandestine activity. My responsibilities were divided, though sitting next to me in the Watch Committee was a CIA representative, as well as the joint military representatives, mostly Army, and the Security Group.

Q: Weren't they pretty much intertwined?

Capt. B.: I often wondered how much they knew about my circumstance, but it was the kind of thing you don't talk about or ask about other alignments. There never was an indication that anyone suspected me of having multiple duties.

In any event my next orders were back to the Amphibious Training Command at Coronado. I didn't know just what I was coming back to, but in any event the orders were modified before I got back and Admiral Speck who had been chief of staff to Admiral Fahrion at ComPhibLant prior to my going to Korea, was now the Commander of the Amphibious Training Command but on a temporary assignment to a joint amphibious exercise,

"Rocky Shoals," working out of Presidio at San Francisco. Admiral Speck was the joint commander of this division size landing, the first that had been attempted by the U. S. Army in the Pacific with the Naval Forces since World War II. Admiral Speck intercepted me and I went direct to the Presidio and worked on the early planning in preparation for this amphibious exercise—continued through the exercise, which was held down the coast at the Hearst estate at San Simeon, California. Then back to San Francisco for the after-exercise reports. All this prior to my reporting to Coronado. I served on the joint intelligence staff through this operation.

Q: This was your introduction to the training school? Would you describe in some detail this amphibious exercise, the combined one? It probably has some corollaries with one that Admiral Struble told me about which took place in the '30s I believe, and in pretty much the same location and it was rather primitive. He described it in detail and perhaps this would be a parallel.

Capt. B.: This was probably the most unique exercise that I have been a part of, though in earlier years I suppose I have been a part of 20 or 30 on the Atlantic Coast. It was unique in this case in that all army equipment had to be transported from the various army bases throughout the country, by land to the West Coast—a very expensive job of assembling their equipments and getting them to their point of embarkation. It probably cost more money to pull this together than half a dozen exercises that we had been associated with in Marine and Navy training on which we would pick up the troops by ship from a Marine base and take it from there.

Q: There must have been quite a motivating factor to do this?

Capt. B.: Well, I think it was a tremendous experience for the army personnel, more so than the navy. As naval amphibians we were quite accustomed to the procedures, the necessities, the embarkation, the preparations and the intelligence. My job headed the intelligence section of the overall staff but we became involved in a little bit of everything. The most difficult task fell to the logistics group in pulling this together. It took two or three months to assemble the forces; they came from Fort Riley, Kansas, some from the East coast; there were breakdowns on the way among the convoys; and it became quite an army exercise of initiatives, of recovery, of maintenance, of bailing them out of difficulties. Some equipments came by flatcar and there were, of necessity, several points of embarkation on the West coast as far south as San Diego and different areas.

Q: Personnel-wise how many men participated?

Capt. B.: A full scale army division. I can't specifically estimate there, but I would say there were at least 10,000 troops, for the navy it was routine. The ships were manned by their regular crews and the overall plan of the operation was prepared at our Presidio headquarters, then passed down through the various group commanders within the navy in the same manner we have always done it. For the navy it was not an undue strain other than movement of ships, embarking and debarking of the troops and the routine conduct of an amphibious over the beaches landing.

Q: Did the idea originate with the army?

Capt. B.: Yes, I'm not fully familiar in that phase as it was completed before I arrived from Korea. The staff had been assembled at the Presidio and the man I relieved, heading the intelligence section, was the officer in charge of the Intelligence School at Coronado, which, I found, was going to be my next assignment.

Q: Could you say, as intelligence officer for the amphibious exercise of this sort, what were your immediate obligations?

Capt. B.: It had a pretty broad scope, ranging from the beach intelligence--hydrographic information, gradients, weather, and the very fundamental over-the-beach phases.

Q: Presumably that would be fairly easy along the California coast?

Capt. B.: Yes. We could accumulate much of the information from existing sources and rely on it. However, we did find in the State of California that there wasn't quite as much information as we had anticipated and we did have to use our demolition teams and work pre-operation reconnaissance as we would in an actual operation. But we did have more backup than you would have on a foreign beach. One interesting point, more advanced than I had previously experienced was the use of photographic intelligence. The army had the aircraft and we photographed the beaches and were working out a new system which did not replace but certainly supported the human physical intelligence on the beaches. We would make runs on the hour, photographically, and then by the overlay on the charts confirmed by rise and fall of the tide, the gradients and, at low tide, obstacles, offshore rocks, reefs and that sort of thing. This was new to me and a good experience.

Q: Did you have any time limit on this, did you have to assemble all this data within a given period of time?

Capt. B.: We had very fixed operational dates comparable to what you would in an actual operation. It seems there is always a scramble no matter how much time you have. With various breakdowns you are always scrambling to pull it all together, to coordinate it as your so-called D-day is being approached.

Q: How did you achieve a situation similar to what you would face in an operation on a foreign beach, where there was the enemy onshore; how did you achieve something similar there on a California beach? Was there any opposition to your exploration of the beaches and that sort of thing?

Capt. B.: Not really. There were many artificialities that

were brought into this exercise. The division size was the most impressive part, but among the artificialities the landing itself had to be confined to the limits of the Hearst estate. The Hearst castle was out-of-bounds as well as, I recall, was a large stack of tile that had been disassembled in Italy from, I believe, a monastery. It had been transported to be re-assembled on the Hearst estate although this had not been done due apparently to the death of Mr. Hearst. This was an out-of-bounds obstacle right in the middle of our assault beach. I don't recall what we named that, whether we named it a church or something inviolable, but there were artificialities of that type. There were additional artificialities which were converted into excellent exercise for the army as it involved the electronic and communication phases. In that area it would have been a great civilian disturbance had we utilized jamming and some of the communications normal to the military.

Q: You mean people would have been deprived of their favorite radio programs and such?

Capt. B.: Yes, that would have caused more furor than a resisting force, I am afraid. It became a very large, land-line communication exercise in which both the aggressor force and the landing force utilized land-line field phones. The figure of 40,000 miles of wire comes to mind, that were utilized and recovered afterward, which was another big project and of major importance for army training.

Q: What about barbed wire?

Capt. B.: There was barbed wire used around many of the out-of-bounds areas, but this was telephone wire on the field phones. Instead of transmitting by wave-lengths, UHF equipment that we would normally use in communications from the front lines, this exercise simulated radio communications with telephone wire. It was entirely an army project, but one of the most complicated that I recall.

Q: Was the local populace aware of this exercise? If so, did they interfere in any way?

Capt. B.: No interference was encountered but there were a tremendous number of army military police assigned to block off the areas. You couldn't cut off the main highways and the MPs had quite a traffic problem particularly after the exercise started, in stopping, holding back traffic then releasing it. This too was part of the land-line communications drill-- almost a stop and go venture. These were unusual artificialities that, in the California area, had to be considered and injected because your main highways north and south come very close to the coast line there.

Q: In a regular amphibious operation there is a softening up of the beach in advance isn't there? What did you do here?

Capt. B.: There was no bombardment. That is a most difficult thing any place on our West coast and it is also on the East coast now. The navy and marines accomplish such training when operating from the San Diego and Camp Pendleton areas. There you normally insert your bombardments at San Clemente or on offshore islands that have been set aside for gunnery practice, and on the East coast at Guantanamo, then inject that into your exercise scenario. So much has been accomplished by increments, but you do get to test all weapons without jeopardizing the populace.

Q: An ingenious arrangement.

Capt. B.: It is really quite complicated. A large scale amphibious operation is about as complex and detailed a matter as you see in the military, though it is a point of criticism that we are always going to simplify. The basic operations orders will very often get to about one inch thick with their various annexes and communications, logistics and overall support functions--quite a preparation.

Q: For an operation of this sort you must have had a considerable number of VIPs from Washington as observers?

Capt. B.: We always had that. I don't recall who all but I do remember some landed in the boats--which makes excellent political photography--some ashore. Usually there is a grandstand observation point for VIP visitors from which they can see the troops coming across the beach, and that is the galmour point of interest. As the operation progresses the troops become so dispersed that there is not much for an observer to see. It is not very impressive to see soldiers snaking on their bellies twenty yards apart--in other words you don't see many of them once they stomp the first hundred yards coming out of the boats. Or, there can be included simulations of gunfire and aircraft and perhaps a parachute drop, that's about it for observers. The rest of it occurs in briefings, telling them what they are there to see, even though they don't see it--the overall strategical and tactical exercise.

Q: Is it to be assumed that your intelligence duties diminished considerably as they began to land on the beaches?

Capt. B.: Yes. We reverted to what might be considered a reporting responsibility. I had an outpost on the beach from which we kept a blackboard account of waves landed, groups landed, reports coming back over the land line phones: was this road open? or what objective had been accomplished-- which we passed on to command and to the observers. It was not as glamorous as a radio report but we gave them a running account of what they couldn't see but what was happening -- more for showmanship and public relations than realistic military procedure!

Q: With the operation, when was the command turned over to the army?

Capt. B.: When a beachhead is "neutralized" and the troops are ashore, control turns over very quickly in this type of exercise.

Q: It's almost automatic?

Capt. B.: Yes, really it is. In an actual operation of course, it could take several days and even then with question as to whether a beachhead would hold, but we knew we were winners from the time we had launched the troops in this exercise.

Q: How many casualties did you estimate you had?

Capt. B.: I don't recall. Of course, this was another artificiality. We had our casualty counts (and a few actual casualties which you always have whether it be broken ankles or vehicular accidents--that type of thing).

Q: This having taken place in 1958, did you use any post World War II type craft?

Capt. B.: Unfortunately we didn't have many new craft in this period. We had gone through a very austere period in which there had been some new craft, mostly replacement craft. Nothing radically new had been brought in during the Korean War, and the post-war congressional restrictions and attitudes had very much restricted naval development. There were some landing vehicles of the combined Jeep and DUK order, in other words, from the water would move on to the land, by the army but I don't recall any real new developments in equipments that were used.

I do recall, going back a few years to exemplify the restrictions on the military, while I was with the ComPhibLant it was a matter of great concern that you could, at that time, procure a new landing craft for seventy-five hundred dollars and it was costing us ten to twelve thousand dollars to repair the existing craft. But congressional authority would not permit new procurement. I am afraid that condition prevailed throughout the '50s. One naval development was a new and larger LCU which would carry more vehicles and supplies than the medium sized landing craft. That's the only one I recall as a new development.

Q: Did you have a very modern command ship?

Capt. B.: They were all World War II types. I think we had one new ship that was the squadron commander's at that time. The changes for flagships were improvised--old ships modified by adding things like a helicopter pad, improved C.I.C., modernized communications equipment--in other words, no radical change in the ships, in their design or propulsion. There were some electronic additions but the basic hulls were getting old and tired, though they had several years to go yet.

Q: That was a fascinating experience and it got your feet wet on the West coast.

Capt. B.: With the report work that occurred after the exercise, it gave a little pleasant time in San Francisco. While we were at the Presidio we spent a couple of months in coordinating exercise reports of what happened, because the dispersal of the troops was just about as complicated as the assemblage had been and report information would come back in from say Fort Riley, Kansas. We didn't work too hard. We had to wait and we were all glad to get to our next assignment. We were all bored with the waiting.

Q: Were there any, not startling, but quasi-startling discoveries in this operation?

Capt. B.: I think it was considered quite a revelation to the army planners and commands, and the experience gained--mainly because they hadn't done it before. The senior officers were World War II veterans with various experiences, but not as the navy is accustomed to amphibious-wise, of having at least one full scale exercise every six months. This had to be considered as basically an army training exercise. It was more or less a routine matter to the navy, although every time you do it, it brings in a little better understanding with more experience. Once the troops are ashore you disperse the ships and the ships are back to their home ports, it is one more phase done.

From there I reported to the Amphibious Training Command at Coronado, as officer in charge of the Amphibious Intelligence School, which was a new experience to me. It was more or less a classroom operation.

Q: How long had the school been in existence?

Capt. B.: The Amphibious Training Command was set up during World War II. It declined, was re-activated or expanded during the Korean war and continued from there. The various schools that were included under the training command involved, other than Intelligence, Gunfire Support, Air Support, Beach Group -- each of these being a separate school. There was boat handling, maintenance -- six or seven different schools. At the time that I reported we were each in a separate barracks type building and they were building a new school building which consolidated each of the schools. We then continued as separate departments in our specialized field but operated in the same building, under the same roof.

Q: Under the administration of the director of the Intelligence Command?

Capt. B.: A commanding officer of the Naval Amphibious Schools, and was directly under the Commander Ambhibious Training Command. That, for several years, was the dominant activity of the Coronado Amphibious Base. The base also headquartered the staff of the Commander Amphibious Forces, Pacific, and several subordinate commands such as Tactical Air Squadrons, Dispensary, Engineering and Repair for Amphibious small craft, etc. But a good portion of our activity involved the moving of the schools under the same roof and establishing a new organization, while meanwhile conducting the training courses (usually two-weeks duration) for both active duty and reserve personnel.

Q: Was that accomplished during your time there?

Capt. B.: Yes. About at the end of my first year we moved

into the new building. Meanwhile our courses included both active duty personnel, for example, those personnel that are being assigned to amphibious staffs and related responsibilities -- these combined with reserve intelligence officers. Most of the courses were set up on a two-week basis and we would alternate sequence. In the Intelligence School we had a series of three two-week courses, or, one six-week course for an incoming intelligence officer. He would take each of the three, consecutively. This would also satisfy the two-weeks active duty of the various reserve officers. It was broken up into two-week courses, and following the six weeks we had perhaps a week off to reassemble and start the same pattern again.

Q: How many students would you have going through your school at one point?

Capt. B.: The intelligence courses were rather popular and we would range around 50 students a class.

Q: These were all officers?

Capt. B.: In rare cases we might have an enlisted man such as photographic intelligence specialist or someone of that type. However, the courses are tailored for officer personnel. I served there until early in 1961 when I was assigned to Amphibious Group One, as the staff intelligence officer.

Q: Before you go on to that phase of your career, would you please say something more about the component parts of the courses that you were teaching? Were you involved with the SEALS and the UDT people?

Capt. B.: Only in student training--selected UDTs. SEALS were not activated at that time. With UDTs, we had selected officers who, as with shipboard, were intended for intelligence officer duties. The UDT training was a part of the amphibious school but simply a department, as we were.

Q: So it wasn't actually under your aegis?

Capt. B.: Not then, that occurred later -- but under the school system, no.

Q: The UDT department there at Coronado, in the course of sprouts they underwent, was it similar to the one on the East coast?

Capt. B.: It was a close parallel. There were some variances but the training came under the administration of the Amphibious Schools and there were counterparts -- Atlantic and Pacific -- under the training commands that maintained a natural liaison. It continues to exist today I think under a very similar organization.

Q: As the head of the intelligence department, did you select your own instructors? How did you do that?

Capt. B.: No, they were assigned by their services. I had four naval officers, a marine and an army officer as my instructors. Of course, I took my turn for various lectures.

Q: I should think you would with your vast background and experience; that you would have something to impart that others didn't have.

Capt. B.: We put in a lot of lecture hours. I had one pitch on Order of Battle in which I covered the entire Far East -- that was a two-hour lecture included in each of the courses. Where they did come concurrently it was repetitious to those students who had six weeks continuous study.

Q: Maybe some of it would bear repetition?

Capt. B.: It did actually become kind of a popular pitch. I must say that I de-classified a lot of otherwise Secret information in coordinating it, but the Order of Battle talk which covered circumstances ranging from Korea to Taiwan to China -- the entire Far East -- was utilized with many command press briefings, and they tossed my talk in for any group of VIP visitors, you might say. It was a little different from the normal thing.

Q: You were kind of a star performer, would you say?

Capt. B.: No, I wouldn't say that but I did it often enough that all I needed was a map and a pointer.

Q: You say you had to de-classify and clean up some of the information you imparted to the students, but they all had clearance, did they not?

Capt. B.: Yes. In your intelligence classes you can label what is Secret. I perhaps cheated a bit and with much of the military classification I could find some place such as _Time_ magazine or _The Wall Street Journal_ coverage that told you the same thing unclassified that was militarily secret, and thus we could justify the inclusion of some of these statistics. In the coverage of Order of Battle it would be limited or incomplete as it covered the weaponry. It would suffice, considering the audience, to explain where we had certain nuclear weapons, without going into any great detail about it. Mostly the number of troops and the number of ships, aircraft and army types, such detail as that, mixed with a few slides and perhaps an accounting that this country had a shipyard and a few bases, and the general capabilities which to a novice would be fairly impressive -- such as, to indicate that there were 600,000 troops in Korea in addition to the U.S. forces there. It might relate to other things in the discussion and explain a lot of points that normally were not clear to a newcomer in the field. We covered various aspects from psychological warfare to photographic intelligence, but in such schools you really only scratch the surface on detail and give a general understanding to the student of the overall responsibilities and its relation, its importance to the overall picture.

Q: Actually he has to go out and learn by doing, doesn't he?

Capt. B.: Yes, and no two situations are the same. The emphasis one time may fall on the reconnaissance and another time it may be the handling of prisoners of war. Each of these aspects we touched upon with a fairly good but general explanation.

Q: What kind of screening was achieved in guaranteeing that these students had the necessary gray matter, so to speak, to cope with all these diversified subjects?

Capt. B.: Well, the assumption that as naval officers or army (we did get army and marine mixed in in lesser numbers with our students) -- I am afraid there is a very limited amount of screening by the personnel desks -- there was the assumption, however, that all officers have the background and the capabilities.

Q: Isn't that a dubious assumption?

Capt. B.: If the interest is there, they can expand from the starting point but admittedly not all are qualified. We have had to screen out some for various reasons. I recall a lieutenant commander coming to me and telling me his problems, which happened to be that he was subject to blackmail from an earlier escapade and he was about to be assigned to a rather responsible position. It was his own concern that brought him to me and I in turn was sent him to his admiral. I hope his problems were resolved but his assignment was changed to shipyard duties other than intelligence and security involvement. That is a rare incident, but things like that do occur.

In other cases when you are dealing with a very junior officer you have to assume his potential though it may appear very questionable during the indoctrination period. But you also must assume that he is not going in to head a department. If a more senior officer intended to head a department or staff division, we often would recommend an additional course--give him more training, you might say a little special tutoring in which we would pull him from the class and set him aside for all day briefings. For example, in intelligence planning and operational plans -- if he hadn't previously been exposed, we could give him enough background for a starting point. There are always difficulties on the matter of personnel assignments and that is not confined to intelligence activities alone.

Q: It is comforting to know that a man with potential assignments of this sort is considered very carefully.

Capt. B.: If the interests are there, the enthusiasm, they do develop rapidly. Curiosity will stimulate. I have always felt, in an instructing capacity, if you can get a group full of questions, that are inquisitive, that's not making it tough, it's making it better for the instructor as well as for the advancement of the student. That doesn't come, as I have observed in some courses, just by telling jokes -- it is not all laughs.

Q: And it doesn't come immediately, does it? It takes a while in a course for this to develop?

Capt. B.: Yes, if you can hit that point of interest it will expand. I found that to be the case regarding psychological warfare, though it is a very interesting subject, to me at least -- and I handled a lecture on the subject myself -- I found that most students have only general ideas as to what all the subject includes. Actually it has tremendously broad scope -- not always practiced by the military, but the assets are there and it requires initiative on the part of these officers to influence and see to it that these assets are included in exercises and operations. These can very easily be omitted or down-played in favor of some basic concerns of the commander of landing troops. As you develop your scenarios, the inclusion of all your capabilities and the exercising of them is very important. Whether or not you need them then, we should not let the capability die, which I think we often tend to do.

You might say that my school experience was not the most exciting, but it was one of the more interesting times.

Q: Perhaps you needed an interesting time that wasn't too much filled with adventure at this point?

Capt. B.: Well, I renewed a lot of old acquaintances, some dating back to World War II. With their later reserve activities

and two week annual active duty, they would come in as students.
I think I told you the story about Judge Archie Brown of
Texas who was commanding officer of his Intelligence Unit.
He was not only a student but the key figure the time that
the admiral's piano was stolen. We had some fun incidents
and I consider the intelligence officer students -- they certainly built up my respect and admiration -- as being among the
most interested of naval officers concerning overall world
developments, current intelligence, and the political aspects.
We encouraged and had some informal meetings, cocktail parties,
for the class, and made effort to know them personally. We
had our fun with it. I think it important to know the people
you are instructing and, as it differs from many aspects of
civilian school life, in a military school you are all fellow
officers, contemporaries, and you can afford to be a little
more relaxed and personal. You need to find out if a man
has a coming assignment that he is not too certain about, to
break down his reluctance, to find out where his confidence
might be a little lacking and give him a hand.

Q: As you say, the interest lies in the fact that, when you
are dealing with intelligence and the intelligence school, the
world is indeed your oyster and all the ramifications of the
world of men is involved in this particular subject.

Capt. B.: I think also, as it differs from many academic type
courses, in a military school there is a place for personal
experience, for relating actual incidents, occurrences, problems,

giving them an idea of the broad scope of things that they will bump into, the surprise elements. I believe this is more appropriate in a military circumstance than in an academic curriculum where you cover the basic facts.

Q: There is a more immediate trust within the group, is there not?

Capt. B.: With your contemporaries, yes.

Q: You are about to depart from Coronado and the schools in June of 1961.

Capt. B.: I then reported to the staff of the Commander, Amphibious Group One. The flagship was in San Diego at that time so that was not a great move momentarily.

Q: I meant to ask -- when you were at the school this must have afforded Helen a much happier period of normal family life?

Capt. B.: We bought a home in Coronado and later got to return to it for another three years. So, until our settling here in Virginia, that was the longest stay in one spot that we had. We retained the house in Coronado and came back to it, so we enjoyed that very much. We both played a lot of golf and you can't really criticize the California environment and Coronado is an ideal spot for a military location. We did enjoy that very much.

Q: And Helen gave up extraneous duties on the outside at this point?

Capt. B.: Well, yes, on the employment side. I guess in the navy you never get away from the Navy Relief extraneous type duties, and there is quite a bit of social life. In each of my jobs it seemed that we had collateral or additional duties with higher staffs so we did have obligations of that type -- from which we have pretty much retired at this stage.

Back to Amphibious Group One -- I knew the man I was relieving, he having spent six weeks in my intelligence school, and we didn't have too much of a relief due to that reason.

Q: He did things the way you wanted them done, is that what you imply?

Capt. B.: He sort of laughed it off when I came on board and said, "Well, you briefed me so I won't have to bother with much of a turnover." He had just made Captain -- John Neff is his name -- and he went to CinCPacFlt, so our affiliations continued throughout his tour there.

Admiral Kirkpatrick was Commander, Amphibious Group One at the time but he was about to be relieved by Admiral Ed Hooper. Though we were based in San Diego, we were coming into a world of rather interesting activities which included first a public relations visit up to the State of Washington for their annual Sea Fair, a one-week operation at which they have their hydroplane races and quite some activity, and the Amphibious Group, actually a squadron of the group, had been asked to appear as a navy public relations venture.

Q: Did they put on any kind of performance?

Capt. B.: Yes, in parading the ships through the harbor and participation in various shore events. Being a newcomer to the staff, I assume -- not having become bogged down with too many other duties -- I was sent as an advance man to assist in arrangements for Sea Fair. I returned, then with the flagship and one of the squadrons, we made the junket. On return to San Diego we commenced preparation for another amphibious exercise with the army in the Fort Lewis area near Seattle. That was another tricky operation -- much politics involved with it in that it had been scheduled at the time of the salmon run, which would have caused tremendous conflict with the commercial fishing.

Q: And you would have had an Indian war on your hands too, would you not?

Capt. B.: It was quite complicated politically and as a result, this was one of the most unique amphibious operations in which I have participated. An agreement was reached that we would operate one day, be off a day, then come back on -- so that we would alternate without conflict with the fishermen and the related commercial activities in the area.

Q: Giving the pseudo enemy an opportunity to regroup?

Capt. B.: Right. There was another complication which made it tricky for navy landing craft in that the landing area was loaded with submerged and floating logs which created some boat hazards.

Q: From logging operations?

Capt. B.: Yes, there are a lot of submerged obstacles in that area.

Q: Was this at the mouth of the Columbia River?

Capt. B.: Right. We had a two-week exercise and the day on and day off made it unusual. On the day off we were quite busy in view of the logs, reporting and, you might say, "log surveillance." Upon return -- I forget the exact date but it was in the mid-fall -- to San Diego we received word that the amphibious group had had a change of home port to Subic Bay in the Philippines.

Q: It was during this operation that Ed Hooper took over as commander, wasn't it?

Capt. B.: Yes, actually he took over prior to Sea Fair. I only had a couple of weeks under Admiral Kirkpatrick.

Q: As I remember Ed's story, he hadn't really been involved in the planning of this operation -- he just had to carry it out.

Capt. B.: The admiral hadn't been involved with the planning, that is correct, but of necessity he certainly became involved when he had to arrange the compromise to a day on-day off basis; that was done after we arrived in the Seattle area. It took quite some doing to perform that without antagonizing all of the commercial world in that area and yet fulfilling the army requirements for training.

Well, as I said, we received preliminary orders to change home port to Subic Bay and that was received with somewhat mixed emotions. I personally was rather enthused and the staff operations officer, Captain Bob Thienes and myself were sent out to Subic Bay to look the situation over, check facilities, available housing, and such details -- as our dependents were to move with us, since we were to be home ported and this would be a permanent move for the command staff, with flagships only rotating on a six-month basis.

Q: Was this a reflection of Vietnam?

Capt. B.: It was a reflection of rather long time considerations. It had been recommended over a period of years but never finalized for several reasons. I suppose the primary one was economy -- to alleviate some of the expense of having ships enroute and returning from Western Pacific as they had been relieving one another every six months. There was considerable expense and wear and tear on ships and some question of the defense coverage of the area during that transition period, as well as the knowledge of the build-up in Southeast Asia which had been occurring. I know my first awareness came from Captain Rufus Taylor, while I was in Korea and he was with CinCPacFlt at the time. He had told me back in 1957, "Keep your eye on Laos and Cambodia, that's the next hot spot." So that had been building up and in 1961 when we went out, still nothing was really happening but the threat was there and alerts occurred, which made the intelligence assignment rather interesting. In any event, Bob Thienes and I came back from the Philippines and we built it up to the staff and to the wives as, "Boy, you're going to love this." With any group of people, I think you'll find 50% may love it and the other 50% would hate it; and that turned out to be somewhat the case.

Q: Where were you being based in the Philippines?

Capt. B.: At Subic Bay. It had its good and bad points. There was good housing there, miserable climate, some nice facilities including a golf course, officer and enlisted clubs, plenty of help, lots of stealing -- problems that you might face any place, but the difficulty for dependents is that you are isolated to that base. The roads would be washed out and, as Helen put it some times, "the only way out of here is straight up." That was literally true, to get to Manila you had to fly. It became a boring situation in many ways for the dependents.

Now, for the flagship, I think most of us thought it was an ideal situation because we kept moving. We weren't in Subic as much as we would have liked. Each quarter we would make the circuit going to Japan, Korea at times, stop off at Okinawa and Taiwan, come back through Manila, Hong Kong, Singapore, we covered the entire Far East. It became a very interesting experience to me and an enjoyable one with Admiral Hooper. I think we visited every temple in the Far East and saw as many golf courses as we could in the same period. In the course of our stay we had amphibious exercises in Taiwan, in Thailand and in the Philippines. We had "alerts" that occurred too. At one stage we were in standby to evacuate American personnel from Indonesia during the troubles in that area. Turmoil was building up in the Far East without actual conflict. We visited Saigon, and we had amphibious landings on the Vietnamese coast during which we performed considerable reconnaissance utilizing our UDTs detachment. Admiral Hooper tasked me as the staff cognizant office responsible for UDTs performance of beach reconnaissance and their support. We did a lot of intelligence gathering on the Vietnamese coast.

Q: This was in the Gulf of Tonkin period?

Capt. B.: Yes -- utilizing our UDTs.

Q: Was this intelligence gathering for the North area?

Capt. B.: No, for the Southern area. We were totally lacking beach intelligence information. UDTs did quite a job there, although you never are finalized on beach intelligence because of the changes that can occur overnight, such as a typhoon.

Q: Silting of the rivers also? Was this data that you collected at this point useful to us a little later?

Capt. B.: At least in its preliminary form. We acquired the general background information which had been lacking up to this time.

Q: There were no topographic maps?

Capt. B.: Not that could be considered accurate. We always had to recheck and update each detail.

Q: Would such maps have dated from the French period?

Capt. B.: Yes, as the most reliable source. The exact date that they were developed I don't recall, but we worked from the French charts, the markings were in French, and the Vietnamese Navy had little or no interest. Their main maritime, I won't say naval, interests were with their thousands of fishing craft and the fishermen worked on the rule of thumb, knew the waters. They hadn't the depth and gradient problems that you have with naval craft. Their interests were only in passing. They were cooperative with us but our entire reconnaissance was conducted with naval ships, with the APDs and the UDTs working from the APDs. They spent a period of two to three months in continuous operations charting the coastal waters.

Q: All this was done with the cognizance of the Diem government?

Capt. B.: Yes, and with the assistance of the naval attaché in liaison with them. There were no real problems in that line -- no withholding or question of authorization.

I can't recall many exciting incidents during our Phib Group tours; as I say, it was a very interesting assignment. The travel and the fact that we were kept in a mobile position, moving from one country to the next, made it most interesting but with no exciting events. The amphibious landing that was conducted in the Gulf of Siam with the Thai navy was a routine operation. We had the usual problems. This was the first time the Thais had been involved in an actual amphibious landing. They had been given several amphibious ships but very seldom had their ships been under way. I understand that we had to subsidize the Thai government with per diem for some of the officers to get their ships away from the pier. They were mostly high ranking officers -- captains in charge of LSTs. The joint commander, Rear Admiral Ching Chulasukum, with Admiral Hooper, was a Thai prince whom I had known previously at the amphibious intelligence school. Going back to the intelligence school, I did mention that we had a very interesting foreign officers' course that lasted for about six weeks. It was conducted each year with representatives from about twenty foreign countries, both European and Asiatic.

Q: It must have been a kind of Tower of Babel, wasn't it?

Capt. B.: There was an amazing congeniality and pleasant contacts were made.

Q: How did you impart the teaching material?

Capt. B.: It was very generalized. Classroom life, I think, was somewhat boring to these senior students, but their personal contacts with one another did a tremendous lot of good and the social life was quite interesting to them -- so I have been told by Admiral Liu Kwan Kai, later Commander in Chief of the Nationalist Chinese Navy.

Again, golf came into the picture. Liu became bored with classroom routine and explained to Rear Admiral Charley Duncan, then Commander Amphibious Training Command, that he had come to this course for at least a partial rest and would like to develop his golf game. Admiral Duncan called me in and said, "I don't play golf, would you mind playing with the Admiral?"

I was glad to cooperate on such an enjoyable assignment, done on week-ends, of course. Helen and I and my army major intelligence assistant, Major Vallentine, played quite a bit with Admiral Liu and established a very strong friendship which was continued in Taiwan during Phib Group One visits. We came to know his family and his five sons who all came to college and postgrad school in the United States. But the admiral was bored with the training.

Q: But he had been exposed in the general sense. And that calls to mind the question about the Thailand navy and their cooperation with this amphibious operation -- prior to that had they not observed some as a member of SEATO?

Capt. B.: Some of them had a background of military schools training and among their Marine and Army generals I believe they had had some World War II, though not combat, military experience. However, the bulk of them are of royalty or are political appointees -- that type background. Very congenial and cooperative -- and I would say among the more willing to learn as we, on a joint exercise, would have them side by side, living as counterparts aboard the flagship. In my intelligence section we had three or four Thais working side by side with our U. S. Navy types. I was impressed by their willingness and interest in learning though they had limited naval background.

Q: A limited number of ships, too?

Capt. B.: Yes, and they didn't spend too much time aboard them. They were very anxious to assist us in touring Bangkok, however, and in shopping and such deals they were more familiar with.

Q: Will you speak of your experiences in Taiwan?

Capt. B.: We had amphibious exercises there which were restricted to a degree in that the Taiwanese did not wish us -- you might say forbade us -- to see certain portions of the island. The landing was conducted on the east coast of Taiwan as opposed to the west from where they launched their offshore island operations. Some of their activities, clandestine commando type operations and defenses against the China mainland, were of considerable concern and sensitivity in shielding them from exposure to U. S. question or criticism.

Q: Were those operations, clandestine -- were they entirely Taiwanese or were they also related to the CIA?

Capt. B.: I can't answer that because I don't know of CIA affiliation. I personally, through Admiral Liu Kwan Kai, had some briefing on their activities, which are extremely clandestine, to the extent of using hoods on their operators to prevent them from knowing one another, or exposure as to who is participating in a raid, or where -- that sort of thing. From my limited analysis of their training, it was thorough and strenuous. I was asked many questions concerning UDT training. I thought, in many ways, their operation was even more demanding than ours in training and qualification.

At Taiwan we visited at Kaohsiung, their seaport in the south of the island. That was their naval base. Just a few miles north of Taipei is their main seaport, Keelung, where transports and large ships can be berthed in a protected harbor.

Q: They did a conversion job on an LST?

Capt. B.: They made it into a command and control ship, putting in a very elaborate CIC and improvised to duplicate as best they could anything they had learned from our flagship and control facilities. I was very much impressed with their conversion efforts and by the accomplishments they had made in developing their own landing craft. They had drydocks and to this day, insist upon their own production of craft. On their commercial efforts their interests at the present time are in joint enterprise. They want to continue and further develop their capabilities within Taiwan, not to receive hand-me-down gifts or such equipment that may be surplus to us, or obsolete.

Q: This is somewhat in contrast with most of the other peoples in the Far East, isn't it?

Capt. B.: At the present time there is interest in joint effort, mostly to obtain technological knowledge and assistance to exploit their own capabilities and developing in-house capabilities. I think for a number of years following World War II and the Korean war, the main interest of most of these countries was in receiving whatever grants of ships and equipment that we could afford.

Q: Didn't we encourage that through the MAAG program?

Capt. B.: Yes, not only in the Far East but worldwide, and they built up considerable forces. The ships, however, more so than army and marine equipment tend to become obsolete and worn out. I think there was a better replacement program, from my observation, for amphibious tanks, and marine equipment of that type. Though the numbers were not excessive the equipment was kept modernized. This was the same theme utilized by the Military Assistance Programs in rationing of equipment and ammunition and fuel to the aided countries to prevent them from becoming the aggressors as Taiwan against the

Communists, as the Koreans against the North Koreans, and so on. The Chinese Nationalists conducted a very effective program from Matsu and their offshore islands with bombardments almost continuously or day by day, against the coast line, and with frequent raiding operations from their PT type craft. Their general capabilities, I thought, were among the best in the Far East. The amphibious exercise in which we participated jointly with them was a very good show.

Q: That was off the south coast?

Capt. B.: Off the southeast coast. As with most of the Far East military, however, age and rank were becoming top-heavy, obviously so, within their services. For example, the admirals and vice admirals were in abundance.

Q: They were mainly the mainland Chinese contingent, weren't they?

Capt. B.: That's right. They had had some experience. Of course, there wasn't a Chinese navy from World War II. That, as you will recall, is one of the jobs offered to Admiral Miles in wanting him to build up a navy. He turned it down but it indicated the respect they had for him and their desire to build a navy. This, accompanied by the continuous threat of the Chinese Communists with their various coastal and radio-controlled craft, the Swatows, and their build-up which was occurring from Shanghai yards and at several different spots along the mainland coastline -- there was a continuous threat against the Chinese Nationalists and they were giving it back, play for play. In my opinion they built up considerable strength.

Q: What relationship did you have with the Taiwan defense command and the Americans there?

Capt. B.: Of course, this was a joint exercise with the Chinese navy and the liaison, the coordination, was supported by the Taiwan Defense Command. We made our calls and exchanged our visits whenever we came into the area.

Q: Can you recall who it was at that point?

Capt. B.: I personally dealt with a Lieutenant Colonel Johnson, who had been my back-up man from ComNavFE while I was in Korea. The Commander, Taiwan Defense Command was Admiral Charley Melson. I believe I have covered all of the amphibious exercises that we participated in under joint command.

Q: You had three, one in Thailand, one in Taiwan and did you have one in the Philippines, too?

Capt. B.: Yes, we had rather a large scale one in the Philippines. Again, a joint exercise in which the Filipinos came aboard the flagship, assisted in planning and worked very closely side by side with our people; they operated their own ships fairly well and they worked as a separate force, but alongside our beaches and craft in the landings.

Q: Where did you have your operation there, in the Mariveles area?

Capt. B.: Yes, it was not a long transit course. There was some concern at the time of the Huks rioting and there was a little confusion during the exercise with their threat but it was uneventful, well coordinated, and the Filipinos had a rather passive attitude but reasonably good capability.

Q: What were your plans for the proposed evacuation of Americans from Indonesia? What sort of stand-by arrangements?

Capt. B.: The flagship was in stand-by for a period of several weeks, during which time we had quite a scramble trying to get hydrographic and intelligence information on beaches and the areas of possible evacuation. It was another circumstance in which, surprisingly, considering our considerable World War II activity there, we had very little on record. Most of this was done by aircraft photography and fortunately we did not have to land any craft over the beaches. It was a tricky thing even for planning because even where you had information the areas may have been overgrown with tropical jungle.

Q: Evacuation would have been from Jakarta, would it not?

Capt. B.: From that area. We had to look over all the coastal beaches with possible evacuation points, and you had, of course, about a thousand islands in the archipelago but no one knew exactly where or how many of these people were there. There was little we could do through our own resources, but through CinCPacFlt we gradually accumulated information on how many people were last known to be on this island and how many on another, and tension existed as to whether the revolt would be to the extent of capturing the people or driving them into the sea. But, it all quieted down.

Q: As I recall the events, it was a threatened Communist takeover, wasn't it, of the islands, of the government? And were you contemplating some cooperation from Sukarno's government?

Capt. B.: Our consideration involved an independent effort. Sukarno's government, as I recall, was shaky enough at the time that it was little to be relied upon. Our planning was done on the basis of an over-the-beach evacuation. I believe the ultimate decisions that never had to be executed were that it would be far better to evacuate them by air pending the securing of a suitable landing field. It was not an ideal situation.

Q: It sounds almost as difficult as the proposed one from Teheran.

Capt. B.: Yes, you can see a close parallel.

Q: Jakarta was a big city and they were going to get most of the people from Jakarta -- it would be difficult.

Capt. B.: Really until you become involved enough to face these considerations, you just don't realize the complexity of it. It is not as simple as bringing in a ship and taking them out. Mr. Carter's trying to talk that way now on Cuba but...

Q: I would think that your job as intelligence officer was far greater for something like this than just reconnaissance of the beaches.

Capt. B.: Well, you never know what to attribute to experience but it is a matter that each and all of us as senior staff officers brainstorm one another for possible solutions -- and often some wild ones come out! If you research and study the problem you get many ideas, then you shake down their feasibility. You do, in support of any commander, have the responsibility of giving him many ideas. It is his decision and it is a lot easier to shoot holes in a proposal than it is to come up with a solid answer.

Q: Were there any other hot spots at that time? Was New Guinea a hot spot, or Timor, or any of those places?

Capt. B.: As I recall the Indonesian flap -- we were accumulating information that there were 300 Americans here, and 20 here, and with so many different islands involved, you didn't know how it might spread nor what you had to pull out. Of course, going back to our earlier discussion of Salerno and Admiral Conolly, an over-the-beach evacuation can be a very hazardous, tricky operation.

Q: What about your cognizance of Singapore and Malaysia? In that day the Malaysians were hard pressed by the Communists too.

Capt. B.: We had no evidence of that. We made a port call at Kuala Lumpur under Admiral Hooper -- we were entertained royally there, literally so. I remember well the entertainment. The Sultan had a buffet dinner for our entire staff on the lawn of his estate and it was followed by not one but two full length movies. We sat on folding chairs on the lawn. They were American movies, but weren't very exciting and it got rather cold as the evening progressed. It was midnight before those movies ended but, of course, the juniors never moved until the seniors did. I don't think Admiral Hooper was any more enthused than we were, but our host thought it was great.

We also visited the Sultan's museum and I remember a display of their precious gems -- jewels -- the personal property of our host and they were as much as any I have ever seen displayed. There were no apparent political difficulties at that time.

The British were most hospitable and we had equally pleasant times in Singapore. Singapore was just coming into its new organization under Mayor Lee. It was a well disciplined city and, as we have seen publicized since, they are very strict on all forms of cleanliness, sanitation, and this makes it a very impressive city.

Q: Very British, too, isn't it?

Capt. B.: Very much so. It was compared to Hong Kong -- calling it the second Hong Kong of the Far East -- that may be so but it is not in the commercial realm of Hong Kong in my opinion -- or it wasn't at that stage. The British Southeast Asia Commander, Sir Admiral Cunningham, was situated in Singapore at the time of our visit. We had a joint golf tournament one afternoon with the British; Admiral Hooper tasked me to come up with a trophy.

Q: Can you do this by command?

Capt. B.: Both by command and by willing effort, I guess. I didn't tell the admiral until later but I had one of my boys steal a life-ring off his barge. We put a plaque in the center of it and had some of our intelligence shop people to engrave the occasion and the Championship Title and the Year. It was a rather unique trophy and I told the admiral a few days later, "We are going to need a new life-ring for your barge." He wasn't displeased -- except for our golf scores -- but I had seen that done before -- and such trophies can be greater conversation pieces than would a fancy metal cup.

Q: Drawing on experience as you often had to. What about the visit to Hong Kong? Was that just R and R?

Capt. B.: Yes. We had no real military activity there. As a matter of fact we had several visits to Hong Kong -- with

Admiral Hooper and later with Admiral Champ Blouin, who relieved Admiral Hooper. Those visits were very pleasant and many of the wives flew over from Subic Bay via Manila. It is rather complicated travel, requiring visas and such through the Philippine government. But the wives came to Hong Kong timing their travel with our ship visits. It had complexities as the wives had to take care of all those details and I have been told it takes a full day sitting around the Philippine office to get such visa clearance. It was not all easy.

Helen made one such trip, arranged by Admiral Blouin on what was called "a dependent's cruise' in which one of the amphibious transports from Subic, which was also scheduled for a direct route port of call at Hong Kong, would take the ladies and children as a dependent's cruise. It became a rather hectic one when the assigned ship was called off to Okinawa for an emergency and its replacement had no opportunity to dress itself other than the troop transport it was -- rigged for Marines. A navy transport is not designed for ladies and the heat and the weather was kind of rough on them. I guess most of them stayed on deck through the night rather than be below decks with limited ventilation and other facilities.

We had a pleasant time in Hong Kong. I think every lady there bought herself a folding chair of some type for the trip back with the intent of not going below deck and of keeping as cool as possible.

Q: What about Japan? Yokosuka was your port of call?

Capt. B.: We had several ports of call in Japan. I don't recall the different ones. There were several different ones and I have lost some of the Japanese names. Yokosuka was the main U. S. naval base. In the course of about a week's stop-over we would visit several Japanese ports and saw a lot of temples!

Q: Was this Hooper's passion, to visit temples?

Capt. B.: Not really, but several of us as staff members concluded that we should see all we could other than the usual bars, and we would take tours -- but it is sort of a standing joke that if you have seen one temple, you've seen them all. We visited in Japan a very unique place where they had a monkey farm and had hundreds of them. We tried to see as much as we could.

It was a hardship tour for the women who were confined to Subic most of the while, but for the men we had a very pleasant experience of covering many countries.

Q: These experiences added to the capability of the amphibious force, would you say?

Capt. B.: The amphibious exercise is good experience gained for even the more experienced U. S. forces. Certainly I think it contributed greatly to the capabilities of the various allied foreign countries with whom we worked. Secondly, and perhaps of even more importance, is the showing of the flag principle. It's not an entire force that makes the rounds each quarter, but the various port calls of the flagship, I think, have an important bearing wherever you may be in the world. Your presence is important, with "open house" aboard ship and an exchange of hospitality, and friendliness can't hurt our international relationships.

Q: Perhaps that is more important than the contribution you had made to the amphibious groups in these foreign countries?

Capt. B.: I feel that. It is a good will gesture as well as it is impressive. Normally when you make such port visits you have visitors aboard -- they swarm all over the ship while there -- but it's showing the flag.

Q: I sometimes wonder when you talk about an amphibious operation in Thailand and places like that, is it a little like doing something on shifting sand? There seems to be rather an impermanence about the contribution you are making -- to the casual observer it seems like that.

Capt. B.: I think it is important that they know you are out there, that you can be there rather quickly, if required. Now there have been several concerns at different times over recent years in Japan and Korea, and even Taiwan -- I believe that is part of the problem at the present time -- when the Seventh Fleet moves ships to cover areas such as the Indian Ocean and there is a responsibility there, there immediately is concern expressed from the Northern Asian countries that we are decreasing our readiness to cover them. They don't dictate, but they protest -- "You are here to protect us."

Q: In other words they like to think we are hovering around their backyard all the time?

Capt. B.: That you are always there. An amphibious ship making a port of call can be a lot more impressive than perhaps an aircraft carrier being in the area. The carrier doesn't come completely into the port, it may anchor off and is not as visible to the local people. That tying up to the pier, I think, is a morale factor.

Q: Is this not building up a kind of dependence -- defensewise -- that is not entirely healthy?

Capt. B.: I would agree with that certainly. As in the case of Japan, they certainly can afford to build up their own defenses at this stage of the game. Admittedly, U. S. influence discouraged that after World War II. But now for many years we have been trying to encourage them to take a greater responsibility.

Q: Actually we wrote the constitution with that in, didn't we?

Capt. B.: That is true. With the numerical strength and military capabilities of the Koreans, with the possible exception of their not having nuclear weapons -- or all they would like to have -- they have numerical strength and outfitting that should be able to counter North Korean operations, barring added support of the Chinese Communists. We have withdrawn from the Chinese Nationalist or Taiwan support, which was our own doing though I personally am not in agreement with the way we did it. I think the dependence we built up in South Vietnam was -- the dependence was too much and the political influences made the military look unjustly bad.

But I think a presence -- it has long been discussed -- but until something has been done about establishing a periodical presence in the Indian Ocean and in the Mid-Eastern waters, we can anticipate threatened troubles in the mid-east. I think this is a very worthwhile effort that we establish some midway bases such as the long discussed yet controversial Diego Garcia.

Q: You say a periodic effort. Would it not also be proper to say a consistency in doing so?

Capt. B.: Yes, that would be the ideal situation in my opinion, but realistically, I guess we have to concede that you can only spread your resources so thinly and it is a big world. Of course, today we might add the same premise in our support for so many of the African countries.

Interview No. 7 with Captain Phil H. Bucklew

Place: At his residence in Fairfax, Virginia

Date: Thursday, 29 May 1980

Subject: Biography

By: John T. Mason, Jr.

Q: I think you want to resume your story with June 1963 when you were departing the Seventh Fleet Amphibious Forces and you had been with them for a period of two years. You were returning to the Amphibious Base at Coronado and were going to be the exec there.

Capt. B.: My orders as exec of the Coronado Amphibious Base were a surprise to me.

Q: They reached you in Japan?

Capt. B.: No, in the Philippines. I am not certain where we were but I was detached from Subic Bay in the Philippines and got permission to come back by ship with Helen, on a military transport. Meanwhile I had a very pleasant, almost embarrassing experience. I mentioned that over the years, starting from Coronado and later at Taiwan, both Helen and I had become close friends with Admiral Liu Kwan Kai of the Chinese navy. We first met when he was a part of the senior officers course at Coronado. The admiral sent an official message asking that Commander and Mrs. Bucklew stop off at Taiwan on their way home. Of course, this was very flattering, and it was official, and it was approved -- but we had no idea of the extent of their hospitality. They had quarters for us in Taipei, a car, and a banner was streamed across the street saying "Welcome Commander and Mrs. Bucklew." I am sure that many Americans as well as Chinese were wondering "Who were they?" but the admiral did it up very well.

Q: Did they have the red-carpet custom in that land?

Capt. B.: We had the red-carpet treatment. As I say, we spent only three days there, but it was more difficult to get out via military transport and on to Japan, and we were so embarrassed by this overwhelming hospitality that we flew commercial just to get away. I made no calls into the Taiwan Defense Headquarters as I had no obligations and under the circumstance I didn't want to. We were the official guests of the Chinese Navy and then flew to Okinawa and then on up to Yokohama where we took the transport home, along with our old dog Porky, who was subject to many official messages in arranging his concurrent transportation home. The Chief of Staff of the Phib group said, "This is getting to be too much." Porky was about 12 years old then and a pretty well-travelled member of our family.

Q: And he was distainful of quarantine and that sort of thing?

Capt. B.: Completely. We did have one major disturbance. Porky was a bulldog -- very friendly to all small animals but he didn't like big dogs. He broke his chain aboard ship to take on a German shepherd that he didn't like, and the ship doctor did a little sewing up on that but old Pork was pretty satisfied. That always seemed to be the way, with his love of battle a few scars never seemed to trouble him. He was well known throughout the ship as 'that little dog that fights the big ones.' That was the most exciting part of the trip home.

We reported to Coronado. Fortunately we had a home there rented in our absence and we were returning and had a place to go. I reported as Executive Officer of the Base, something completely new to me in administrative detail; I had an interesting, rather hectic indoctrination, studying files, personnel matters, civil service, and administrative responsibilities that were completely new to me.

Q: This was by design I take it, so that you would have this training and experience?

Capt. B.: I really don't think so. As I learned later, Admiral Blouin wrote some letters of protest, that at this time a person with Special Operations background could well be used in that field. He didn't say I wasn't an administrator but he might have thought it. In any event, I was selected for Captain about that time and Admiral Eph Holmes was then Commander of Amphibious Forces, Pacific. I had served under him years before in the Atlantic. He called me in and said, "I am nominating you to form this Special Operations Group, which will include the Underwater Demolition Teams and the SEAL teams, a Boat Support Unit, and you will coordinate the training and command of the special operators."

Q: While you were there as exec?

Capt. B.: Well, going from that job. It would be my first assignment on becoming captain. The exec was a commander's billet so I would be transferred. The timing was excellent with this commissioning of a new unit. Admiral Holmes was very anxious at that time to get the Pacific unit commissioned and active in advance of the Atlantic. This helped me considerably, coming back into what you might say was my home field.

Q: Would you say, however, a little more about this five months in Coronado?

Capt. B.: It was quite an interesting time -- much of it doing routine base administratin duties, but it was at a time when austerity was in full bloom and the base was poverty stricken. I served under Captain Stumpy Baker who was a pretty shrewd operator and he fought his way through a lot of obstacles by threatening Washington. For example, with the various cutbacks that periodically occur, and did during this 1963 period, it was found that we did not have enough money in our base operating accounts to even release civil service workers. We couldn't pay them off in their accumulated leave. We had to have an augmentation of funds to let people go. We didn't have enough guards to man the gate watches. One of the first things I uncovered was that the base guards were working on 12-hour shifts -- 12 on and 12 off. Stumpy Baker, who as I say was pretty shrewd, would send a cryptic message back to the Bureau of Personnel like, "We'll have to shut down the dispensary if funds are not made available by such and such a date." And you know we wouldn't shut down our infirmary. So the funds came through. But it was by dabs. This was an interesting period; it had its hectic moments.

Meanwhile at the Naval Base, San Diego a spinal meningitis epidemic broke out. This disease and its causes I believe are still difficult to determine the source. But one theory implied that overcrowding in the barracks might be a cause. The Coronado Amphibious Base volunteered and set up a tent city and we moved a large portion of the recruit training center into tent city at Amphibious Base, Coronado, until the epidemic was cleared and Naval Base, San Diego was properly sanitized and approved.

Q: Were any of your men victims?

Capt. B.: No, we had no problems there but across the bay in San Diego it had gone up to I think 30 or 40 cases and they feared the beginning of an epidemic. We had much liaison with the Bureau of Medicine in Washington -- people coming out, decisions were hastily made -- not unlike today with the refugees.

It was determined that the Bainbridge Naval Base was inadequate, run-down and could not be rehabilitated for immediate action and several different so-called mothballed bases were ruled out -- therefore we became a tent city.

Q: Isn't it true that this disease is not a primary infection but is secondary to some other disease?

Capt. B.: There was much speculation although no real determination was made to my knowledge. We asked many questions on it and had much concern. Of course, there were a lot of details in setting up water and toilet facilities and all the necessities for taking on a large number of men overnight. I would say during the summer months and prior to my reporting to my new assignment, this was the major concern, along with the continuing resolution of finances and logistics. It was quite an informative period to me.

Meanwhile, Admiral Holmes had made a "deal" with the Bureau of Personnel that if I would be assigned and if immediate commissioning would be authorized, that he would make me available for a selection board. They apparently were having a very difficult time to locate a Captain with Reserve Officer status, which, of course, I was. We commissioned the Naval Operations Support Group in October of '63 and one week later I came to Washington to be a part of this Selection Board.

Q: Selection for captains?

Capt. B.: No, for lieutenants. It required 10 or 12 captains on the board. It was a critical time in two ways on the Selection Board in that we were still in the cutback period and attrition of personnel was involved with Selection Board recommendations influencing the action, and two, there was such an inequality of grading. It was very difficult because 75% of the eligible officers may have all been in top-grade category, so we had to in great detail go through each record and break down what you might say were "perfect" records.

Q: Something less than perfect?

Capt. B.: And, in the midst of this Selection Board came the assassination of President Kennedy. We got the reports of it while in session. Of course, we observed the funeral and the ceremonies during this period, from our building, the Navy Annex, as they came across the Memorial Bridge toward Arlington Cemetery.

Q: So there was a postponement in your selection?

Capt. B.: Upon completion of it -- this was a "hurry up and wait" then rush to the next seession -- of the work of the selection board, I returned to Coronado and the following day (or night in this case) was called to Admiral Holmes office and told I would be going to Vietnam as part of a study group of the situation there.

Q: Before you had a chance to organize the Special Operations Group?

Capt. B.: At that time we had a one-room office. We were commissioned, but that was all. I had been given a Chief Staff Officer and our other officers were being drawn from the five commands that we were to coordinate -- two Underwater Demolition Teams, the SEAL team, the Beach Jumper Unit and a newly formed Boat Support Unit, so there would be five commands that we were coordinating. We drew our officers by using/coordinating the commanding officers and had a temporary.

Back to the Vietnam Study Group: Under the command of Admiral Paul Savidge this small group was to go to Vietnam, report en route to Admiral Felt at CinCPac for instructions, take on additional personnel that would be provided through CinCPac and CinCPacFlt, and continue to Vietnam.

Q: What was the background for that sudden assembling of the team?

Capt. B.: It was the concern about the infiltration of the Viet Cong, the North Vietnamese, by seas and waterways. We were to explore this problem and give our opinion and recommendations concerning it.

Q: For how long a period were you expected to study this?

Capt. B.: It was rather indefinite. It was first thought to be a six-weeks job, but additional responsibilities were added, as usually occurs, as we went along the line. We reported to Admiral Felt in Hawaii, and spent about a week there with general indoctrination briefings from the CinCPac intelligence staff, and in reading Vietnamese files that were sent in from the advisory groups. It was an ideal place to start in that not only is that a joint staff but we could get pretty good input from army, navy and air force and marines at that one command, as opposed to a single service briefing.

Q: Also the State I suppose?

Capt. B.: Yes, and the CIA also.

Q: What did Felt reflect in his remarks to you?

Capt. B.: We had a general discussion on infiltration -- on the overall problems and Vietnamese attitudes, estimates of their capabilities and shortcomings, but I always remember Admiral Felt, on the final day prior to our departure. I posed the question indicating that I wasn't really clear in concise terms what our mission was intended to be. Admiral Felt, as he sat in his flight jacket and with his moccasin shoes on the desk, put it to us very concisely. He said, "I don't know exactly what I want you to do. I want you to tell me from what you see after covering this area, what you recommend, what the problems are, and what should be done. In a nutshell, I want to know why all I get from Vietnam are glowing reports of our accomplishments and meanwhile we are getting the hell kicked out of us. That's your job."

Q: Those reports he was receiving came from what source?

Capt. B.: Advisory groups, ambassadors, CIA, and they didn't make sense. It was easy to see why once we got there.

Q: Was there any discussion or any investigation regarding the British experience in Malaysia with infiltration?

Capt. B.: We were briefed by some of the British on staff liaison, and did considerable reading and research. But as is too often the case, background experience seemingly was ignored. Each new group that comes in, particularly in an advisory capacity, knows how to do things better and ignores the past.

Q: At this point Diem had been assassinated, so the government was in a chaotic state?

Capt. B.: In fact it was overthrown once again while we were in Vietnam. The chaos continued, not in the violent sense that it did under Diem and with his assassination, but there was complete confusion. There was not a close coordination between the American elements and those Vietnamese whom they were advising at the top staff level. They were across town from one another -- the Vietnamese headquarters on one side and the Americans on the other. With field advisers it is a different situation. They live with the troops and had a much closer association. Staffs had quite a breach -- quite a sensitivity in requesting from one another even the smallest of normal military exchanges, let alone not coordinating or even keeping one another informed of plans or intentions.

Q: Just a bit more to get the picture, the background of what you were stepping into. The government was in disarray. Was Lodge there as ambassador? Was General Harkins there as MAAG?

Capt. B.: Lodge was ambassador and Harkins was Chief MAAG and had the overall command. We had a naval advisory group and an old friend of mine, Captain Joe Draknik, became chief of it about that time. Mrs. Diem was living at the quarters of the then chief of the naval advisory group. She hadn't left the country.

Q: That was the brother's wife, Mrs. Ngo-dinh-Nhu, because President Diem didn't have a wife. She was a very vocal woman.

Capt. B.: I guess it was the brother's wife -- I never saw her but she stayed in isolation at his quarters. At least he told us that while we were visiting there -- she was upstairs. We discussed many of the details and got as much input available prior to starting an actual survey and reconnaissance. We talked to individual commanders and made our rounds, both in military protocol and in quizzing them.

Q: This was all in Saigon?

Capt. B.: Right. We started from Saigon. We travelled throughout the country during the course of the survey and had actually started this when Admiral Savidge developed some heart and health difficulties. I was very much concerned and took him into the hospital. From there on I did not know too much about it but orders came from CinCPac to return him to the United States and I would take over the Team. My liaison increased and prior to leaving Saigon I would have morning coffee with General Harkness who was a very kindly but frustrated commander at that point.

I had occasion to observe some of his political difficulties with the embassy. For example, one morning following a military coup that had happened during the night, we were having coffee and General Harkness was trying to reach Ambassador Lodge by telephone. I heard the whole conversation when the ambassador finally did get on the phone and the general gave him a concise report of the coup -- of the tanks and where they were stationed; that there had been no casualties -- it was a bloodless coup. I can recall Lodge's chuckle saying, "Did you just find out about this? I knew of it a week ago."

General Harkness said, "You mean you had such information and did not pass it to us?" And the ambassador commented, "Well, that's up to you to find out things for yourself."

To me, this was indicative of the whole relationship and problem that we were facing.

Q: Was this a personality conflict or was it more than that?

Capt. B.: I would have to say it was more than that. There were other small things that I observed. For example, I recall, at a reception while Admiral Savidge was still there, all

Ambassador Lodge wanted to talk about was asking, "How do you think my chances are for the Presidential election?"

Q: Oh, politics as usual.

Capt. B.: Politics as usual. It was a deplorable situation really and there was no concern of this being a possible war situation. It was taken too lightly. The build-up was coming very rapidly for the military. During this period we started visiting different base areas; we travelled up the Mekong to the Cambodian border. We weren't allowed to cross it but we laid in wait during the day and observed some of the activity.

We were aboard a Vietnamese ship at the time -- a gunboat and small craft that we used for closer observations than from the ship. We made general observations and we stopped at different military bases up and down the river to discuss their existing problems. We travelled down to the coast, and to the southern islands, and up to Danang at the northern border.

We had excellent cooperation from the intelligence staff of MACV and General Harkness's staff. They set us up for most anything we would like to see. We had informal discussions with the various unit officers in charge, and it became my firm belief that these men best knew the problems but were not often listened to. We wanted to get their opinion. Most of it stemmed from lack of communication and lack of supplies, and some were in very sad situations.

I remember one young man, a naval lieutenant who happened

to be the nephew of Senator Margaret Chase Smith. He was alone on an offshore island in South Vietnam. I had quite a harsh exchange with the young man and though I admired his actions I didn't think his approach was right.

Q: What was his mission on the island by himself?

Capt. B.: He was there to help the Vietnamese, to serve as an adviser, and he had little or nothing to do it with, including communications. He was out of touch with the rest of the military. When he explained to me that he was getting medicine and getting supplies from his Aunt, Senator Smith, because he couldn't get them from the military, that's where we had our harsh exchanges.

I said, "You are not helping the situation. You are not clarifying the problem in so doing. You may be finding an immediate solution, and I don't blame you a bit for that, but you've got to get it on track. These things must be made a matter of record."

We did, in our report. But we found that sort of circumstance to exist in so many places with advisers -- that they were just isolated, out of touch, on their own -- and with their willingness, desperation and enthusiasm they would go to any means available to them from writing home and outlining their needs, to whatever, as this boy did with his Aunt.

Q: That is one of the charges that has been levelled at the Washington end of things. They didn't publicize or didn't want the lack of supplies known in this country, did they?

Capt. B.: Later, when I was in the Pentagon, I heard so many times, quoting the Secretary of Defense, that we weren't allowed to include any inflationary costs in our budgeting, that war should not cost us any more than our peacetime operation. We had occasion, throughout later years, and throughout this war, to see just what happens from some of the stockpiled ammunition and duds and obsolete weapons and poorly conditioned things that were left over from World War II -- that they were being thrown into combat as an economy measure. The whole logistics situation became a very difficult obstacle for an adviser to make progress in training. It was very frustrating to each of them -- also it was hazardous.

To pinpoint the fault: some was a lack of communication from the field into Saigon where there was this political turmoil, both with the Americans and with the Vietnamese, and with even routine field operations being controlled and requiring authorization from the Washington area. You couldn't give the time of day out of Saigon without getting permission from Washington. Any field operation had to be cleared first from the field, into Saigon, from Saigon to Washington and back again.

This we saw for the next two years. If you are going to make a counterattack in the field you have minutes, at the most a few hours, to react. An approval decision that takes two to three days to get from Washington makes the whole operation a lost cause and a hazard. That remained the biggest problem in Vietnam in my opinion until the end of the war.

We moved from base to base. We gathered comments and opinions, and added our own on different tactics and possible solutions as to means of protecting the many river and water ways. There are many hundreds of them with the tributaries throughout the central and south land. It is jungle country and, of course, we couldn't see them all. We had to study the existing charts and maps -- documents that were left behind by the French -- and recommendations they had made. We touched upon everything from psychological warfare, the logistical needs and procedures, to different types of barricading and blocking of the river and water ways at strategic points. Ultimately, in our report which became known as the Bucklew Report, since I had taken over, we made a separate report, an addendum in which we did include (there was only one copy of this and I turned it over to Admiral Felt) many of the harsh criticisms and observations that we made that were somewhat beyond the military expectancy -- and with our recommendations.

Q: What was our intention at that stage, in 1963, when you were there? To what extent were we planning to be involved? Or was that apparent to you as you made your study?

Capt. B.: The army was expanding rapidly at that stage. General Harkins was pretty much on his way out. I discussed his future intentions with him at one time on a personal basis, and he said, "If I can get away from this mess I will retire and I'll never want to speak another word about it."

To my knowledge it has been that way. When his relief came in -- General Westmoreland -- it was evident that policy changes would soon occur. Westmoreland travelled the country, quizzed everyone, including me, wanting to know in advance of our report.

Q: Who has spoken his piece?

Capt. B.: The general's room in the Rex Hotel when he came in as deputy commander was next door to me. We had lunch several times and discussed different observations that we made and he sat in on different briefings that we gave as well as attended. Major General Stillwell was the operations officer, very cooperative and very much concerned about what was going to be in our report and he did everything but ask me to submit it to them before releasing it. But Admiral Felt was a little more shrewd and just called me back to Pearl Harbor with my report overnight, so no one in the army saw it. Admiral Felt returned the following day to Saigon and he asked if I wished to accompany him. I told him I had a new command that I really hadn't taken over. He said, "All right. Your job is done, go on back to Coronado." I did.

As to the buildup, you could see staffs increasing in size, a rather typical headquarters maneuver, unfortunately. The army works a lot differently from the navy in the sense that the bigger staff you have, the more prestigious. And I think it is a well known fact that the army attitude was that for promotion's sake you had to have a tour in Vietnam. This could be the only combat circumstance or exposure of an army officer's career, or this era of it. That was building up a top-heavy rank structure. The more your staff structure built up, the more your logistics and support units built up. And even during our time in country, which was only a couple of months, you could see Saigon bulging with American army-- yet, there was a feeling of restraint which came from the Washington level, that we are not in a combat position. Certainly the big staff was not advising or training but it was inevitable that there would be an integration and ultimately, by impatience, participation.

Q: Was the picture confused in any way by SecDef's insistence on the so-called Hamlet program?

Capt. B.: I don't know that that would be a confusion as much as another alphabetical project. It didn't seem to be a very effective sort of thing. As we travelled on the river ways and by helicopter over many of these areas, it was somewhat ridiculous to see hamlets, barbed wire enclosed, one wearing a Communist flag and the next wearing the Vietnamese flag. These were almost side by side, particularly in the river areas. There was not the real division of the peasants of the countryside -- very little political thinking on their part.

As with China, from years before, if a son is attached to

some unit, either guerrilla or one faction or another, and he comes into his village home, he gets support. In these hamlets the unfriendlies provided the cover for the many Cong that would infiltrate by night and, as the saying very logically went, the entire war was fought by night throughout Vietnam. They came by night and they left by night. They disappeared into the swamp, the wilderness. They did their damage. It was hit and run and they received support from as many hamlets as were protected from them. As in the case of any civil war, and from an American viewpoint more so than in the Orient, there was no way in the world you could tell friend from foe. They dressed alike, looked alike, spoke alike. And as we said with the fishing boats, you can only identify friend from foe when they start firing at you.

Q: In talking about the hamlet program, am I to infer that it was a diversionary thing on the part of Washington, which really wasn't very helpful in pursuit of our overall purpose, if we had one?

Capt. B.: It wouldn't be fair for me to make a long-range analysis but I personally could see no benefit. It was a waste of effort, materiel, and it was ignored as a necessary nuisance to the Vietnamese themselves. Someone's whim.

Q: In your visits around the country, investigating with your committee, did you have any brushes with the Viet Cong? How active were they in the areas where you went?

Capt. B.: We had no close contact brushes.

Q: Later on it became very dangerous, didn't it?

Capt. B.: Yes, it became much more prevalent in later times. In '63, as we came down the Mekong aboard a Vietnamese gunboat there was considerable gunfire on the shore. I went up to the bridge and wanted to know what was going on. "Don't we do something about it? Don't we assist? Don't you turn your radio on to find out what this is?"

In courtesy to me they let me play with the radio to monitor, but in that language I didn't understand what was going on. They merely passed by -- we're not involved. It wasn't a matter of can we assist, we've got firepower here -- but there was some fairly heavy artillery working in the swamplands along the coast line. The attitude was if I'm not ordered into it, it's none of my business.

Q: This being the Vietnamese attitude.

Capt. B.: I lived at the Rex Hotel which had an officers' mess on the roof and night after night the gunfire would be almost like a fireworks display which we could observe from the mess at Saigon. It was a very casual thing. No one really concerned about it, none of the attitude that I had always known in the past, like hadn't we better get back to headquarters -- shouldn't we know what this is about. And it happened night after night.

Q: So it became commonplace? Was this the attitude of the American military there?

Capt. B.: Oh, yes. Of everyone.

Q: You went up to Danang? And the Marines were there?

Capt. B.: This was a transition period of Danang in early 1964 and the Marines were not there at this time. Some of my SEAL teams were, but I hadn't really taken over yet. The base was operated at Danang at this time by the CIA and our SEAL teams were assisting. It happened that an old friend of mine who headed the CIA detachment in Korea, Tucker Gugleman, had set up the Danang base. I met with him there and he remained until a turnover of control occurred with the military, with a Saigon based headquarters command known as MACSOG -- Military Assistance Command and Special Operations Group -- taking over.

There were several colonels in command in the period of the next four years, the last being Jack Singlaub, now General Singlaub. The detachments at Danang came under MACSOG in their linkage of command and MACSOG was a subordinate command to MacV, the supreme commander, and this was a strong political army command with many problems of control. Navy was committed, as with CIA, to provice boats, SEAL personnel, and the actual operation of the Danang Base. MACSOG wanted to build and did build. They always wanted more and more PT boats (in later years -- getting ahead of my story) and they built up their own individual air force and fleet (in later years), separate from the MacV command -- but under MacV. The relationship there, as it was near the end of the war, Jack Singlaub lived in the same house and billet with General Westmoreland, so that the linkage was as much personal as it was military.

Q: Militarily I think it might have been an irritant to MacV?

Capt. B.: Well, if there were personality conflicts, it would have been. But Singlaub and Westmoreland seemingly got along fine. Some of Singlaub's predecessors, however, had their difficulties and left as frustrated as General Harkness.

Q: Later on this existed in Danang, side by side with the Marine set-up, did it?

Capt. B.: The Marines came in a little later, after my first visit. Once the Marines made their landing at Danang they set up an air base there, I think in 1964. But from that time on the Danang area was dominantly Marine as opposed to Army, though they came under this same MacV overall chain of command. Once assigned to Vietnam, all component units were under MacV.

Now, across town in Danang was a Vietnamese base -- PT boats and our base for SEAL teams and for their Vietnamese counterparts. This all came under MACSOG command with a separate base for the Marines. I don't say there was no contact but no real military tie-in between the two -- the SEAL/Viet base under MACSOG was "clandestine" for operations in North

Vietnam; Marine activities were "conventional." In later years when I went to Danang from Saigon I would come in to the Marine base and people would come to pick me up and it was as if they were separate entities.

Q: Would you talk about the naval aspects of it as this was a part of your study in '63 -- something about the Vietnamese navy as it existed? It was under a captain, was it not?

Capt. B.: Captain Kang was the Viet CNO. I was impressed with him as being a very capable officer and doing a creditable job of reorganization after the turnover from the Diem administration. But he later got into political difficulties and was (I don't know if he was assassinated ultimately) relieved of command. A confusion existed continuously thereafter regarding the navy. I thought that Kang was quite aggressive and wanted to help in every way that he could. He did have ships under his command but not necessarily under his control. He could patrol his ships but he could in no way intrude in an operation under another's control. There was a lack of coordination between not only each province, but each little sector within the province.

Q: And the Vietnamese navy was certainly not co-equal with the Vietnamese army?

Capt. B.: Certainly not numerically but some of the ships and craft they had gave them more fire power and they were continuously being dictated to as to where they would provide the army firepower and back-up support. I blame our U.S. command and the army command specifically for insisting upon this being a land war, which we had always insisted that we would never get into on the Asian continent, and I certainly felt we had brought it on ourselves.

Q: Was it also possibly a reflection of the traditional attitude of the U.S. army toward the navy as a means of conveyance, much more than anything else?

Capt. B.: That's probably true. The conveyance was a necessity for any landing of troops in the different sectors. They couldn't go overland so navy boats, whether Vietnamese or U.S., transported them to their objective and stood by waiting for them. Conveyance had to be an important concern.

In fairness, I have been critical of the army and have long been critical of tne top-heavy controls that I have observed. (It has long been my opinion that the army with approximately one fourth of the troops that they had in Vietnam could have done a hundred per cent better job. They built up so much, supportwise and Pentagon East as their huge headquarters was known -- a huge headquarters -- and their staff and their career promotional ambitions of serving in such a thing.) But meanwhile, within the Navy there were many of our top level people who were determined that the Navy would never become involved in muddy-water operations.

Q: Later known as Riverine Warfare.

Capt. B.: Riverine warfare, coincidentally, the man who put such statements in writing was Admiral Rivero. He objected vigorously when he was VCNO -- "the navy will never" -- he put it in writing, so the navy came in as a support function providing this conveyance, as you say. This was with a willingness of our Pentagon staff -- up to a point.

Now this attitude changed, but before it changed the army had developed this tremendous and top-heavy command and deployed more and more troops. A significant influence of that was "so we are in a war." The policy developed, as continued throughout, that men would serve one-year tours in-country and be relieved. Well, that will never work in any war. In such circumstance, whenever men are deployed it takes an indoctrination period to find out what is going on regardless of their training, their briefing, or their past experience. They are gradually integrated into the operations and by the time six months have passed and they are just getting their feet wet, they are counting the days until they go home. And in such nasty circumstances, you can't blame men for avoiding exposure and being as cautious as they can.

Q: Did you make this observation a part of your report -- the fact that we were not in a declared war and we had this policy of one-year tours?

Capt. B.: No, not as part of our report. Of course, in 1963 it was not really a combatant situation as yet. We were declared as "not being part of it" and trying to avoid being a part of it at that stage.

Q: You spoke earlier, as a part of your charge, the fact that you had to deal with the problem of infiltration by sea into South Vietnam. What about the Tonkin Gulf coast, did you travel that with your committee and what did you discover?

Capt. B.: We found no more than three or four incidents that could be, even questionably, proven as sea infiltration. There were a few incidents and I forget the specifics of them, in which coastal craft were encountered that were laden with weapons, demolitions, ammo or something of that nature, that we felt were intended Cong support. It was quite evident, however, that the riverways coming off the jungles were being used; they were stockpiled with ammunition, with food supplies, with all of the necessities for the guerrillas to move. It was readily learned that in the movement of troops from North Vietnam, or from whatever surrounding country-- Laos or from wherever they came -- that such movement might take as much as thirty days. It was a patient, slow-moving operation, and "hit and run" when they came into an objective area or a resisted area. It was not a mass movement down the rivers but by night with one or two boats moving through with a handful of operators.

Q: Is this Oriental approach to things a philosophical approach to a struggle of this sort? Was it really appreciated by our people? Did they understand this? It is so in contrast to our own approach and our culture.

Capt. B.: No, I don't think it has ever really been understood. It takes many years and the whole basic philosophy of the Oriental is based on patience. I think they can exercise patience with aggression, and by such infiltration -- move and wait, move and wait -- maybe even working in the fields as they go along. We learned many things, that they assembled their ammunition after they got to their destination. They assembled their weapons, their weapons were broken down so that they could be carried in a sack of rice on their backs. They were in small bits. This is very unlike our concept of infantry warfare.

But, when they reached a destination they had their weapons, and for this reason you had to have search posts -- watch posts along the line. It was part of our recommendations that we should have on these small tributaries many well positioned watch posts, and we recommended waterway barricades to be closed at night, and where you had a sentry, it would also assist him. The Vietnamese, as opposed to our concept of boats and transport, used these long canoe-like klong craft -- silent, high speed -- they can make over 20 knots in them. We recommended the use of them ourselves. You could buy them in Thailand for a cost of about 900 dollars!

Q: Manufactured by whom?

Capt. B.: In Thailand you could get all you wanted. I thought they were very practical, but it was not the concept that was later adopted by the army. Their idea was that we needed craft with armor plating, old amphibious boats with heavy pipe and plated armament -- bullet proof, noisy perhaps, but that would carry 30 or 40 men -- that is the concept that we adopted. We intended, quite obviously, to overcome by numerical strength, and it was not as effective as hoped for.

Q: At that stage in the game we hadn't really come to appreciate or understand guerrilla warfare even though it had been practiced for generations. We simply hadn't come to understand it, had we?

Capt. B.: Well, certainly the French learned it the hard way and I don't think we ever profited by the French disaster and experience. We always felt we could do it better and that we had the right idea.

Q: Did your experience as a Beach Jumper and all your training give you additional sight, so to speak, in appreciating this technique the Orientals were using?

Capt. B.: I think so. And I think this applied more so to me and to all of our participants over these later years of the UDT and SEAL people. They were trained and experienced in working in the water, at night, and in stealth. I think they understood the problem far better, and though we took our casualties it wasn't in the manner of the plodding infantryman who wades on and on into the fire.

Q: I can't blame you for indulging in a commercial like that, nevertheless I appreciate that answer.

Capt. B.: Well, I think you can see it in this article on guerrilla tactics. The man cites -- his years were not the same -- but, as a commercial...

Q: I'm sorry to have put it on that level.

Capt. B.: Well, it is quite true, but it also is a matter of record. Our SEAL teams in the later war years had men that had as many as 12 deployments to Vietnam -- six months in-country and six months home. They learned a lot in that time. Their greatest problem was controlling a new man. Of the casualties we had, it was that young, hard charger who sees a target and bursts forth to do something about it. He takes the hit.

Q: He hasn't yet learned patience.

Capt. B.: Patience, hold your position. It didn't happen too often. But to control your new men was the most difficult thing cited to me in debriefs of our returning men. But I tried to talk to each of the men as we rotated them. I regretted very much that they had to go back as quickly as they did, though they were all volunteers and their reluctance to return did not show. They felt the job had to be done and they felt they could do it better than others. That is ego but they were capable.

Q: Going back to your report period in '63, you made one very brief reference to the fact that you and observers went up to the Cambodian border and were not allowed to go over. But what you said was pregnant with meaning. What did you observe?

Capt. B.: The ridiculousness of the activity across the border -- enemy craft within sight from aboard Vietnamese craft. It is difficult to understand why you don't do something about it, if this is the enemy. It was not unlike things in China where I watched the Japanese as they planted rice during the day. There was sort of a peaceful co-existence between enemies during the day but when night came the attacks came also.

Of course, you got into new trial and error tactics as the war progressed. I suppose the most popular coined word was infrastructure, and the infiltration of enemy people right into the staffs in Saigon, the enemy leaders within bases and headquarters -- that sort of thing. It is a natural and continuing problem when you can't identify friend or foe by appearance or language. Who knows what an individual's political beliefs are or where his orders come from?

Q: You must have discussed some of these subjects with the army command in Saigon. What kind of satisfaction did you get from them, or what frustration did they build in you?

Capt. B.: I probably learned more from one individual who was the N-2, their intelligence head who happened to be an old friend of mine, a Marine from China, back in SACO -- Colonel Dutch Cramer. Dutch briefed me very much in detail on transportation of weapons and supplies, movement and personnel foot routes. He gave me his opinions as often opposed to higher command. It was the prevalent belief of the army top level that these people must be coming by sea. They couldn't be infiltrating right through our protected areas.

I agreed with Dutch Cramer. They were not coming by sea. He showed me supply dumps. He travelled with us on several trips to point out and to assist. He was nearing the end of his one-year tour, and having lived with it intelligence-wise knew a lot of details which certainly we tried to incorporate into our thinking and ultimately into our report.

We did the same with each of the field advisers met. As I have said, the most critical problem was a lack of communications that frustrated nearly all advisers. I suppose any place in the military if you ask their complaints they will want more equipment of some type, usually more weapons or more sophisticated items. But communications equipment and spare parts was almost a unanimous cry at this stage.

Q: Was it seemingly a lack of communications between the army's own intelligence officer and their understanding, at least? They didn't accept what he told them?

Capt. B.: That is correct. On a personal basis Dutch gave me a lot of opinions, but I think his opinions were well founded and convincing. I remember General Stillwell saying that the infiltrators must be coming from the sea -- they "couldn't" come from elsewhere. We would go through the evidence that very few sampans had been captured that carried any military equipments; the illogical travel that they would have to make by sea; and, relating this to where the concentration of force and equipment was known to be. We could not be convinced that they were coming by sea.

However, over the period of the next few years, I must say that the navy couldn't be convinced either. When the army would make their requests and their logistic demands from Saigon, it was not army alone. When Admiral Zumwalt went to Vietnam he clamored for more and more coastal craft. The effectiveness of these craft was questionable although they were provided, about 180 of the 50' SWIFT boats. The SWIFT boats were built here in the United States.

The Norwegian NASTY PT boats were utilized by our SEAL teams and their Viet counterparts from Danang going on North Vietnam operations. They were purchased on the basis of a third country being the provider -- which was not a very convincing circumstance, since they were being manned by Vietnamese and by our SEALS trained and from Danang. The fact that the boats came from Norway I am sure didn't convince the Communists that the United States had nothing to do with them. We did get our first six boats from Norway, followed by six built in the U. S. that were called OSPREYS that were of the same basic characteristics as the NASTYs but were of aluminum hull construction, whereas the Norwegian NASTY is a mahogany hull, high speed PT type.

Q: Dealing again with the report and your study in preparation for it, what did you incorporate in terms of the political and diplomatic? Did you include that in your report? Did Admiral Felt expect this?

Capt. B.: In the addendum to the report, of which I said there was only one copy which I gave to Admiral Felt, we made comments, not in great detail, but that there was a division of authority, there were political conflicts observed that handicapped the whole organization, there were radical differences of opinion between the embassy and the military commands. These comments we made as discreetly as possible, but I don't think they were wasted on Admiral Felt. He made his comments. I briefed him on the patio of his CinCPac quarters on a Sunday morning, a private briefing with two or three members of his staff. Admiral Felt speaks his mind -- and he cross-examined me.

Q: He wanted to be certain of his facts.

Capt. B.: Pertaining to some of our recommendations, I recall he said, "Do you feel it is right to subject American personnel to things you are recommending?"

I said, "That's why we recommend them, for training and putting men in the field."

We recommended getting our advisers closer with the troops, living with them. He questioned that and I said I thought it was excellent training and had been done before, that we had all experienced that in World War II and our men were just as capable today.

He said, "I hope so."

Some of the recommendations, though I forget now all that was included in the report -- there was a time when I kept score -- I think every recommendation was ultimately implemented. However, as was the complaint of my entire group, if they had implemented even within a period of six months, we felt confident of effectiveness. But when you implement over a period of four years, one little thing at a time (and these were not major or expensive actions that we recommended) I think they lost their purpose.

Q: During that interim of four years the press had gotten its licks in. During your survey there, did you have any contact with the American press?

Capt. B.: No, not directly. They were permitted to attend many of General Harkins's briefings -- not all of them, because they were misquoting and there were certain individuals they were very much incensed with. I have heard the General's comments concerning some of them, regarding distortions that were occurring. Other than the General's immediate staff I don't think anyone was really aware of our purpose until we completed the assignment -- and even then the report was labeled "Top Secret." Many of the reporters lived in the same hotel billet that I did and I knew them by their garb.

But I avoided association with them.

Q: Did you attempt to talk with any of the Vietnamese governmental people?

Capt. B.: Only military. Of course, most everything was military.

Q: With a general as president, I suppose?

Capt. B.: Yes. During the coup while we were there, General Kuong took over.

Q: But you didn't derive any intelligence from the government officials that was worth incorporating in your report?

Capt. B.: No. Other than the criticism we had of the lack of coordination between the State Department and the military we avoided comment or criticism. It was rather common knowledge and feeling among many of the U. S. civilian workers -- industrial employees. I don't know what all they were -- all types of civilians were there in the different billets. (They were there with their families still -- many advisers also had their families there but they departed soon afterward. It was pretty good living at this stage.)

Q: Did you get down to Camrahn Bay? And what was your estimate of that?

Capt. B.: Yes, but there was not a base there at the time.

Q: Just the natural facilities?

Capt. B.: It was a small Vietnamese military base. Of course, that was before the huge U. S. Navy build-up.

Q: Would you say something about your committee. I think you said there were 12 or 13 members of the committee. What was the complexion of the committee, their background and experience? Was there a general consensus of opinion on the various points you incorporated in the report?

Capt. B.: I would certainly feel we had a consensus of opinion but there were many controversial opinions that, around the table, we thrashed out. As in any group, you didn't have immediate agreement until we discussed the pros and cons. There were the usual arguments over one wanted more impetus put on his specialized field.

For example, of the personnel involved, two of the people later became a part of my special operations staff. One was Dave Del Guidice, who was then commanding officer of SEAL Team One and later progressed up the line through the Pentagon routine to head of the Special Operations. And Bill Thede, who later became my Chief Staff Officer with the Naval Operations Support Group. We had two intelligence officers from CinCPacFlt, we had two advisers from the field, from the Naval Advisory Group, stationed in-country at the time -- one was Commander Arnie Levine, adviser to the Viet amphibious task force. Levine was very strongly in favor of psychological warfare and we did include a limited comment in our report on psychological warfare in deference to his strong feelings, although we did not feel that it applied directly to infiltration.

Q: Was it too sophisticated for that situation?

Capt. B.: No, but his concepts of what was needed, were more related to the "People to People" aspect and he firmly believed in it. But, as I have said, it did not apply to infiltration and the stopping of it.

We included comments as to the benefits that might accrue from different types of psychological warfare and help the overall problem. We had a couple of photographic intelligence types one from CinCPacFlt. And we had available to us selected MACV staff personnel that might assist as we needed them. In addition to the interviews and visits that we made, we called people in and sat down and discussed, round-table, with them their field problems, seeking their versions of infiltration specifically, as well as getting their opinions on logistics and other pertinent problems. The most prevalent complaint was lack of communications. The advisers went out and were isolated along with their assigned troops.

Q: Did you fan out as a group, did you have different missions or did you go as a group?

Capt. B.: In travelling from base to base we went as a group. We had a plane assigned to us, sometimes a helicopter, sometimes a light transport, scheduled in rather than special flights. We would be out a couple days here and there. MACV provided us office space to ourselves. In other words, we had privacy and could get our administrative work cleared without interference. We did a lot of our own typing, which you usually do in an intelligence job.

Q: Did you have any typing staff, any yeomen, with you?

Capt. B.: No, we did a lot of writing longhand. And where typewriters were available, we all had a little experience, and we roughed it up and coordinated it, and as is usually the case, at the last minute we pulled it together.

Q: It was a period of sixty days? Other than the reactions from Admiral Felt, which you said were positive, did you get other reactions, from the DOD by any chance?

Capt. B.: No, but I was well quizzed for several reasons by Admiral Holmes, who had meanwhile moved over to ComFirst Fleet. He wanted to know a lot about Admiral Savidge's illness. I was quizzed by Admiral Sharp at CinCPacFlt. First Admiral Felt, then Admiral Sharp, then Admiral Holmes. They got the report back at Washington.

Q: Not the complete report?

Capt. B.: Not the complete report. I don't know whether Admiral Felt ever showed the addendum, other than the discussion on his own patio at his quarters. We never went into the office with it and he left the next day for Vietnam. I heard of some of the sessions he had on arrival in Vietnam and know that he expressed our opinions very curtly.

Q: Maybe it was a good idea you didn't go back with him?

Capt. B.: I was ready to come back to Coronado, but it was probably just as well for army friendships that I didn't go to Vietnam.

Q: What was Sharp interested in?

Capt. B.: From Washington they received the basic report and apparently also from CinCPac discussion. They quizzed me a lot on the telephone. I think some distortions of my opinions came from that. It was the old story -- the navy person at the end of the line had his opinions so he might shape the comments accordingly. They quizzed me from Washington to Coronado on the entire report, but due to my having the new command -- that was used as an excuse -- they didn't bring me in to Washington for thirty days or so, saying, "You've got your hands full there getting organized." And of course, we were going to be used for these same activities in Vietnam support.

Q: Yes, but if the report was that important you would think they would want a face-to-face discussion of it in Washington.

Capt. B.: Well, I thought so as momentum built up. I had never heard of this as the "Bucklew Report." We didn't use that name but it became labelled that from back in Washington, and it was handled like a hot potato. On a Secret and even Top Secret basis, and some of the points that I had made were even more sensitive to CNO policy. Admiral Rivero, I am certain, did not concur with all of our recommendations with his feelings about riverine warfare.

Q: Did MacDonald react at all?

Capt. B.: I never talked with him on the subject. It came up several times once I was back here and, of course, in discussion of different craft and boats and that sort of requirement. I made quite a few comments. I was organizing then our new outfit. We volunteered and were made responsible for boat training before CNO set up additional boat training bases on the west coast. My people took it on routinely and trained the new crews as they were assigned.

We were then also taking over the base in Danang which had been operated by the CIA. The PT boats were arriving from Norway. The SWIFT boats -- Mr. McNamara came out during my visit at Danang and ordered the build-up of SWIFT boats, 20 more immediately -- and by the time I ultimately ended up in Washington, the number had been built up to 180 of those boats. The newly assigned commanders wanted more and more.

Q: Would you take a retrospective look at the report and the recommendations you made and say something about the implementation as it developed in the next four years -- specific implementation?

Capt. B.: I believe that the succession of commands, army and navy, that occurred within Vietnam, along with many personal ideas that these commanders would originate, the points made in our report were revivied, or they occurred as "original" within the staff and were ultimately implemented. The manner in which they were implemented probably did not derive from our report. It would be my opinion that within the MACV staff, as they looked it over they might say, "Well, that's a good point, we'll use that, but skip this one," as is usually done. It is significant that ultimately each of the recommendations were implemented, probably at someone else's instigation.

Q: I suppose with a specialized study like that, much of it has to be anticipatory and eventually comes to be obvious. If it is a truthful observation to people who focused on the problem later on, it becomes obvious to people who are involved.

Capt. B.: I certainly think that is true. We also have to remember the resistance factor over this whole Vietnamese situation which was building up at that time. You might say it was only the beginning but it had started. It was an unpleasant circumstance for all. The Navy -- from the Chief of Naval Operations side -- looked at it as, "This is an army situation." I don't believe it was taken adequately seriously in the early years and it was more an attitude of, "There will never be need for aircraft carriers out there, so we'll give them the support that we can and steer clear of it." But, the requirements increased tremendously. I was later sent checking different types of ships that were in mothballs, made a few visits looking at repair ships in the Philippines, checking on different LSTs -- how badly are they in need of repair, can they be repaired. Some of them were so rusted that you could stick your fist through the hull.

Q: Bad mothballs?

Capt. B.: Yet they were pulled out, refurbished, and they did a tremendous job in logistcs support. They weren't combatant ships but they hauled supplies back and forth from the Philippines and became the work horses supporting almost any task in moving equipment, troops, or in providing back-up support.

Q: Another question: at that stage in 1963 when you were there for observation, was ROLLING THUNDER in its early stages in operation?

Capt. B.: It was in the planning stage. I don't know of the implementation on it. I knew a little bit about it but not much.

Q: In the early stages, I understand it was largely photography and intelligence observations.

Capt. B.: To the best of my knowledge that is all that was occurring. There were dozens of plans going on within little isolated groups. I suppose everyone had a theory.

Q: Contingency plans?

Capt. B.: For the Vietnamese and contingent upon their willingness to accept or do, or to meet the requirements.

Q: That is the nature of the military, that's the training.

Interview No. 8 with Captain Phil H. Bucklew

Place: At his residence in Fairfax, Virginia

Date: Thursday, 19 June 1980

Subject: Biography

By: John T. Mason, Jr.

Q: When we broke off you were back in Coronado having completed your survey and investigation of the situation in Vietnam and you had written your report which had been forwarded to Washington and which later became known as the Bucklew Report. Did you return to Vietnam immediately?

Capt. B.: No. My immediate job was picking up the straws where we had left them on the formation of this new command which was known as the Naval Operations Support Group -- there being some objections from the Pentagon to calling it Naval Special Operations, which they later did.

Q: Why?

Capt. B.: Because of a fetish at the VCNO level -- "We don't want Special Operations within the navy."

Q: This was Admiral Rivero's hand?

Capt. B.: Yes. So it became Naval Operations Support Group

which implied that we were a logistics organization -- by the name. Actually, we were consolidating five different small commands: two underwater demolition teams, the Boat Support Unit, which was newly formed for Vietnam, the Beach Jumper units, and the SEAL teams. Naval Operations Support Group thus was a headquarters command for these, conducting their administration, providing for the personnel commitments for Vietnam, and for the logistics and training of personnel which was greatly increased. It being a rapidly expanding new command, we had the problem of housing and did a lot of it ourselves. We took over barracks, ultimately a large portion of the Coronado Amphib Base, refurbishing the buildings into offices and billets.

Our Underwater Demolition Teams were on the other side of the road, so to speak, but had their own new construction building, and we were adding to that. We had quite an extensive program going on for the next four years as well as providing for the new developments and requirements that were occurring in Vietnam. Probably the most urgent of these involved the Boat Support Unit to man and maintain the many newly constructed craft for which we just didn't have people trained -- in Danang of responsibilities for clandestine operations in North Vietnam.

Our SEAL contingents would train Vietnamese SEALS and supervise. They were not allowed to go north of the demarcation line, though they did at times -- but the Vietnamese were intended to man the boats. There was a considerable expansion in the navy boat program with the innovation of what was called the SWIFT boat, an aluminum hulled craft that had been designed for crew boat work with the oil companies. Being of simple nature and high speed capability the SWIFT was better than anything the navy had at that time. We ultimately had 180 of them in Vietnam.

Meanwhile, a project which had been initiated by our CIA predecessors, we received 6 Norwegian NASTY type PT boats -- a very sophisticated craft. It was with considerable difficulty that the Vietnamese were trained to operate them in a very short time. Maintenance was another story.

Q: Due to a lack of technical knowledge?

Capt. B.: That's right. In fact, we didn't have sufficient in the U. S. navy and we had to develop it, but our people were more adept at picking up such training. We utilized the shipyard at Subic for major overhauls, any major maintenance and repairs necessary, and set up a complete base at Danang that was jointly shared and operated by the Vietnamese SEAL components and our U. S. SEAL teams. This became our major combatant problem for the next several years. We rotated SEAL personnel on the basis of every six months. However, before the end of the Vietnamese operations many of our men had been there ten and twelve times.

Q: They would be there for six months and then go home for six months.

Capt. B.: Back home for six and then back to Vietnam again. This was on a voluntary basis. I didn't really approve of it, but the SEAL teams were as highly motivated a group as I have ever known. They took their casualties, but were relatively low in fatalities. It was another type of operation comparable to that which I described earlier with Admiral Conolly in North Africa. The training on the spot became very important. In working in a newcomer with a group of old hands, it was necessary to keep the newcomer suppressed and held down with the realization that these were more "sneak and peek" cautious operations than they were "charge." Casualties that occurred were more often from too much determination -- hard charging.

Q: The new recruits were gung-ho then?

Capt. B.: The gung-ho had to be held in check because that is where you get hurt in guerrilla operations -- exposing yourself instead of waiting and watching.

Q: As a part of the story, will you tell me what was the state of the SEAL teams when you came into command?

Capt. B.: Their proficiency was developing rapidly. We had SEAL Team One as the Pacific Unit. They were not under me at the time but they had been participants in the Cuban operation and had received a very versatile form of training, all of which did not apply to Vietnam. The program for the SEALs was a most ambitious one, including ski training and all types of military operations including parachuting, weapons play and guerrilla warfare and tactics. We even worked our SEAL personnel along with the Customs people on the Mexican border for training, working them at night and helping out the Customs people where help was a much needed thing.

Q: The Rio Grande isn't very deep is it?

Capt. B.: Well, it wasn't very wet. It was a dry river. But this was more for night operation training, although it was amazing the number of wetbacks captured. That part of training helped the SEALs get the feel of it. However, as I have said, the on-the-spot training in general warfare is the most beneficial.

Q: In the locale where they are going to operate? What are the qualifications for a man who wants to be a SEAL?

Capt. B.: He must first have the background of Underwater Demolition Training, so he has that -- the demolition and the swimming, and more often than not the parachuting. From there you expand into weapons work, living off the land. A good portion of time is spent in training other military services, such as the Army Special Forces.

Q: In terms of intelligence gathering, what kind of training do they have there?

Capt. B.: A portion of the work there is done through the Intelligence Schools. As these groups were being formed, in which I had an advisory part back in the '61 and '62 periods when SEAL teams were coming into being, we outlined a broad scope of school training, and intelligence was a major part. It all related from the demolition and swimming and beach reconnaissance, which was a primary responsibility of our demolition teams. The men had that part behind them. The jungle operation, however, was quite different. It is a mud operation rather than a sandy beach.

Q: What is the average age of the SEAL?

Capt. B.: I would say the average would run from about 23 to 24 years, however, we had some remarkably well conditioned men who would be in the 40-year-old category.

Q: They would have to have real stamina?

Capt. B.: There is a type of man who makes a career of this type work. I can touch upon that later. I spent much of my Pentagon tour that followed in establishing a career pattern and program for these specialists. This had always been in the back of my mind, having observed it from World War II where at the end of the war the specialized personnel were disestablished from their organized units. Then the Korean War came along and it was necessary to reactivate, to call the veterans out of reserve, and start over again. We continuously avoid the lesson of retaining a nucleus of such special skills and personnel.

It so happened that over my career period I was the most senior person in this type of work on active duty. I believed in the navy's need to retain a nucleus of these special skills, and to accomplish this there must be a program offering career opportunity. We later set it up so that there could be a rotation of specialized personnel in billets and in different specialties ranging from basic demolition, to SEAL team and intelligence billets, to including assignments into the logistical pattern supporting their own specialty of boat programs. At the present time, if the cutbacks haven't damaged them too badly in the last three or four years, we have a rather broad pattern in billet structure establishing and retaining a nucleus of career personnel for Special Warfare. The name has been changed to Special Warfare, the rank structure includes several captain billets and -- one day -- it will open up for flag rank opportunity.

Q: And you've got a different VCNO.

Capt. B.: That's right. As I digressed, a good portion of our time back there in '63 and '64 was not only in the deployment of our initial units in the river operations and into the clandestine north Viet operations from Danang; training the boat crews and as boats came into our possession; of giving support in Vietnam; and meanwhile to build our buildings, conduct our own training, and develop our organization back in Coronado.

Q: That certainly was a mammoth job. In terms of personnel, what did you have?

Capt. B.: In over-all strength we ran about a thousand men. Officer percentage is perhaps a little high in this type of work, but with the type of personnel you need, most have come through officer candidate school. They are college graduates. I neglected to mention before, language training has always been a part of our SEAL team training, though you have to be rather lucky to hit the right language for the situation at hand.

Q: It seems to me that each man is almost the equivalent of a one-man army. He has so many different facets to his training and preparation.

Capt. B.: That's true, and those comments have been made at the Bureau of Personnel level, to the effect that unless there occurred some disciplinary problem, these officers certainly should have no problems with promotion. The advantage of the training and experience gained -- that was the importance of setting up billets and having a place for them to progress to. In my own case we ran out of billets. After I had headed the Special Warfare Program, where was there to go? And with my seniority I didn't care to go to any field other than the one in which I had spent all the years. I was not intending to be a hanger-on in the navy -- but, there was no place to go beyond.

Q: You mentioned just a short time back that language study is a requirement. How many different languages did a man master or was required to master?

Capt. B.: Most of the training was done in navy schools and that, in effect, controls the number of languages. The usual trend is to follow where the hot spot of the moment is. So we had people trained in Russian, and many of the exotic languages, and many times you hit the basics such as Spanish and French, as problems might be occurring in South America and Central America. I would say that it was advantageous to many. Some we had in Japanese and Chines language school, but that takes a longer period and it is not usually included within the naval system. We did have problems on these longer periods of training in that it is also difficult to predict a man's period of service. We made considerable effort, with some limited success, in drawing Naval Academy graduates into the program.

Q: Through publicity at the Academy, or how?

Capt. B.: There was a resistance on this at the Bureau of Personnel level although we solicited all the help we could to draw them in. The midshipmen themselves seemed quite interested -- it was an exciting thing to them. We gradually have succeeded and were allocated five or six one year, and they are moving up the line now.

I recently met a lieutenant commander in the Navy Exchange that we had a hard time fighting for. We felt that the duty would be suited to him and he fought his way for the opportunity. It takes two-way cooperation to manage this. But it was my opinion and that of our key people who were working for this career program that this just had to be to assure the continuity of the program, that a career person would require, and you assume that academy personnel would be career inclined. (Percentages didn't always back that up in the last few years.) I had the conviction, initially handed down to me as advice from Admiral Spike Fahrion, that if you stay operational in this type of work you needn't worry about being cut out, and I think that has been the case.

Q: It might be a good idea to cover this very complicated command by taking one category at a time, instead of during the period you were with them. Would that be advisable?

Capt. B.: You mean the different commands? I have touched upon the SEAL teams.

Q: Yes, but you haven't told me much about their actual operations in Vietnam -- if you can?

Capt. B.: The majority of our SEALs were deployed from our base in Danang, being close to the border. Their entire program was the training of the Vietnamese SEALs and for harassment tactics against North Vietnam.

Q: The Vietnamese SEALs were known as PHOENIX, were they?

Capt. B.: No, that was a group down in the river operation -- more of a CIA type operation.

We also had to provide personnel in support of the CIA operations. It wasn't defined as such, but we would have to provide so many men, maybe 2 or 4, for specific operations. Most of this reassignment would be done from Saigon so our administrative channel would be sending the men to MACSOG, which was the Military Advisory Command Special Operations Group. They rotated their commanding officers. The last one was Jack Singlaub (Colonel) and the MACSOG command progressed to having (loosely saying) several thousand personnel. It was hard to define the difference between routine army operations and special operations, infantry, and whatever.

We had a numbers game of having to fill army billets in Vietnam and our men might be redeployed as they arrived in Saigon. Presumably we were sending those that were selected for specialized purposes to our own Danang base, which also came under MACSOG control in Vietnam. This group operated until the end of the war and took over several of the facilities that had been developed by the CIA. Ultimately they asked and received more and more Navy boats (high speed PT types) that were used for raiding purposes and had many successful operations and some that were not -- none were publicized.

One of the amazing incidents was the Tonkin Gulf one which was highly publicized (for an entirely different reason) than as we knew it. The actual situation was that our PT boats had operated against a Vietnamese island base one night and had successfully completed a strafing and incendiary rocket operation. The following night the MADDOX and one other destroyer had not been advised of this. They steamed into the area unaware of the PT action. The MADDOX was attacked by North

Viet SWATOW craft who presumed another attack on their base was being launched. This was one of the hazards and weaknesses of separately controlled special operations clandestine work. The MADDOX did not know that it was in hazardous waters and the Vietnamese boats that came out to attack them, to our knowledge, were merely defending themselves, having been strafed with incendiary fire the night before. This was turned around politically to appear that two innocent steaming destroyers were attacked by the Vietnamese, but there was good reason from the Vietnamese point of view, who thought they were being attacked again as they had been the night before.

Q: Did they make any effort to press this point?

Capt. B.: Well, politically it was used as justification for further U. S. actions and the SEAL team operation was not acknowledged. (It was the Vietnamese operating the boats who had done this from the Danang base. These were always Secret.) None of the SEAL operations were ever publicized on a specific basis. They would be covered by special reports to CinCPac, who would pass at his discretion detailed reports to JCS in Washington, D. C.

Q: How were the Vietnamese as SEAL teams?

Capt. B.: Some were outstanding. Most of them were limited by experience, particularly in the boat operations. They made their mistakes and they grounded boats, but they didn't abandon them. They lost two PT boats in the period of about four years. There was one incident that they opened fire on one another, not that these things are impossible for American craft. Where there is fighting between small craft in an area that may include as many as a thousand deployed fishing boats and you cannot identify friend or foe until they open fire on you, many tragic things can happen. It takes considerable skills in recognition, as well as experience and calm, calculated control to be successful. I thought the Vietnamese progressed remarkably well considering the limitations of their previous experience in high proficiency type power boats.

Q: Was their motivation comparable with the high motivation of the American SEALs?

Capt. B. Not to that degree. I have had considerable discussions with our SEAL personnel in debriefing them and they backed their Viet counterparts to the hilt. But in comparison to our own men I couldn't say they were motivated in the same manner. Our men were keyed to get the job done and get the war over with. My impression of the Vietnamese has been that they expected it to be a lifetime ordeal. A number of the Viet SEALs had dedication, but they also had a contentment in that they were well fed, paid, and their families were nearby. Military life had become a way of life to them. They were not of the peasant farmer types that were avoiding all aspects of war. These had a motivation for military life.

Q: Were they college men also?

Capt. B.: Some. I couldn't speak for the personnel records of the Vietnamese. These were rather well guarded by the Vietnamese and as it occurred in Saigon between the major levels of command, there was a separation between them, closely guarded.

Q: Why was it so closely guarded?

Capt. B.: I imagine that derived from the whole political scheme. I recall when I was first in Vietnam on my reconnaissance study, I heard so often the complaint from the American headquarters, "Well, all we can do is ask them!" Since this was not our war, we were their advisers. That U. S. lack of control continued until the end. This was one of the major contributing factors to failure.

American troops when on various field skirmishes for the army, if they had Vietnamese with them, yes, they pushed them, prodded them and in many cases had them out front and working as a team. But it was not a matter of control as it was throughout European warfare where you had one commander. Throughout Vietnam there was the American and there was his counterpart. There might also have been the Australian or the Britisher as additional counterparts -- which does not ensure field disciplines that require firm control and single authority.

Q: What role did you have in the development of the individual operations involving SEAL teams? How was this effected? What went into the consideration of an operation?

Capt. B.: Our SEAL officers could make recommendations. I am speaking now of using Danang as an operating point. They could make their recommendations. They could gather intelligence. They could foresee or project activities, suggesting counter actions but they had no authority to execute. They had to go first back to Saigon, to MACSOG. If MACSOG considered approval beyond their authority, they had to go to Washington with an outline of their plan and await approval or disapproval. For an immediate reaction in the field it would take approximately three days to get authority, which, of course negated most counter actions or actions deriving from spot intelligence acquired, from actual field observations. With such restrictions by the time authorization was received from the Washington level, the opportunity had usually passed and there was nothing there.

Q: That must have been a morale problem, wasn't it?

Capt. B.: It was a tremendous frustration to all troops. Of course, their own lives were hazarded every time they would go into the field or go over the waters in their boats. They could not help but consider their actions so often a wasted effort when belated authorization came through. Much of that, as I later learned, was controlled from the U. S. Secretary of Defense level and for those operations that were into North Vietnam, authorization, in many cases, went to the Presidential level. It was done through the liaison and a special office under the Joint Chiefs of Staff. Their messenger, a Navy captain, would go to the "Hill" or to the White House to seek approval. Very often it would take them a day to get their hearing and by the time decision got back to the field the opportunity was lost and often casualties could be attributed to such preposterous control.

Q: The SEALs operated largely in the northern part of South Vietnam rather than down in the delta area?

Capt. B.: The majority of them. Our Boat Support Units worked both on the coastal areas with the SWIFT boats and with the river boats. Their craft were used both as personnel carriers and as back-up fire power for operations in the rivers. As I have said, the war was mostly fought at night and the boat people were there. We gained considerable experience in that field, much of which has gone over the dam now, although Navy still has three small boat support units -- one working down in the Louisiana Gulf area, and one on each coast -- at Little Creek and at Coronado. But they haven't boats. I was told recently that the Navy has six remaining, with next production expected in FY 82.

Q: They are not so terribly expensive are they -- boats of that size?

Capt. B.: No, certainly not relative to aircraft, tanks and such. You know my personal retired occupation is in part representing a builder of small craft, and the foreign nations that we supply are really far better equipped than the U. S.

Navy in high proficiency small craft. This is quite an annoyance to me.

Q: For the sake of the record here, do you want to go into some of the lessons the support people learned in Vietnam?

Capt. B.: That is a difficult thing to do with specifics -- progress was made on a day by day basis. For example, on the boats, there was much improvisation. Our SEAL teams with the PT boats improvised to meet a need by combining a 50-calibre machine gun, even a twin 50-calibre, with an 81mm mortar on the same mount so that one man could operate either, the purpose being that the flare from the mortar would go out and light up the target so you could identify friend or foe while your MG weapon was ready to fight or defend, as the case may be.

This took several years but is now approved equipment in the U. S. Navy inventory, although now they don't have the boats. It is called a Piggy-back weapon. For four years piggy-backs were built in the field by our SEAL teams by welding parts together, and hoping for authorized weapons to be produced at home. We had other equipments which I managed to obtain on the basis of test and evaluation.

For example, there is the Stoner System of automatic weaponry which, with one weapon you can modify it to accommodate maybe ten or more different requirements. The Marines tried for years to get the Stoner System, and I don't believe it has been accepted to the present day. But I had ten units of it with my SEAL teams on the basis of test and evaluation.

We would write reports and send them in about once a month, and I had good support on what you might call an "under the table" basis from the Weapons Systems Command. They knew what we were doing and with the limited operational funds that field units could provide, they did their best to back us up.

As developments would occur, the men in the field would usually have the imagination and capability to do something about it. Their uniforms, their boots, on all types of things -- they made their changes to suit the immediate need. Some of the rigs that they would wear -- ammunition belts and the like -- you have never seen on a military base I am sure. There was not the rigid discipline as in Patton's day of uniformity comparing anything in the jungle.

Q: Was that perhaps a detriment, in the long run, to the continuation of the units?

Capt. B.: No, it should have been a justification. Unfortunately within the Navy there are so few senior officers who have even observed let alone understood the land aspects and the guerrilla aspects. Naturally, they are sea-going types, shipboard and aviator types, but they have had limited exposure to field operations.

Q: Well, they are not blind?

Capt. B.: No, but they are not close to it. They are more accustomed to being 50 miles off the coast. They can read a report but they can't really visualize how much these activities accomplish. It isn't that they don't give credit, but they have not fully understood. And if you will recall there was that initial high-level resistance to the Navy becoming involved even in muddy river operations.

On many of these things, as they developed, our type of special warfare units worked more closely with Marine and Army units than they did with our own navy. They were so assigned and remained so.

When I speak of equipments we received, Admiral Eph Holmes came back from CNO to Coronado and informed me, "I am sending out three Air Cushion Vehicles. I want you to check them out here hurriedly and get them out to Vietnam." So we had the first three in the military service. We trained crews to operate them at Coronado and deployed them. They were unsatisfactory for naval use because of the noise factor -- to work at night on the rivers with their gas turbines you could hear them for 5 or 6 miles in the quiet over water. They were beautiful equipment for going from the water up over the land and pursuing, though we had to improvise further after getting them to Vietnam. The army wanted them for personnel and for the type of warfare that they were in, this capability of coming from the water and pursuing on through the bullrushes and the swamps was ideal.

We had to rig catwalks to give additional support and to strengthen them to carry troops. After a short period of time, I don't recall exactly although we must have had them in the field for about six months, we turned them over to the army direct considering them more appropriate for their operations where the pursuit of the enemy goes on over the land.

There was much accomplished in new equipments of that type. As I suppose it always has been in war, there was less planning than what you could "adapt," to your existing needs. Some of it was good, some was bad. Unfortunately a good portion of this is lost for lack of documentation.

Although the Navy today is dominated by the carrier force and the submarines, there continues to be a place, more so in the Navy and Marines than with the Army, for capability in this type of operation. They have already cut back on it, but I don't believe this has come about due to over-extending of capabilities as much as due to limited funds and somewhat the attitude -- as a recent CNO has often been quoted -- "If it can't fly, I don't want to hear about it." Insofar as budgets and personnel were concerned, he absolutely would not listen.

Q: What about helicopters? Did your men use them in any way?

Capt. B.: We had none assigned to us although MACSOG did. MACSOG had small aircraft and helicopters and our men were utilized with them. On any type operation utilizing the Vietnamese, an adviser accompanied them unless authority completely forbade it, as it was forbade that Americans go into North Vietnames waters -- but it was done.

Q: In the advisory capacity?

Capt. B.: Riding the boat, reassuring them. You had your boat captain, the Vietnamese captain and you assisted him in every way possible from maintenance, from checking out his supplies, from briefing his troops, from planning. But being at his shoulder during such operations made it that much more effective. So normally one adviser would accompany a team of Vietnamese. This same would apply whether it were helicopter or PT boat operations and whether or not the Vietnamese were responsible for command. As far as the SEAL teams were concerned their task was against the North Vietnamese and operations in that northern area.

Q: When a man went along with a Vietnamese team as an adviser, what was their attitude toward him? Was his advice really more than advice -- possibly in the nature of a command at times?

Capt. B.: As far as you could go, tactfully. I will say for the Vietnamese officers, most of them had a great respect for their counterparts -- our SEALs. It was sort of a big brother relationship. I mean big brother in the sense that our men were physically bigger. Our men were more experienced and were recognized for that too. And their presence was reassuring to the Vietnamese. Advisorship is closely parallel to leadership, within the limits defined for you.

Q: A matter of semantics? You said on a previous occasion that two SEALs could have been more effective in blowing up bridges and things of that sort, than high level bombing from out of Thailand. Was there any incident of this sort? Did they ever attempt this in an advisory role?

Capt. B.: Not to my knowledge of specifics. I wouldn't say it didn't happen because many things happened in the field to get the job done that were never publicized. They took their chances, they sank boats, they attacked shore installations. I did make that statement and I think it applies to both the UDT capability and the SEAL capability. But the problem is more often with the military commands in control and their reluctance to utilize or recognize capabilities at hand. Many times such proposals have been pushed forward, and not just at the tactical level. I mentioned it of Admiral Moorer in the blockade of Haiphong and the discussions of it. It is brought up time after time and those who can visualize and know the capabilities of their own men can consider it a very simple task, while others say "that's ridiculous; that's impossible." Our SEALs and demolition men never considered it impossible to move up a river clandestinely. They are trained and they are strong and they can carry their demolitions. We felt that much might have been done in Vietnam with accuracy where bombs failed. But that has been a long time argument and there is a philosophy with the Special Warfare type person that you are so much safer in the water as an individual than you might be in one of those flying machines or on a boat. It's an old story. We know he is up there but he doesn't know we are here. We can move and we can do it by various propulsion sources.

Q: Were the SEALs ever involved in rescue operations of pilots who were shot down? Inadvertently, I suppose?

Capt. B.: Yes. That's been a rather common occurrence. I couldn't cite many illustrations on it but it has occurred often enough to be considered routine, pulling people out. I think I told of some incidents that occurred during World War II and they continued on. They are hardly worthy of reports. I am quite prejudiced that they are great outfits.

You asked about the other units -- the UDTs. The UDTs were deployed mainly aboard the amphibious ships to be available for reconnaissance and, of course, conducted that in any landing preparations or movements over a virgin beach. Beaches are always checked in advance or during landings, and we have on a continuing basis a detachment deployed with the WestPac Amphibious Force. They rotate every six months and are used for whatever tasks, mainly landing exercises, although there were major amphibious landings in the Danang area as that area was opened up. Our base was there before, but later, 1974, it became a Marine base and airfield after we landed our troops there. There have also been UDT detachments assigned to the river groups, mostly for reconnaissance, but available for any special demolition type operations.

Our Boat Support Unit, I touched upon. It became a most versatile group of boat handlers and maintenance personnel, probably the most experienced that the navy had.

Q: How large did that grow to be?

Capt. B.: About 200 men. They could operate any of the type craft that we had -- not that that was such a complex thing -- it's like driving an automobile. You drive one and you have the basics for most. Maintenance and experience in maintenance is always a problem -- maintenance and repair. They had their components for that.

The fifth unit was only used for a few experimental operations -- the Beach Jumpers. One of the factors: there was the language barrier, the second was the limited communications -- sophisitcated communications -- used by the enemy. Our communications were a little more exotic, but I don't think much more effective. Deception tactics were not employed in any major way.

Q: But there were small instances where they were? Could you cite any of those?

Capt. B.: Mostly the Beach Jumpers were used in an advisory capacity on communications. They attempted some deception operations but working more, at the Vietnam field level, almost with the old walkie-talkie type equipments. There were no reportable operations of a spectacular nature. Now, we always had Beach Jumpers deployed with the Seventh Fleet and there were personnel aboard ship there who specialized in deception work. Most of these operations were in the form of monitoring communications rather than offensively working a deception program.

Q: Would they be up in the Taiwan area?

Capt. B.: Wherever Seventh Fleet was deployed, in the Taiwan area, in the Korean area or throughout Southeast Asia. We had some with the Amphibious WestPac Detachment, which of course is part of the Seventh Fleet, and their activities were mainly in the highly specialized field of monitoring -- you monitor, you tape, you analyze.

Q: The techniques they mastered, have they been passed on or have they been absorbed into NSA?

Capt. B.: They have worked some with NSA. I am not certain of this, but I believe the Beach Jumpers may now have been administratively shifted, their control having been passed to higher levels in NSA at this time. That occurred since my retirement. Within the Pentagon they pulled BJ out of Special Warfare and put it up in another shop with intent that it be utilized to better advantage with the fleet controlled tactical units and NSA related operations.

Q: So their experience hasn't been entirely lost then?

Capt. B.: No, and I think much fleet indoctrination and understanding was accomplished over the period of years from our reactivation back in the early '50s. For example, in naval war planning, we developed the Naval War Plan (NWP) there and the NWIPs. There was a concerted effort to document experience gained, digging back into World War II and the progressive developments after.

Within the electronic equipment inventory many exotic capabilities have developed. Navy developed the very exotic Cruiser NORTHAMPTON back in the '50s, long since mothballed. But it was loaded with electronic equipments for this purpose -- monitoring, jamming, deception, the entire scope. Of course, many of the NSA type operations, such as the PUEBLO, have taken over many of these responsibilities. The LIBERTY, as well as the PUEBLO, were publicized for their difficulties but that type of operation is very comparable and within the Beach Jumper capability.

Q: I can see that much of what they learned in Vietnam has been dissipated but I can see a positive note that it has been incorporated higher up and elsewhere. I was thinking in terms of the Boat Support Units. Their techniques as they acquired and learned them in Vietnam would be almost unique to that topography, would it not? And couldn't it be transplanted elsewhere in the world and used?

Capt. B.: In boat operations, there are so many little things gained by experience. As an example, it has always been difficult to train high speed boat operators to accept the philosophy that his speed is best used for exit or for emergency. That his approach to a target is best done at the slowest and the quietest movement to encourage the surprise of the attack. Then, when he has to get the hell out of there that is when power and speed and running is valuable. You have to experience that to appreciate it, I think. Slowing down and moving quietly in approach, the old hand will do. The new man wants to gun the throttle and charge.

Q: Then it boils down to the fact that this is almost an individual experience, a learned experience. How do you pass that on to the next generation?

Capt. B.: I'm afraid that is more often lost than not. You gain experience that you never lose, but with the turn-over of personnel it is not readily available and on call because it is a specialty. Perhaps a more simple one and less respected, but I am sure it is the same situation with aircraft although on a more sophisticated basis.

Q: I see this as very typical of the navy with its rotating commands. A man on a particular job acquires a certain amount of knowledge which he didn't have prior to that job but then he is transferred elsewhere and somebody else comes on in the change of command. He briefs him before the change but does he really impart all the knowledge that he has acquired while he was there? I don't think so.

Capt. B.: More often than not, I think the relieving officer feels, "Don't tell me any more, I'll run this show when I get my hands on the throttle." The other is anxious to leave and get to his next assignment. However, I think in most phases of military life, though a broad general experience is ideal, we have passed the time when you can have experience in all fields. It becomes generalized. You cannot be a specialist in electronics, communications, computers, weaponry, in each category, though they are related. I think it is a rare instance today that a man comes up through the navy with experience in destroyers, amphibious ships and cruisers, before finally, an aircraft carrier. More often than not, an aviator comes from his squadron to become exec of a carrier and may never have operated from a ship until that time. He often may have difficulties, but the old tradition of the well rounded naval officer having covered the entire scope as he came up the line, I think has passed us.

Q: As a comparison I think it is relatively rare to find a doctor now who is a practitioner of general medicine.

Capt. B.: True, the surgeon doesn't know much about the measles.

I think it was inevitable where I was going next.

Q: First, would you talk a little more about your personal experiences while you were in Vietnam, until December of 1967?

Capt. B.: I made three brief return visits after my initial reconnaissance survey experience. Mostly it was to inspect our units, show your presence. At one time I was to be assigned there. They called me out to CinCPac (Admiral Felt then), discussed my assignment in the Special Warfare Section and I personally had planned to go. But Admiral J. B. Colwell,

ComPhibPac, was of the opinion that it was better for the field teams to have me in the backup position. He felt more was needed that I could best support our operations right from Coronado, and this extended my tour there about two years.

I was never assigned with specific duration of tour but he felt I could do more in equipping and providing men, and already had a basic knowledge of the area. Although it probably would have been career advantageous to have the assignment, I feel that it was a wise judgment, as was my later move from Coronado to the Pentagon in the Special Warfare Division. I think when you put men in unindoctrinated, the same as in the field, and they don't understand, it takes six months to even analyze the requirements, or to understand why they need it. You don't learn the sources overnight. I made my visits, once with Admiral Colwell -- we covered you might say the whole circuit -- Korea, Japan and Taiwan, before going to Vietnam. I went again with Admiral Roeder and again later as a member of a Joint Chiefs team to document much of the Vietnam history, operations, and procedures. That occurred during my final six months in the Navy. My last visit to Vietnam was from Washington and this was a several weeks junket in documenting the activities of MACSOG and clandestine operations. About once a year I would be included on a two or three week tour back into Vietnam.

Q: With these period visits to Vietnam, what was your attitude toward the conflict there? What convictions were you developing in these different periods of time?

Capt. B.: I was no doubt biased in my opinions from the beginning that I had. I would have a natural interest in what had been done with some of the recommendations we had made back in the '63, '64 period. Had things improved? I was perhaps quite cynical regarding the expansion of personnel (I am referring to the army) and it seemed more of a service situation than a combat operation. There were troops everywhere. In Saigon they were building a new headquarters -- Pentagon East. It seemed to me they could cut the troops in half and get more done -- the age-old story.

I found even greater frustration in all the camps I visited. The frustration was 100% more in '67, '68, '69 than it had been back in the early days. A few of the old hands had been there for many tours and the new hands were reflecting the cynicism that was developing here at home. They were thinking about getting home before they arrived there, and there was definitely the attitude that the less we do the less chance of being hurt. Overall, the frustration seemed to increase year by year.

My feeling from the beginning was that it could all have been closed out in a six months period, without the casualties. I regret that there seemed so little you could do about it. You say the attitude of many -- "I have to do this for my career." But they were doing too much -- that's when you get hurt. We saw the post exchanges expand, along with black markets and civilian opportunists. Comparable to the Chinese in World War II -- "When this show is over we've got our own to do." I thought Vietnam reflected that.

Q: Did you notice the buildup of supplies?

Capt. B.: There were more aircraft. Helicopters were the dominant force and well used for night patrol, and the maintenance of them was a major supply problem. Other supplies seemed to be more administrative. There were troop messes all over the place and plenty of bars.

Q: But at the same time your men weren't getting more boats, were they?

Capt. B.: They were building up. They didn't want more boats as there was no justification seen for them. That was coming from Washington. I had experiences after I came back to Washington to that effect -- you couldn't stop it. I had one hurried experience in the Pentagon when an admiral who had to brief on the "Hill" in 15 minutes demanded, "How many more boats do you think will counter the infiltration actions we are having there?"

I responded, "We haven't had record of infiltration since 1963."

He said, "I don't care, I've got to answer how many more boats will help."

I said, "I can't honestly say we need any more boats."

But before it was over there were 180 of the 50-foot

SWIFT boats in country. We had 385 boats including the river craft. We built our own PT boats, the OSPREY class with aluminum hull but patterned after the Norwegian NASTYs design and I don't recall anyone other than Admiral Zumwalt wanting the PGs, the gunboats (which also came under our shop cognizance). We gave them all away afterward.

Why they wanted them then -- we recommended strongly that they not be deployed until they had a thorough shakedown in the United States -- but they wanted them and they went out where they laid at Subic mostly. Boats and equipment seemed to be thrust upon people. The operators never understood this -- those I was associated with, including army and marines. They all felt that small units could do a better job.

On equipment and weapons there are circumstances where you need a limited number of unusual types. I mentioned the Stoner weapon, but we did not need anything really that good. Operators in such an environment think more of what they carry, that is what they have to live with, and the Mark 16 is as good as any. Very often where patrols are concerned, the operator feels he can do with five men much better than twenty. You are more of a target when you have a huge logistic backup behind you. I suppose you can consider it "comforting" to have that but you are more of a target and top-heavy. I am very much a dissenter on the way this was politically handled. It seemed to be entirely on rotation basis -- rotating of draftees, rotating the career requirements of people, get everyone in the act but don't bother to win.

Q: Did you have any problem with drugs?

Capt. B.: To my knowledge, none. In fact, I am completely ignorant on the problem. I have asked many questions before retirement and since, because I have been told by those who did have the problems -- in Saigon, and drug availability everywhere -- but unless it was well covered, and it could have been, I didn't have a single drug case within the entire Special Warfare group. SEALs and Demolition people are different types, however, they are known to drink pretty well but they certainly keep themselves in top physical condition. They have to, it's imbued in them and I would say the majority of them loved doing that. Drinking, yes -- but as far as drugs, no. I had a couple of black market cases and had to pull a couple people out -- girl problems, difficulties of that type -- but never physical disability.

Q: The lack of record of such things in your special units, would you relate that to the high motivation and the fact that they were busy most of the time?

Capt. B.: It certainly is related. That, and there is a team brotherhood of taking care of one another. I had that pointed out to me one time when I was going through records of the men -- this while in Coronado. I commented to my Chief Staff Officer to the effect that, "It's peculiar to me but I have never known a case of VD in these outfits."

He smiled and replied, "Isn't that something you take care

of on your own?"

And I probed, "You mean the corpsmen don't record?" and was answered, "I don't know that, but I imagine they take care of their own."

Now that could be a parallel to drug incidence but there has never been a tolerance among the SEALs or UDT people. When there is a shortcoming, and they did occur, when a youngster is a little too impulsive, an eager beaver, hard charger, the old hand may pull him out and let him cool his heels until he readjusts to the necessary disciplines. "You jeopardize my life as well as your own, so cool it before you go out with us." That is the attitude. Anything like a drug related nature would be countered that way. There was no hesitancy in dealing with the young officers and discipline, to send somebody back, pull him out of the outfit, send him home. There is pride in their outfit, but they would never cover for a man who might jeopardize the lives of others or of themselves.

Q: So there was a constant culling effect which they instituted themselves?

Capt. B.: They had their prejudices and in-house fights. I have wondered how much was taken care of by fists. I recall that in my World War II operating days I had a young bos'n mate in North Africa. He was young, about 19, but he had those troops in shape every morning. I would go down the line looking them over and might see a few black eyes and ask him a few questions. The only answer I would get was that he had had a problem, "But we settled it." I concluded -- don't ask too many questions. Everybody seemed happy and I think that "policy" may apply to a lot of these physically inclined outfits.

Q: Small outfits and not within the mainstream of the military regimentation?

Capt. B.: I couldn't prove such things but you seldom had a complaint from any of the men.

Q: There is a saying about 'the proof is in the pudding.' Do you want to talk about the involvement of your units in the Tet offensive which happened in January of 1968?

Capt. B.: I can't report much on that. They had special assignments. One or two men were assigned to other agency groups and their reporting was much less documented and through channels other than our unit. When we rotated our teams back to the States, we would compile almost diary-like reports on them. But, the men were often restricted in reporting by agency policies when they went with individual units. We talked to them as individuals later and we might get some "sea stories" of incidents and how they countered "six here, and twelve there," and that sort of thing. But nothing that I could factually describe. They had a lot of hairy incidents and told good stories of them but not directly related to the overall operation. They assisted in planning and worked on a very cooperative basis, both sides. There was good team play on these -- penetrating the infrastructure (the key word of the time, you know).

One of our overall navy complaints which certainly existed until Admiral Zumwalt reported and he asserted a little more independence for his naval operations -- all of which we didn't agree was needed -- but the controls were taken away from us as soon as they wanted our personnel and from that point, "It's none of your business." They were required to make more reporting back to CinCPac and it didn't always come back through naval channels.

Q: What kind of skills were they seeking from your groups?

Capt. B.: Our SEALs had a reputation for their versatility and were held in high respect and reputation by the army and other services. The army always asked for SEALs whether they wanted boat people or for whatever assignments. We would send them what we thought appropriate, and never had any complaints. Our boys did become probably the most decorated single outfit in Vietnam. We had Presidential Citations and Meritorious Unit Citations, a lot of individual awards, and they were very popular with the Vietnamese. The SEALs were well liked. I am confident they did a tremendous job in training and working with the Vietnamese. They knew what they were working with, they got the most out of them, and were understanding, if not tolerant, in some cases for their problems.

Q: There is one story -- I have seen it in print somewhere --

and I would like to hear the official version. The raid on the Viet Cong gathering down in the Delta area when the SEALs burst in on their meeting.

Capt. B.: My memory of specific details on that is fuzzy. But through SEAL gathered intelligence, they learned that several Viet Cong leaders were to be in disguise among the funeral procession of a deceased village leader. They had come into this village and the SEALs taking their own action, which I suppose was rather harsh interrupting a funeral procession, captured several of the leaders of the Cong from that group. That is about all I remember, though it was quite a coup at the time. They just swooped in on them, there wasn't a shot fired. They took them by just plain physical strength.

Q: This was verification as to the kind of intelligence they gathered.

Capt. B.: At that time this infrastructure play was being concentrated on to break it up, and it was commonly known to the operators that Cong controls and leadership were concentrated in the heart of these villages. This wasn't always accepted by the higher authorities. So many things in Vietnam the reaction would be, "No, it just can't be." But it was. Nearly all villages were penetrated by the Viet Cong and the whole complexion of things changed by night when they went to work. By day they would be respected villagers insofar as American knowledge was concerned. It was a difficult situation the major problem again being the inability to identify friend or foe.

Q: Was there any thought at any time of utilizing the SEALs or any of your other contingents in a rescue effort for some of the POWs?

Capt. B.: Not to my knowledge of any really planned efforts. There were many plans conceived but not implemented at that time. In fact, this continued after my retirement from active duty at which time I was approached for an action of that type from right here in Washington. Ross Perot contacted me before his attempt there and I was receptive but didn't agree with some of his concepts. He later tried it by just taking a plane in.

Q: He was financing it?

Capt. B.: He was financing it and had very patriotic intent. But, in my opinion, he was not very familiar with the environment and the circumstance. I was not interested until he obtained White House endorsement, which he never did. How well he was received I don't know, but I briefed him on some of the problems, how things were, what I disagreed with, but that specific effort was never carried out. There was plan after plan and, of course, a major concern at all levels was gaining release of the prisoners of war -- not unlike the circumstance in Iran today.

I am certain there was talk of SEAL actions as well as

Army Special Forces. Either nothing was authorized by the White House or the plans were not carried that far. Colonel Bull Simons, the man who completed the successful rescue of a couple of Ross Perot's men in Iran was my counterpart in Special Operations, my counterpart on CinCPac Staff at that time. He was a very enthusiastic parachutist and I am confident that he developed a dozen plans as to how it might be done. He was a go-go man.

Q: That is more difficult to implement, however. You were called back to Washington every month or so while you were stationed in Vietnam?

Capt. B.: Not from Vietnam, from Coronado. For each step or change, or addition of troops, I would have to come back for meetings here and then implement from out there.

You asked about cooperation and equipment and that sort of thing. I would feel we had every cooperation from the military levels on "what do you need?" basis. That wasn't really the problem logistically, nor was money. But some of the high level devices conceived were impractical and forced on the operators for research and development experimentation. There were some wild ones.

Q: Were you hamstrung in much the same fashion as the air force was in their directions from the White House? Were your operations scrutinized in that way too?

Capt. B.: Very much so. I mentioned the time element it would often take to get authorization to carry out a task or mission. This was a tremendous annoyance and a hazard to the men in the field.

Q: You did mention that. Does it then imply that the White House itself -- the staff there -- had a finger in this pie and such operations were authorized only if they said so?

Capt. B.: That is correct. All authorizations did not go to the level of the White House, but many did, certainly any border crossing operations would require White House clearances. Most of them went to the Secretary of Defense level or I should say to his office. There were many pseudo-militarists involved there in civilian clothes that were "decision makers" and responsible for many of the problems to those in the field by the time lag.

I would say from an operator's point of view that is one of the greatest of frustrations, to see opportunity at hand and have it pass you by, all caused by waiting for an authorization from some control source thousands of miles away. I have known many instances in which the target was apparent, the men ready to go, but have been forbidden such movement until authorization was received. Since most movement and activity occurred at night, this might entail an additional 12 hour delay even after approval came in. Men would be standing by in a state of readiness just waiting, waiting, waiting, and losing all of the potential impact.

Q: I would think that an outfit such as yours would have been even more vulnerable to this kind of interference in Washington because the operations were relatively colorful as well as secret and therefore...

Capt. B.: That is quite true. The navy did not interfere but monitored a channel that came in to the Joint Chiefs. A friend of mine happened to be the JCS courier that would go to the Hill to pass along information. He would have to brief and explain. Certainly from his position with the Offices of the Joint Chiefs his understanding was limited to the concise message request received. You can't throw a full operations plan into a cabled message and include the detail and the interpretation of it. With each step it can get distorted a bit and there was yet another link going through CinCPac before the Joint Chiefs, or before going to whomever at a higher level, whether SecDef or the White House itself, for approval. Then, response comes back through the same channels. As I say, a three-day lag was typical, even on an urgent request.

Q: Did SecDef ever visit your headquarters out there? He came out occasionally.

Capt. B.: Yes. I was present when he and Admiral Sharp visited Danang. I recall this with some amusement and cynicism. That is how we got into the 50-foot SWIFT boats. It happened that the agency had ordered three of these SWIFT boats which had been originally designed as crew boats. They were of simple construction, with aluminum hull and a speed of a little over 20 knots. The first three of these had arrived at Danang about three weeks before a visit by Mr. McNamara and his staff representatives.

As he inspected the base facility, he asked our Chief Bos'n Mate, "How much maintenance does that boat require?"

The chief was hesitant in talking with the Secretary of Defense, but said, "It hasn't required any, sir."

Mr. McNamara said, "I know, but when did it have its last overhaul?"

The Chief answered, "It hasn't required an overhaul, sir."

So without telling Mr. McNamara that the boats had been there only three weeks and had only been used for supply runs to an offshore island, McNamara turned to his aide and said, "I want 21 of those boats."

The aide asked, "Sole source?" and he said, "Yes, sole source."

That was the first contract let for 50-foot SWIFT boats. It happened that the same company got the later, follow-on contracts, because naturally after you have built so many increments you should be able to outbid the others. But they built the first 20 on sole source basis and the next three increments, which amounted to a final total of 180 of these boats -- and they were all ordered from that beginning. Fortunately, they were effective craft but not ideally so. There were many design modifications that would have greatly improved their capabilities.

Q: And they did require overhual occasionally?

Capt. B.: Certainly they required overhauls. They were not large enough. Today the same boat is built on a hull of 65 feet which makes it much more seaworthy and habitable for the crew. It was the plan, at that stage, to use them on coastal surveillance and that hopefully, we could send crews out for a week at sea, and then relieve them. There were no problems on the stability of the boats and the ruggedness of them. This possibly attributed to the simplicity of design and lack of sophisticated equipment involved. But unfortunately, the crews on 50-foot boats hadn't the endurance to hold up for a week -- about three days was all they could manage. The boast were successful and unfortunately were left to the North Vietnamese, the Cong, when we pulled out.

Q: And there was...

Capt. B.: From what I have heard, they have suffered from lack of maintenance and spare parts. They have deteriorated a lot, but there are some in use at the present time, I learned recently, involving the Vietnamese refugees in the Thai camps. Our own SWIFT boats have been involved there.

Q: What happened to the NASTY boats? There were only six of those did you say?

Capt. B.: There were six of the Norwegian procured NASTYs and six of the U. S. built OSPREY class which was of the same design and propulsion but on an aluminum hull. The NASTYs, I believe, were all left there. The OSPREYs were brought back and there is one still down at Little Creek. The Navy has considered modernizing and modifying this PT but they ran out of money this past year, I understand. They have had a project under way to rework the boat for the future, once funds are available. It is really a top grade, high speed torpedo boat but very expensive to operate and very sophisticated with the British built propulsion system.

The difference between the OSPREY and the Norwegian NASTY is in the hull. The Norwegian boat has a mahogany double hull as opposed to the aluminum in the OSPREY.

Q: How does it happen the Norwegians developed such a sophisticated kind of boat? Was there a need for that?

Capt. B.: I think throughout Europe there is a greater appreciation for the smaller patrol craft and a desire for the emergency high speed. The engines are British made in the Norwegian boat and they are monstrous. We had much difficulty with our U. S. naval support and overhauls had to be made in Subic Bay (major maintenance work also). There we had technicians from the manufacturer. Our people at the maintenance base at Danang developed very creditable capability, and trained the Vietnamese with close supervision from our own people. Some things you can do on the spot, other things the boats have to come out of the water for work and damage access.

Q: Did you have anything to do at all with the Korean contingents down in Vietnam?

Capt. B.: No. I met a few during my visits and they were a highly respected force. They were hard chargers. They wanted more action than they received but I have no knowledge of their problems or restraints. They were much welcomed when they came in but they were also rather frustrated with limited activity.

Interview No. 9 with Captain Phil H. Bucklew

Place: At his residence in Fairfax, Virginia

Date: Thursday, 26 June 1980

Subject: Biography

By: John T. Mason, Jr.

Q: Your tour of duty in Coronado and Vietnam had come to an end late in 1966 and you were preparing for an assignment in Washington as head of the Special Operations Branch.

Capt. B.: Yes.

Q: Now tell me the circumstances that brought you back to Washington on a permanent basis.

Capt. B.: Actually my tour as Commander of the Naval Operations Support Group had been extended to about three years. I was due for relief and it was timely that one of my old special operations associates from the East coast was available as well as the obvious next step for me was to Washington -- to the Pentagon -- as head of the Special Warfare and Special Operations Division, OP-343.

Q: I suppose one might observe that the Bucklew Philosophy, in terms of these various operations, seemed to prevail because it was always people who had served with you and had been trained by you, who had taken over from you?

Capt. B.: This is quite true. Basically because there were very few of us with long term experience. It happened that Frank Kaine, who relieved me in Coronado, dated back to World War II as well. He was with the demolition teams at that time and it was a natural transition to follow back to the support groups. In special operations it is a little more difficult than in some aspects of the navy -- to move people into command position if they do not have an understanding from experience. In other words, it is much better to have been grounded in the small boat operations as opposed to larger ships, and in demolitions and small unit work.

Q: I would certainly think that would be just a common sense feature of the thing and something the people who give out the assignments would be very cognizant of.

Capt. B.: In that respect, during my Pentagon tour, along with several of my associates and assistants, we worked up a career program for these specialized officers and managed to push it through. To do this we researched and pinpointed various billets in the various ranks and grades that men could be moved to -- a career program for special warfare officers -- and this was accomplished with much cooperation from the naval personnel people.

Q: Did they adhere to this scheme?

Capt. B.: With perhaps some resistance at first, but I think with the help and endorsement of Admiral Charley Duncan, the Chief of Naval Personnel whom we also had known over the years. We received maximum cooperation and in about two years time such a program was authorized and is now in being. We designed a specialized career, comparable you might say to what they have in the intelligence field, although we did program that some of our people be rotated at certain periods of their careers to intelligence billets, to operations staff, and to give them a balance of experience but always returning to their basic specialized field.

Q: Is it possible at the present time to achieve flag rank by this route?

Capt. B.: Our billet structure has only gone through the captain grade. There has long been jealous guarding of admiral billets in the navy and, as you are familiar, there have always been a number of these billets unfilled, authorized but unfilled within the navy. They are closely guarded by the aviators and we were not successful in building beyond captain, but we do have several captain billets. I think it is inevitable over a period of time that flag rank will be a target and opened to this specialty, but in the interest of the growth and the pyramid structure from which you must build a career program, we thought it was premature to fight too hard to "shoot for the moon," so to speak.

Q: As I recall it was only in the post-World War II era when intelligence broke through and achieved flag rank.

Capt. B.: That's right and I believe today they have at least three flag billets.

Q: Sam Frankel was the first.

Capt. B.: That's a good target but a difficult one unless you are into wartime expansion. I think that the door will open at such time that military expansion occurs, and assuming that the special operators will again be required in the many areas that we claim. This "career program" was not the primary work during my Washington tour but related as we worked on it, on a continuing basis and accomplished success in approximately two years time. A slow and tedious researching and, I might admit, a little politicking on the side.

Q: Were the regular line officers in the fleet helpful to you in this capacity in Washington as head of Special Operations Branch? Were they hostile; were they indifferent?

Capt. B.: Sort of a combination. We had considerable senior flag officer assistance. We felt, and I felt very strongly on the subject, that we needed to bring in more naval academy trained personnel. There was considerable resistance to this. We did attain I think five per year ultimately, but there was resistance along the line.

Q: By what contingent?

Capt. B.: Certainly not from the midshipmen. They were attracted to the program and thought it was a great idea. But the competition from various other specialties, from aviation, from marines and submarines, and from those in command at the naval academy who were normally large combatant ship and destroyer types -- a destroyer type will never concede that you can be a naval officer without a maximum of years in destroyers, I believe. We had no real antagonism but at times you need a push instead of a block to get things through, so it was a slow process. Hence, today the majority -- I would hazard a guess -- would be 49 out of 50 are from NROTC and Officers Candidate Schools as opposed to the Naval Academy. Some of the boys are recruited.

I met one recently in Washington who is now a lieutenant commander from the Naval Academy, who has had his entire career thus far with special warfare units and is quite enthused for the future. There are others that have qualified through UDT and SEAL training, then go back to ships, then return again being brought in, say, as a lieutenant commander to prepare for command of one of the units. This is an effective procedure too, and we certainly had no objection to shipboard training. We felt that it was desirable and in many ways almost a necessity, as long as we could pinpoint our men to come back into the program.

Certainly the shipboard experience and the understanding

of the basic navy is advantageous in coming back to specialization. When men get away from a specialty and there is the question of promotional advantages, either for personal reasons or for navy's requirements it is often difficult to get them back in to that specialty when you need them most. In any event, the basic purpose of our career program was to maintain a nucleus, a point from which you could expand as required in wartime or emergency. I think we have attained that.

Q: In this branch of Special Warfare youth is almost a paramount requirement, isn't it? And the blush of youth passes off and then they want to get somewhere else? Family interests might draw them away.

Capt. B.: That is quite true. They are strong physical specimens up through their lieutenancy but from that point on, and they resist it somewhat when they really like this sort of activity, for their rounded experience and knowledge they need to be pushed into staff routines or command structure -- lieutenant commanders are the normal commanding officers of the smaller teams -- and to work into the administrative side of the navy as well. Of course, when you reach the commander and captain ranks you are pretty familiar with staff routine and responsibilities, operations, intelligence, logistics or whatever chosen specialty there.

Q: Can you give me some idea in terms of numbers, the number of personnel involved in this whole operation?

Capt. B.: As a ball-park figure, the various teams -- Demolition Teams, SEAL teams, Beach Jumpers, and the like, the basic complements of each would be around 100 men. They would expand at times of need, assuming they could qualify them through their training programs which are always highly competitive. So the command units would fluctuate in size between 100 and 150 men, with approximately fifteen and maybe even as many as 20 officers with each command. The figures were determined and dependent upon the success of the training programs. I think we discussed that there was considerable screening out in these programs.

When you are going through the basic training for demolition there is no rank. The enlisted men and the officers are doing the same things together. For qualification you cannot always tell how many officers you will have, as opposed to how many enlisted men. In overall structure then, this would amount to approximately 600 officers and enlisted men on each coast.

Q: For all of these different operations?

Capt. B.: Overall I would estimate an average for peace time would be about 1200 men in the various components of the Special Warfare Group, two demolition teams on each coast, a SEAL team on each coast, and Beach Jumper and Boat Support Units.

Q: I would take it then, as a result of that, that your budget requirements were fairly small. Did it remain intact or was there an attempt sometimes, when there was a shortage elsewhere, to try to make inroads on what you had available in your budget?

Capt. B.: Yes, there was always a demand. For example, on the West coast we always had a demolition contingent assigned to the amphibious group in WestPac and serving as a reconnaissance arm and that sort of thing. The same applied on the East coast for the Amphibious Group Mediterranean detachment. So this puts a strain on the units in providing for all services requested. One of your teams is always in a state of deployment, leaving only your second team on each coast available for the various contingencies that may occur.

Regularly scheduled assignments include the amphibious exercises in which our teams are always employed, others may include emergency tasks that range from life saving to salvage work. Detachments have gone on the polar expeditions, and they receive reconnaissance calls around the world. So you maintain a state of readiness for deployment and have one team attached to the East coast and one to the West, these falling under the administrative command of the Commander of Amphibious Forces, both Atlantic and Pacific, and are based with them at Little Creek and Coronado.

There are many staff requirements which we can satisfy though always trying to hang onto our people by putting these on a temporary duty basis -- in other words, by keeping the strings on them. In some facets of the career programming they will have complete tours. For example, we have a liaison officer completely toured with the amphibious groups and he serves as the staff representative there. Whereas the deployed detachment may not be physically located near the flagship, they will always be represented, in readiness and available. On the west coast, supporting Pacific forces, they may be ashore at Subic Bay. They might be needed in Vietnam or Taiwan or wherever, and could be put on a plane and quickly be at the spot needed, but they remain under the control of the amphibious force commander.

Q: There is a strong esprit de corps, isn't there, among these men? That should be a binding influence.

Capt. B.: Yes, that develops from the rugged training program that they go through together. It is almost like a fraternal organizatin after they have successfully completed training. In fact, although I didn't attend, they have annual reunions of their people. I just had an invitation to one down at Little Creek, on the East coast. They get together and the detached come back for the affairs. Also, those who have left the active service make a concerted effort to get their two-week reserve training with their old units. They have a lot of fun as well as hard work with partying and whatever. But it is almost a fraternal attachment -- life long.

That's one facet of it. But back to Washington. One of my primary goals was to achieve some type of a career program for the program. With the war going on in Vietnam, the

Pentagon life was rather hectic. I have heard it said many times and firmly believe it -- your Pentagon time is completely reactionary. It is hard to keep that side goal, that side issue of a long-time build-up, when you are fighting all the message traffic to support a wartime operation. Whether these be the daily requests for materiel, logistics support, weaponry, more personnel, coordinating with your east and west coast units and moving people, answering questions -- why did this happen? and why did that? -- that becomes the Pentagon routine. It takes a minimum of a half hour each morning to scan through the morning traffic to see what happened the night before and to get to the first conference to explain your portion. Everything is "urgent." Time is at a premium.

Q: So your objectives had to be secondary very often?

Capt. B.: That's right. You have little research time and programming to push these side issues. It takes much longer than one would imagine in putting through a program. But that is the overall Washington way.

Q: Nevertheless you obviously achieved something. How much of your desires were put into effect?

Capt. B.: I was satisfied with the career program as we developed it and as it was accepted by the Bureau of Personnel. To the best of my knowledge it has been a good beginning and they have lived up to the purpose. For example, at the present time within the Washington structure, there must be ten officers assigned specific billets, several in the Pentagon, some with the Weapons Command and some with the Ships System, so that you have representatives around the circle.-- in addition to those staff billets with the major fleet and field staffs, the operating or team billets in your command structure, and the like.

I was pleased with the ultimate Navy acceptance of this career program and I think our overall personnel were more than happy. That is evident by the service retention rate. In previous years the loss of personnel could have been attributed to the fact that a man was being pulled from a team and sent to a ship or some duty in which he had no interest, and he would decide instead to get out and try his hand at civilian life. If he does have career incentive and has chosen this field, he now has the privilege of sticking with it or knowing that he will be coming back to it after a two-year tour. He has much greater incentive and opportunity for a career in the navy. That has been proven in the last ten years.

Q: Is there any relationship as to bachelorhood or the married state on the retention rate in this particular special operations branch?

Capt. B.: Yes, I think throughout the navy that would have to be recognized. The continuous deployments and long term deployments are hazardous to marriage. I think it may be a little less in Special Operations, however, because the wives too seem to get the spirit of this thing. There is a bit more understanding of what their husbands are doing and of the need for it than is often the case (it has been my observation) related to routine shipboard duty. They do experience considerable worries for the hazards of the business, but seem to recognize that it's their husband's choice -- and accept it.

Q: That would be obvious but it is much more colorful and can be understood much more readily than the pedestrian life on shipboard.

Capt. B.: I think that's quite true. Over the years, we have also had an advantage of hazardous duty pay which helps the junior officer and his family in particular.

Q: What is the percentage?

Capt. B.: All men that were qualified and in an operational position -- this does not apply to staff billets but they can be reinstated when they come back to be operational -- both the enlisted men and the officers receive a demolition pay bonus of $100 a month, and as parachutists, $100. That pay advantage of a couple hundred dollars a month can be an incentive today. It is very helpful in the case of junior officers in getting over that initial hump in the navy. When they reach the middle grades, their pay -- though it's evident today it doesn't meet inflationary standards -- the middle grade to the senior officer can get along. He may challenge many of these career points as compared to those of his civilian counterpart but he is not hurting. The enlisted and the junior officer are greatly helped by the pay.

A number of men, as we have always encouraged the junior enlisted, when their tour is up, go on to college, then come back to a Navy career. The opportunities are greater. We have had a high percentage who return. If men have come through training as petty officers -- second class and up -- they are more inclined to complete their career in the Special Warfare field. They consider that it is less opportune for them to resume going to school or have growing families or that they are happy to have "found a home." We have, within our program, encouraged the juniors and seamen though they may be attaining the petty officer rank soon, if they are so qualified we tell them to go to school -- come and see us in a couple of years. I assume this policy is still in being.

Q: Would you talk about various areas of involvement -- more specifically the relationship of this special set up -- with the marines?

Capt. B.: We always worked with the Marines on amphibious operations and the Marine Reconnaissance Units and our UDTs have parallel type backgrounds and responsibility. Sometimes they work on the beaches as a team and then the Marines rejoin their units. The Marines have had problems similar to ours in trying to retain an integrity to their reconnaissance units, but have been reasonably successful. They are a component to their force the same as ours are with the amphibious forces.

Q: What about the army?

Capt. B.: The army has their Special Forces Group -- the Green Berets, as they are often known. They received a tremendous push during the administration and through the interest of President Kennedy. They took full advantage of it in building a very fine school down in Fort Bragg -- new buildings and outstanding facilities. They have had an outstanding publicity program, although it isn't commonly known or acknowledged, we train many of their personnel. We have trained them in demolition work and in any diving or water work that they do. (They don't always give credit to the Navy. I know when I visited a Fort Bragg demonstration and heard the little speech on it, then asked the good sergeant, "Where did you get your training?" It turned out to be one of our navy groups.)

Q: I suppose that is human nature.

Capt. B.: Yes, and it's friendly rivalry and competition but I think it is significant today that in the new Mobile Task Force being set up down at Tampa -- and I might say rather slowly set up -- now under command, in its formative stages, of Marine Lieutenant General Kelly, his Chief of Staff is Captain Norman Olson, who was originally one of our UDT commanding officers and later my Support Group ops officer. I don't happen to know of others, but the MTF is equally divided, including army and air force components. The publicity on this force has more or less been attributed as an Army Mobile but it is not. It is a joint effort headed by a Marine general and a Navy captain. They work well together and there is a great need for them to do so. One of the major handicaps at the present time, I understand, is their lack of lift capability -- the lack of ships or aircraft to move them quickly. I think it is a great thing, however. It is the cement that will hold together these special programs, the special warfare capabilities that are important to each service.

Q: What about mine warfare, how does that fit into your picture?

Capt. B.: It is a separate field. During the time that I was in the Pentagon and we were forming the career program, it was initially conceived that the Explosive Ordnance Disposal Units would become additional components to this same program. By their own choice they wanted to go their own way and it remains so. I don't think that was too wise a decision but it was on their part and they felt they were moving a little more rapidly and advantageously toward keeping their own group together. They asked to be excluded.

Q: It has been the history of their element that in peacetime it has virtually disappeared.

Capt. B.: That is true. Then, when emergencies occurred, they drew a lot of people from demolition teams and they were calling for help. I personally felt it would have been much better for the austerity of the navy and the protection of all these career interests, that a pool be maintained that could move and support the needs of the various special units. I would have liked to have seen all specialized units under Special Warfare. It came as a surprise to us as we were working on the program and had ordnance disposal people working with us. The facts of the case were that following change of command the new Mine Disposal commanding officer believed, "We can do this on our own." So they backed out while we were well along the line. Perhaps one day they will come back together because I think our overall group have the advantage.

Q: It is interesting, I had a letter just today from Ken Veth who at one point was head of mine warfare, and he said when he was in Vietnam he was opposed to the mining of Haiphong at first and was opposed to the use of mines in any operation of that sort -- not because of its effectiveness, because he knew how effective they could be -- but because he was afraid the Russians and the Chinese might step in and mine some of our harbors, places like Danang, and nullify our efforts. But after a while he came around to another point of view.

Capt. B.: I think that concern was nullified by the lack of naval and air presence of the enemy. Of course, they didn't show and we controlled the air. But had they done so, it could have been a complete mess in the Mekong river and such areas.

Q: I am mindful of the ability the Italians showed in World War II when their real talents seemed to be demonstrated in what they did -- underwater warfare at Gibraltar and Alexandria harbor and so forth. I wonder at the extent of our development in that area and even today what protection we have for some of our ships in Diego Garcia or places like that?

Capt. B.: The state of the art has been continuously improved although I would place the Italians still at the top of the list. We have had exchange with the Italians of visiting personnel. Various figures have come in -- for example, Cousteau (French). Cousteau would visit our demolition teams, display his equipment and the exchange has been good. There is a fraternalism, you might say, between all of these underwater people.

The Italians have closely guarded their capabilities, however, and, in exchange of visits, I think only one of my people was really taken into the inner circle with them. They prefer to show you only what they want to show. That is brought on somewhat by our own security measures. I am sure we do the same thing as it pertains to electronic equipment and fire control and nuclears -- that sort of thing. And there were certain phases of our underwater program that were restricted from any foreign or allied observers.

We worked closely also with the Israelis and I would consider them at about number two in this field today in the world. The Israelis through their own initiatives have developed underwater equipment and midget submarines that are comparable though equally guarded on a security basis, to the

Italians. Those two have done the most.

The British have continued on an austere basis as we have been, within the United States Navy, rather restricted by the various economies. The initial U. S. midget submarines were built within the demolition units by our own men. They improvised, copied and patterned after advice of their foreign friends -- with perhaps more tools to work with. And we have some fairly sophisticated two-man and one-man submarines today within our units. They are used in establishing capability for the fixing of limpet mines and for transporting divers with limpet mines to their targets (where they disembark from their submarine and place the mines on ship hulls or whatever).

We have never been very well informed as to the Soviet capabilities in that field but we know they have it. They haven't been a threat to our ships, a concern, but not a real threat due to their distance, as in Vietnam.

Q: The unknown quantity?

Capt. B.: Yes, the threat is there and the threat was always present with the Viet Cong for improvised mines, limpets and water-borne demolitions. In several instances they were successful in damaging some of our craft, along the rivers, even with floating mines, as well as hull attached units. This was effective but not disastrous.

Q: Why are the Italians so skillful in this area?

Capt. B.: I would attribute it to their successful efforts in World War II. They have simply retained the capability and exploited it further. My first awareness came while working with the British in the Mediterranean. The Mediterranean is an ideal situation for this type of operation and equipment, so the Italians have continued.

In 1943 when I worked the reconnaissance of Sicily with the British from Malta, the British sent back with me (I believe I have mentioned this) the equipment that they had improvised and hoped, "If we could just get this in U. S. production it would be much more effective and efficient." I was turned down completely when I took it to ComNavNaw at Algiers, who said, "We are just not interested in that sort of thing. We know the British want it but we would rather not get into that."

Q: It was too exotic?

Capt. B.: And small. We were thinking, as we have been for a generation, of getting bigger, bigger, bigger, and significantly, the British mid-size submarines had full responsibility for the Mediterranean because our submarines were too large. We had Pacific responsibility and they took, with their medium sized and small submarines, the Mediterranean responsibility. The British expanded on this program. They developed during World War II the X-1 submarine which carried up to a five-man crew. I visited them up in Scotland one time to give an opinion for its usefulness in reconnaissance on Normandy and was impressed with the submarine, but knew it was not going to be within our inventory. And I think the British regretted having used it later. They made one play on a reconnaissance run on Normandy during my operating time there, and it was a disaster.

Q: They lost the submarine?

Capt. B.: They lost everything. Due to the shallow gradient of Normandy beaches and the rapid rise and fall of the tide -- the submarine got bogged down high and dry, like a statue on the mud. It was an unsuccessful recon and the crew was captured. That knocked the X-1 out, for that type of gradient at least. But the British continued with the development into the '50s, and we then brought an X-1 submarine to the United States and conducted test and evaluation at several of our naval bases. We tried to find a place for it within our reconnaissance and demolition team operations.

Q: You experimented down in the Caribbean, didn't you?

Capt. B.: Yes, at St. Thomas in the Caribbean. We had it at Little Creek at one stage but due to various economies and considered difficulties in lifting the craft to objective area, no enthusiasm developed. The Italians have continued their operations, and I am sure that the French have with Costeau's efforts there (although most of it is private enterprise on his part). But where interest is so generated, the military certainly shares with it.

Q: How does that tie in now with Sea Labs and things of that sort?

Capt. B.: On the west coast while I was at Coronado, the Sea Lab tests were held off La Jolla, California, and our SEAL and UDT people did most of the work and supervised the control on it. It was much publicized as a program for the astronauts, but our people did all the basic work.

Q: Wasn't Scripps involved in it?

Capt. B.: It was just off the coast from Scripps that the tests were conducted with official request for approximately 20 of our people to provide support, for which as military people, they got little more than a "thank you." We had some interesting experiences and, I am certain, shared in knowledge gained.

My officer in charge was Warrant Officer Ken Speck, whom I consider one of the most authoritative people on midget submarines in the United States. He had some difficulties with Commander Carpenter -- the astronaut, a fine fellow, when calmed down. But he did learn a lesson the hard way. Carpenter came to me, along with Ken Speck, about a week after commencing the tests, to make known that he now understood all necessary details and would take over as CinC. Of course, he outranked Warrant Officer Speck and tended to be quite authoritative with his actions. Ken Speck, with his experience and knowledge, was a strict disciplinarian on safety precautions and procedures.

Carpenter overruled Speck with, "That's all right for some but it doesn't apply to me." In effect, he "threw rank" and as a result of his own actions got a case of the "bends." He was a big enough man, however, to come to my office at Coronado with Ken Speck and apologize for his actions. He said, "I don't know the whole thing but I know a little more about it now. I want you to know that I will go along with Ken in any procedure."

We had 20 men working there throughout Sea Lab, much of which involved delivery of test participants by the two-man submarines and providing the backup of safety, having our divers on-station for any emergency action and that sort of thing. But that part wasn't publicized.

Q: Now, would you say something about the relationship between your Special Operations and Salvage, or some elements of Salvage?

Capt. B.: A division came between Salvage and Special Operations at approximately the time, December 1966, that I came back to the Pentagon. A separate CNO shop was set up -- I forget the number but it was under OP 03 and the direction of Rear Admiral O'Brien. I recall that because of the PUEBLO incident, which we have discussed before. It was transferred deliberately to Admiral O'Brien's cognizance for liaison with Congress and the various details of the investigations which were coming up. This was done primarily because that shop had no background in the specifics nor of the correspondence that came in from the Commanding Officer, PUEBLO.

So Salvage combined with Mine Warfare and became a new shop within the Pentagon and separated from Special Operations, though it had been intended to coordinate them with the advent of Bill Searle from Service Force Pacific. That didn't work out and Captain Searle ultimately became Supervisor of Salvage, but worked under the Chief of Naval Materiel cognizance instead of from the Pentagon. The separation was made on that. Other than those normal rescue operations that are assigned to SEAL and Demolition teams such as downed aircraft and that type of salvage, we had liaison, but little overlapping of responsibility.

Q: Did you have anything to do with the H-bomb that was lost off Portugal, or anything of that sort?

Capt. B.: I am not certain whether or not any of our divers were involved in that. We did not have cognizance of that from our shop. I do believe that the deployed demolition team divers in the Mediterranean assisted, but my memory on this is very fuzzy because control and cognizance of the salvage operation was not under us.

Q: Very probably they did because it seems to me they called on all our resources.

Capt. B.: Yes, it was a matter of considerable concern and the UDT divers are normally called in. They have done a tremendous lot of work over the years in locating aircraft which, rather shockingly -- I was aware of this on the west coast -- our mine detection equipment would fail to locate. So, the UDTs would have to make physical search dives, which they can accomplish up to 200 feet in locating downed aircraft. During the 1960s, in my time at Coronado, there were several aircraft lost between Brown Field and North Island and our divers were often called upon to search.

It is a very tricky operation in that depth of water and to locate a sunken object is often like searching for a needle in a haystack -- and there are currents to contend with. But they have been successful. Sometimes it takes a week to locate a downed aircraft. This circumstance has occurred around the world and wherever all assets are called upon, the UDT divers are among the first.

Q: What relations do you have with the regular diving shcools, the navy diving school?

Capt. B.: No direct relationship. This area was also considered for coordination under Special Warfare but it did not occur. There has been a long term -- well, not really rivalry because they are not that closely related -- but between the "hard hats" and the "scuba" type divers. In other words, the demolition teams are considered more shallow water -- from 200 feet to the surface -- "scuba" types. The "hard hats" are designed not for mobility or combat effectiveness, but for deep-sea and salvage type operations, using the hood, the mask, and various equipments. There is a closer relationship of "hard hats" with salvage, explosive ordnance disposal, and the deep sea diving. Their school, of which there is one at the Washington shipyard, is completely separate from Special Warfare.

Q: Is there any exchange of ideas and techniques?

Capt. B.: Yes, there are annual seminars and exchange on equipment and new techniques, diving medicine, safety, etc. Much of our equipment for test would come into their laboratory, their schools, here -- in testing them for depth capabilities, pressure tests, and the like. There is good coordination but basically I would say, and they might not agree from the "hard hat" side, it is the difference of combat and support type diving operations.

Q: Were you drawn in, in any way, to the development of the atomic submarine POLARIS?

Capt. B.: I don't recall any exercises in which our men worked with POLARIS, though we have toured, visited, and there may have been some coordination of training exercises in the Little Creek area.

Q: What about your operations in cold water areas -- in the Arctic with the ice and the handicaps which areas of the world like that offer? How do you prepare for this?

Capt. B.: Back in the '50s there was considerable concern and preparation. This was the period when the first Polar operations were being conducted with the submarines and there was much exploration both at the South Pole and up in the Greenland area. Nearly all special operations personnel, though I was not involved in that, were given cold weather training including ski operations which related to some of the European problems -- Norway, concern with the Soviets, Alaska -- time was devoted to include that training, but it was never required.

The scenes change and during the period of my direct involvement in Southeast Asia there was little concern for the snow countries. Many of the exploratory adventures of the '50s, however, included deployments of the demolition teams into Greenland and Iceland and the Polar areas. And UDT contingents were included on the South Pole operations. I had no direct involvement with that.

Q: The NATO exercises have concentrated very often on that part of the oceans, in colder areas and up around the north of Norway. Do your elements get involved in any NATO exercises through the Atlantic Fleet?

Capt. B.: They have been involved in several NATO exercises. Whenever U.S. ships have been involved, our UDT type detachments have been deployed with them. Our Beach Jumper Units with their electronic experience participated in many of the Baltic and operations North, mostly on a monitoring capacity.

Q: Did you get involved in any way with the early attempts

to overcome the effects of the Aurora Borealis on communications?

Capt. B.: No, I had no involvement there.

Q: It presented great hazards with communications.

Capt. B.: I was aware of the problem, but our people were not directly involved.

Q: One more question about the cold waters areas: In the '50s when you were working in that area, how did you cope with the actual underwater operations when a man is not capable of staying in this water more than a few minutes?

Capt. B.: It is a difficult matter and we did not have the proper clothing equipment until the astronauts and their programs developed and improved equipment. Probably the coldest situation I experienced was during my Korean tour back in 1957 when a Globemaster U. S. aircraft crashed in the Han River -- literally into the ice. As adviser to Korean Navy Intelligence, we instituted a UDT and they were called upon to assist in the salvage. Those boys worked under ice in trying to free that aircraft with only the protection of rubber suits and did a tremendous job, but that is a hazardous and difficult task that can be tolerated for very few minutes.

Today there are thermal underwear and various warming assists that help, but in the old days the best equipment we had came from the British who, in World War II and in their various reconnaissance ventures, had developed protective suits but more by thickness -- it was quite cumbersome. You wore heavy underwear and it was particularly hard on hands and feet, causing many problems with frostbite. But that was the best we had up through the '50s.

Q: Calling upon your experience in warmer climes, how do your people cope with problems in that area -- in tropical waters? They too present their problems in terms of coral reefs and sea monsters and such.

Capt. B.: I suppose the continuing and most common threat would be sharks, and regardless of teaching and the confidence of experience, there are very few divers that have a great enthusiasm to work in shark infested waters. They can tell some pretty hairy stories as to how close the sharks came and what was done about it. There have been many antidotes, so to speak, solutions to contaminate the water or weapons to frighten them away. But to the best of my knowledge the best solution today is to clear the water as quickly as possible. There have been no UDT casualties from sharks, but they have been fought off and frightened off -- and have frightened the divers pretty much as well.

There are many other infections and irritations affecting the skin from being in the water too long. You are quite right on the coral infections that have occurred.

Q: Many of your UDT operations have been near island shores, have they not?

Capt. B.: They have been in many areas where they worked on reconnaissance, setting demolition charges and even in assisting on construction projects. I think it is inevitable that you will get cuts and scratches, and the greatest concern is the care for them and sanitizing them as soon as practicable. Regardless of type of boots and other clothing worn, coral is a cutting substance. There were many problems in Vietnam from over-exposure in the water which in some cases caused foot and hand diseases. Again, it is the care and the emphasis on drying out, I might say "curing" the skin in some ways. There is considerable merit for sun bathing and drying out of a diver.

Q: You would have to have worked with a dermatologist and have knowledge in these areas.

Capt. B.: Yes, and in those swampy Vietnam river waters there is every contamination available. It requires maximum attention and care where you do have cuts. It is surprising the things you are not aware of until exposed to that slimy type area -- back waters.

Q: Do you know Bill Batters? He told me he was operating as a diver in the Philippines and was down at considerable depth when he suddenly became aware of all these things swimming around him. At first he didn't realize what they were. It turned out it was a whole school of water moccasins and he was diving right in their midst.

Capt. B.: I have had an aversion for snakes all my life. I think we talked about them from the jungle training of Scouts and Raiders at Fort Pierce. But if it is not necessary I wouldn't care to associate with them. That goes for rats, too.

Q: One has to conclude there are so many hazards in this specialized occupation it is almost impossible to list all of them.

Capt. B.: It is different from shipboard living. But there are many excitements and pleasures to go with it too, or the enthusiasm would not remain as high as it does.

Q: There is one area I think you haven't said much about -- that is counter-insurgency.

Capt. B.: That remains somewhat of a nebulous field. I suppose you can put almost any category of operation in that. It is pretty hard to draw the line. It should be the exact opposite of insurgency but in its application through the Vietnam era I found it difficult to define that difference. We could include the various phases, the words that came into being: "infrastructure," and break it down.

There were many people involved in this, directly and indirectly, and there was considerable attempt in briefings and schoolings to make them understand the problems that existed. But it remained command assignment -- go do such and such. I don't think the individual in our type of operations ever categorized. He did his job and what he was assigned on missions as they were outlined. It falls to a higher level of philosophy and definition to single down the subject.

Q: Yet in your capacity as head of these Special Operations you must have had some delineation.

Capt. B.: Not among people. In my opinion, the entire Vietnam operation from the United States viewpoint could have been considered counter-insurgency, but we know that it went beyond that. From the time we were there in advisory capacities, we were literally countering the Viet Cong operations against the people of South Vietnam. To me that is all counter-insurgency. But the tide reversed and there became aggressive activities -- controversial and otherwise -- in which we were moving against the Cong. We were on the attack continuously. Our people were carrying the attack into North Vietnam.

It is that borderline where I find it difficult to draw the line. Where did counter-insurgency stop, and where was the change over to aggressive attack? Counter-insurgency can include so many things, from economic (where we were not involved) to the out-and-out military efforts. We were labelled counter-insurgency. We were labelled that from the Pentagon to the field. I repeat, I find it difficult to draw the line.

Q: When you contemplate this last assignment and the scope of it, how would you say it fits into the present picture for our own means? And how is it viewed by our potential enemies?

Would you care to discuss this general area? Has it gained in importance for us since you were there in '69, or has it lost importance?

Capt. B.: In my opinion, it is continually gaining in importance. Whether or not that is recognized in our United States concept, I think nearly all of our allied countries and certainly many of our potential enemies concentrate on this type of special effort -- and their confidence has been bolstered by suspicion of our weakness.

It certainly applies in the Middle East at the present time. And, if we had had positive involvement, presence, which we are trying to avoid obviously, in the African countries -- the developing countries -- this, I think, based on my Vietnam experience, would have far more importance than any other facet of our military capability. Our preparedness and willingness for this is limited. We have qualified personnel but they are not well equipped. There were tremendous losses of equipment, the leaving behind of equipment -- boats, weapons, ammo and even people -- in Vietnam. There has been austerity since that in the U. S. Navy, and from my understanding and my discussions with other U. S. military forces, they are not much better off. They have not been replenished in boats and equipment that are applicable to the situation. I point out, for example, the Angola problem. We could have done a lot of good for the anti-Communist cause by a presence there and we certainly shied away from it.

Q: That was a policy thing, was it?

Capt. B.: Policy of course governs dollars. Within the U. S. Navy, it has been notoriously favoring large aircraft carriers and aircraft for this past generation. I think the feeling still exists "We have no need for small craft." And there is still the feeling, "Keep our forces out of the rivers." There are very few countries where this is possible since the river ways are the major mode of transportation.

In the past month, I have received from the Naval Sea Systems Command a communique on anticipated small combatant craft procurements. In the next two years they are programming, although they do not have the funding, for 12 Special Warfare craft, boats of the 65-foot category.

Within the U. S. Army (I have worked on some of their boat requirements in the past year), they are programmed, if and when they ever receive the authorized funding (unfortunately that money was promised to them on the basis of an oil tax which hasn't occurred), they are programmed for only 20 boats that were urgently needed during this past year, and the shortfall is slowing down their operations. The Army Special Forces are more and more reliant on aircraft delivery of their people and arrival either by parachute or over ground. And the Marines have clamored for years for their lift.

This becomes quite a problem upon analysis of worldwide emergencies or threatened disturbances and what would be needed to cope. I think there has come to be a recognition that we can't do it all with bombs and aircraft. That in spite of the reluctance and avoidance of involvement, we still must put manpower in direct contact to resolve the prevalent problems in these developing countries; to assert our presence and intent. The situation certainly exists in Central America. There they are procuring small coastal patrol craft, a category of craft that are no more than 100 to 150 feet in overall length, but are capable of delivering inshore the troops, including the fire power, that would counter these less sophisticated and guerrilla type operations.

I feel there is probably the greatest need ever for this type of capability in offsetting major warfare, in averting the huge build-ups of Vietnam with infantry type troops and huge back-up supports. I feel very strongly that the small, versatile groups can accomplish far more effectively counter-actions that may occur.

Q: The fact that we have in existence an organization like the CIA which in the past and hopefully in the future, will engage in covert operations aboard. Does this mean that that agency has pre-empted some of the needs that ordinarily would go to these Special Services in the military?

Capt. B.: It should not mean that. From past experience with CIA operations, their tactics, of necessity, have been to very often employ retired or discharged military personnel, to over-night step in and perform capabilities that they had learned, but are possibly not current. Such was the case going back to

Korea. When this tremendous responsibility was thrust upon the CIA, they recruited nearly anyone they could get with World War II experience to conduct their operations.

Q: I think you said there weren't many that were available.

Capt. B.: This has occurred around the world. Though we speak of clandestine operations, and I certainly think there is a necessity for them, I don't think it pertains to the true combatant type operation. There is a line to be drawn and the CIA is basically an intelligence collection group with, in my opinion, tremendous capabilities. Research, scholarly, diplomatically, and you can go on. They have some of the finest talent in this country. But for the combatant type operation, that is a different matter that should fall to the military whether it be coordinated with the CIA or under separate command and control procedures.

Q: But in actuality, the point of my question was the fact that they do engage in operations that are quasi-military at times. Does this mean they have pre-empted some of the money that normally would have gone to the Navy Special Operations, or to the Army Special Operations?

Capt. B.: I don't feel that they have pre-empted as much as perhaps our Congressional supervision of these allocations has lacked full consideration of the picture, or knowledge of it. I feel that something has been lost in tasking the military to conduct and to accomplish the required tasks. There is the tendency to direct and control the military in almost every capacity. I think between Congress and the White House and their system of controls, as indicated if not evidenced by the recent Iranian incident, the military prerogatives were very much restricted in how to do their business.

Until our recent generation and throughout World War II it was more traditional to task a military commander with doing a job and letting him do the planning, developing of his requirements, logistic and otherwise, and outlining his way of doing that which he is experienced and trained to do. But with all the political controls today, and the tasking to different departments such as CIA (and the loose use of the term clandestine in their operations as applying it to an intelligence operation), then they may have more of the monies -- but I think even our allocation of funds now is more determined by Congressmen than it is by military commanders.

Q: From what you said, I get the implication that more responsibility might be given by the Congress, in terms of appropriations and so forth, to the Special Services in the military if they knew more about them and their capabilities. While you were the head of Special Services in the Navy, did you make any attempt at a PR program to inform members of Congress about your activities?

Capt. B.: I would have to admit, no. There was much accomplished. Our units received Presidential Unit Citations, Meritorious Unit Citations and much small talk. Our boys -- I attended one such presentation with President Johnson on his very last day in office when he gave our SEAL team the Presidential Citation -- had an open discussion with him. The boys surprised him by giving him a plaque as he gave them their citation and he chatted with them considerably.

Q: Was he knowledgeable?

Capt. B.: He handled it very well but I think he was surprised as most people in that position would be. The presenter usually reads a citation and wonders what is this about? They deal only at the Joint Chiefs level -- and Congressmen are in the same category.

As this pertains to Public Relations, I often recall my very first day in the Pentagon when I was called in and censured for a statement which the press picked up out in California upon my detachment, that SEAL teams wore black berets. I was told that in the navy there were only white hats, you don't talk about such things. And we don't ever want to hear that again. Well, that's a small thing, but you can look at it the other way -- that a little publicity could have helped the cause though we weren't promoting it. My comments were made only in answer to "Do you have such a name and do you wear Green Berets?" I said, "No, but as a matter of fact they wear black berets." Publicity in the navy is desired only for those at top level andppolitically dependent.

Q: The reason I asked is because I know that various branches of the Naval Service do make a concerted effort. They are always taking groups of Congressmen out to an aircraft carrier and indoctrinating them into the operations of that carrier.

Capt. B.: I think you have put your finger on it. That is specifically what they do. They take them to the "biggest" and where they want funds allocated. I think that the navy is the most stodgy and backward of the services in publicizing their overall service capabilities and requirements. I think that is one of the problems of morale.

If you are not in the glamour position in the navy, if you are assigned to an LST, you become a workhorse and little appreciated. You may do a tremendous job, have more work hours and more time deployed possibly than any other type ship, with very little credit -- because there isn't much high level gain by publicizing the workhorse.

This applies up and down the line. It hasn't been desirable at our command levels, to bring out the accomplishments of many -- not just Special Warfare Groups -- but many of our smaller ship components and the men on the spot. I don't think it was ever brought out about much of the shore and river work that was accomplished in Vietnam by the various patrols, and the work they did so successfully. The Stars and Stripes, being a service paper, is the only media that I have seen that has ever given real coverage to such things. Now, they did bring out accomplishments of other services. There is very little that Army Special Forces, the Green Berets have not been acclaimed for, even with exaggerated praise. (That brings the funding support as well as helping recruiting!)

The Air Force had a special force, but it has not been built up so much and it is a little different involving electronic play as conducted by their aircraft crews -- thus differing from the organized components of army, navy and marines.

Q: Is this perhaps one of the impediments to greater publicity about the operations of the Special Services? The fact that some of the operations are necessarily of a confidential or secret nature, and can't be exposed too readily without doing damage? Of course, you can say the same thing pertains to all services but not to the same extent. I think more is in the open there.

Capt. B.: Naturally there are certain security problems. The secrecy of operations must often be preserved, both to ensure success and the safety of personnel. But I don't think that applies to the overall picture. My honest appraisal of it, looking back over the years and with ten years of retirement behind me, I would place the blame within the navy, on jealously guarded personal publicity. As the higher levels of promotion occur, a commanding officer, just as the correspondence he signs whether he wrote it or not bears his signature, any publicity as well as overall responsibility must come to command.

I don't think that lack of recognition is appropriate or

advantageous -- or necessary. There are so many that are deserving of much more credit, whether it be in mine clearance -- a very treacherous job -- what credit have those people ever had for clearing the waters? And they have hot stuff on their hands at all times. You can glamorize a UDT type operator, but once his operation is told you have said it once and for all, they seem to think. The fact that he has so many different responsibilities ranging from reconnaissance, to beach clearance, to combat operations -- this is seldom touched upon -- and is not known or understood by the incoming generation.

I think this is of significant concern, and I never accomplished very much with it. I don't think it is known today but our SEAL teams are probably the most decorated naval force of Vietnam, and with the highest casualty rate. But it was pretty much ignored because we don't talk about that. This has always been the navy attitude -- "That is not our job. We are the deep water navy"-- or, "We are the air force that can dominate the world." Public relations, as it has been controlled from the top levels, I think has ignored the smaller components. This does not apply to all the flag officers, by any means, but the overall trend from top level command has been to that effect.

Q: Still thinking in terms of publicity, underlying all of it you have within the Special Services and the kind of things they perform, a group of heroes and heroes always appeal to the general public -- so you have a built-in capacity for great publicity. It doesn't have to be tremendous. These are individual exploits performed by a single man or a group of men. This is potential news if only it could break through the shell that surrounds them.

Capt. B.: Exactly. "If" it could break through. Now if you are running a football team, their record, their team play, their individual performance would be acclaimed until they were All-American or recognized throughout the reading world. So what does it take -- a public relations man specializing in football or is it mainly recognized as having news value and interest to the public?

I don't think that the public relations personnel are lacking, by any means. But I think the controls of what they are permitted to release may be the problem. I haven't said that within the navy credit has not been given to individuals. But I did not see one word of publicity, for example, on President Johnson's Presidential Unit Citations to the SEAL team. It certainly was not in the Washington paper and it occurred in the White House and I was present. They took pictures, routine photography and so forth. My people searched for it in the west coast papers too, but never a word appeared. I don't know what stopped it and I felt that my office should have done more about it. We checked with Public Relations and they said, "Well, we sent it out."

I think much more can be done but the approach is negative. What do you read today? You read that our army has gone to pot. It has lost its capability. They are below the high school intelligence level. In the navy, we read only that we are not retaining them. Same for the air force. Pilots are leaving, our qualified navy personnel are leaving. I have never believed, as has recently been publicized, that it is pay alone that provides the incentive for continued naval career. I remained a reserve officer for thirty-one and a half years and it certainly wasn't pay that kept me. I was nine years as a lieutenant commander at a time that people were dropping out like mad. I believe in and liked the navy, considered it important, and was needed by my country. Statistics of a few years ago, when I knew them, indicated that we are retaining only between 5% and 10% of our Naval Academy gradutes. We are lacking something in stimulus for those people and I think a great portion of it is credit, not dollars.

I get rather steamed up on that but I don't think that the navy does a very creditable job in acknowledging the value of its people, their sincerity of effort, their devotion to duty.

Q: You are not only steamed up, you are rather eloquent.

Capt. B.: I received just last month from a World War II friend of mine, who was in my outfit in China, a Scout and Raider,-- his son was at Purdue University and two people got up at an athletic game and waved a Communist flag. His son not only stopped that, but wrote an editorial for the University paper. Though I hadn't heard from the man for years he sent me the clipping and said, "I'm proud of my boy." And I wrote him back, "I'm proud of him, too."

There are people out there that feel very strongly but they feel that we are not doing what we should for the public. I don't know -- this liberalism gets my soapbox on duty, I'm afraid. There are so many of these volunteers from World War II and the Korean War that feel as strongly today as they did then and just can't understand the "Hell, no, I won't go" attitude. I think the services themselves have a greater responsibility of putting the message across. I don't intend being on the pedestal or talking for the draft -- I'm getting old. But I can well remember when there were waiting lists to get into this man's navy with a quick six month wait ahead. We don't have that kind of appeal at this time and I can't see why, other than for our own shortcomings. We are not selling, we are asking, we're begging, when the recruits and officer candidates should be knocking on the navy's door.

Maybe that doesn't make sense, but I believe it.

Q: In connection with your duties in the Pentagon, 1967 to 1969 and we were talking about publicity -- tell me about your tours and your speeches.

Capt. B.: Well, it was a continuous thing, though very often I think it is a buck-passing matter. I suppose any naval officer with his regular duties doesn't welcome additional duty assignments. However, I think there is a tremendous responsibility involved. During my Pentagon tour I was so tasked. Of course, there are many conventions and conferences around the Washington area that somebody has to attend, even if it was only a presence in a uniform. And I think it was worthwhile.

I was also tasked to talk to Navy League groups. Once out in Youngstown, Ohio, a very impressive time to me, I described to them Vietnam operations and I was held, after my talk, for more than an hour by questions from that group. Most of the people involved were steel workers.

Q: The sort of thing you people do has a built-in appeal to the populace.

Capt. B.: This group worked me over pretty well, but at that stage most of the questions that they hammered at me were, "Is there any fact behind a withdrawal in Vietnam? Is it possible that the United States would withdraw without winning? Is there any reason we can't win? What can we do to assist?" This was the attitude that I saw from the middle west. I had a comparable experience in St. Louis and I was almost being criticized for being in a uniform and not able to answer "Hell, yes, we'll be in there and we will win." I was not in a position to explain the political restrictions were controlling each operation.

I had a similar experience in Fort Lauderdale, Florida. I must admit that many of the meetings that I attended Washingtonwise were very routine and everyone "knows" the real facts, the truth, and they are not really as interested. But, throughout this country I, to this day, cannot believe that the American public is reconciled to the Vietnam withdrawal which, they would have us believe, we were almost forced into. I don't believe it.

Too many friends from over the years wonder, "What has happened to us?" The World War II veterans feel this. I, too, criticize the teenagers and now those in their 20s and even their 30s for attitudes that they express. The mass of this nation -- it is unbelievable to me from the exposure I have had -- that they can ever accept such a debacle as we politically got into. I cannot blame the military one particle for Vietnam.

Q: You have echoed a note emphasizing the fact that R&D is constantly going forward in terms of small boats.

Capt. B.: Once the navy recognized that it was in the Vietnam war, they belatedly did their best to support the people in the field. Requirements came in from the imagination of every field commander, whether it be river boats -- they were designed through the different research agencies within the navy -- fiberglass river boats, shallow draft, water jet propelled that could go in one foot and they claimed could in six inches of water -- these were small 28-foot craft.

There were coastal craft. The SWIFT boat was one of the best developments in that small craft category over the years. The patrol gunboat, the PGs, came into being, but were too hastily sent off to Vietnam. When I say too hastily, it was recognized by the Pentagon as well as by Ships Systems Command that the boats needed a thorough shakedown. They had some very sophisticated equipment -- propulsion, fire control and ordnance. It takes a little longer perhaps. They really needed about six months of shakedown. But there was a clamor for them which came from Admiral Zumwalt -- "Get them out here and we'll take care of that here." This downgraded the boats. They spent more time in Subic getting their equipment shaken down when keeping them here a little longer could have resolved the problems with greater credit to the equipment and its use.

There were various improvisations that occurred with amphibious craft for river operations, for troop carriers, and in providing support base developments. It required tremendous initiative on the part of all concerned. I think the navy did a creditable job. A little late -- had they started earlier, it might have been more effective. I think, however, they overextended themselves with exotic equipment which unfortunately were all left behind. Many of these requests did come through our CNO Special Warfare shop and working in coordination with the Ships Systems Command, we seemed always to be fighting for funds. But, in fairness, I will have to say financial support was adequate though not in some preferred categories. For example, some equipments were forced upon us that we didn't feel need for and no more did the people in the field. That also was a problem of research -- for anyone who had something to sell, this was an opportunity to push it.

This went on in continuing basis during my CNO tour and

on a reactionary basis there were also many other flaps that occurred around the world. We were pulled away from Vietnam at times with PUEBLO type operations, with casualties and threats in other parts of the world which from the office of the CNO you certainly have your responsibilities and cognizance worldwide. We had an equal concern with outfitting the Atlantic people and ultimately we were drawing on Special Operations people from Little Creek to support the rotations that were going on in Vietnam, trying to take some of the strain off the Pacific units from Coronado. We used SEAL team components from Little Creek as well as from Coronado, which we had not done earlier in the war.

There were various new equipments that were developed. These ranged from hydrofoil craft to air cushion vehicles, which we ultimately transferred to the army. We had various types of weaponry -- rocketry and small arms, and also in Korea, a support function. From the CNO level the policy was "get 'em what they need, if you don't have the money, fight for it."

Of course, and meanwhile, probably the bane of the existence of anyone assigned, is the budget system on which your people on a year-round basis are working -- changing requirements, justifying them, and at that time we had to (foolishly, but part of the McNamara policy) have three studies to support any new project and these couldn't be prepared by any overlapping or single source.

This, I think every officer involved thought was a

waste in dollar cost for the studies -- first, you had to provide all the background and support for those contracted to write your own thoughts, and the whole justification of going outside the military force for such studies was that you didn't have the time to do it yourself, or that you might be prejudiced in your beliefs -- and these unbiased people should prepare such recommendations.

Once you got through one budget cycle, you go into the supplemental budget cycle -- and in spite of the contention of the Secretary of Defense that it cost no more to run a war than a peace time operation, there was considerable need for supplemental budgets. These things take a tremendous amount of time.

I may have told you this of my first meeting with Admiral Arleigh Burke at a reception: I was introduced to him by former Chief of Staff of ComPhibLant, Rear Admiral Henry Briggs, who said, "Captain Bucklew has just arrived in Washington on his first tour here."

Admiral Burke commented, "Well, Captain I think this will probably be one of the most interesting experiences of your life. You know, I had three, or was it four, tours in Washington and I have been thinking about them since I have retired. There is one thing that crosses my mind -- why in the Hell couldn't you, Burke, have accomplished a few more of those things that you always said you would do if you ever got to Washington? You might think about that."

No truer words were ever spoken. Everything is reactionary

in that Pentagon and it is so difficult, whether it be a career program or whatever, to follow through and get done on a day-by-day basis some of those things that from the field you thought were so important and all of them controlled by the never-never land in Washington.

Q: That you felt were important and obvious?

Capt. B.: Important and obvious in the field and discouraging that there aren't enough hours in the day when you are pushing messages and going to conferences and fighting for dollars.

Q: Thank you very much, Phil, for your time. And for your kindness in making your reminiscences a part of the Oral History collection of the U. S. Naval Institute.

Index

to

Series of Taped Interviews

with

Captain Phil H. Bucklew, USN (Ret.)

USS ALMAC (AKA); takes on commando survivors from the LEEDSTOWN, p. 42;

AMOY, China: destination of Bucklew on his long trip through the mountains disguised as a coolie, p. 132; proposed raid on island of Amoy, p. 148 ff;

AMPHIBIOUS COMMANDOS: Bucklew joins nine others in special training at Patuxent, p. 34 ff;

AMPHIBIOUS GROUP ONE: Bucklew reports to staff (June, 1961) in San Diego, p. 290 ff; Public Relations visit to State of Washington, p. 291-2; a joint amphibious operation with army near Seattle - need to avoid conflict with salmon commercial fishing, p. 292-3; transfer to far Pacific with homeport in Subic Bay, p. 293; amphibious operations on Taiwan, p. 300-304; an amphibious operation with the Filipinos, p. 304 ff; planning for evacuation of American citizens from Indonesia, p. 305-6; p. 311-13; Bucklew detached and returns to Coronado as Exec of the Amphibious Base, p. 315; p. 318;

AMPHIBIOUS TRAINING COMMAND - CORONADO: Bucklew reports in 1958 as officer in charge of Amphibious Intelligence School, p. 280-290; p. 298-300;

ATHLETICS: Bucklew's participation after graduation from Xavier, p. 13 ff; two years with Cleveland Rams, p. 13; Cincinnati Bengals, p. 13; forms a new team in Columbus, Ohio - the American League, p. 14-16; barnstorming tour of the West Coast- the Los Angeles game of Dec. 7, 1941 - entire team enlists, p. 20; after WW II Bucklew returns to Xavier, p. 21; on to Columbia University and work with Lou Little, p. 24 ff;

BEACH JUMPERS: p. 381-3;

BEACH JUMPER UNIT II: Bucklew goes to Little Creek, Va. to take command of this new unit (1951-56), p. 197 ff; p. 204; commissioning, p. 205; early struggles, p. 206-8; electronic interference exercises, p. 210-11; test and evaluation efforts with various types of craft, p. 213-14; cooperation with UDTs, p. 219-20; BJUs maintain in training a physical conditioning program, p. 221-2;

BIZERTE: Conolly headquarters for Sicily and Naples operations. see entries under:
CONOLLY, Admiral Richard
and
SICILY
and
SALERNO

BLOUIN, VADM Francis Joseph (Champ): p. 310; relieves Adm. Hooper in command of Amphibious Group 1, p. 310 ff;

BOAT SUPPORT GROUP: p. 380-1; also see entries under:
SPECIAL OPERATIONS GROUP

BRISCOE, Admiral Robert P.: ComPhibLant at Little Creek, p. 197; his ideas about electronic warfare, p. 200; p. 212;

BRITISH INTELLIGENCE WORK AND TECHNIQUES: p. 101-2;

BUCKLEW, Captain Phil H.: family background - early interest in athletics, p. 1-6; the incident that convinced him to apply for a commission in the navy, p. 39.

BUCKLEW REPORT: name given report of the special group sent to Vietnam to study developments and make recommendations; see entries under:
VIETNAM and
SPECIAL OPERATIONS GROUP
and
ADMIRAL H. D. FELT

CHINA THEATER: Bucklew and his small group of Volunteers enroute to Adm. Miles in Chungking, p. 125 ff;
see other entries:
MILES, VADM Milton E.
and
SHANGHAI
and
WEDEMEYER, Gen. Albert C.
and
TAI LI, General

CHUNGKING: The Scouts go to Chungking, headquarters of Admiral Miles, p. 145; p. 149;

CIA - in KOREA: p. 436-8;
see entries under:
KOREA
and
TAYLOR, VADM Rufus
and
NAVAL ADVISORY GROUP KOREA
and
KIM SE WON - Captain

CLARK, General Mark: p. 69; p. 74;

CONOLLY, Admiral Richard (ComLanCrabNav): Bucklew assigned to his staff, p. 54; insists that Bucklew's men should be trained in the Mediterranean, p. 56-7; Conolly pleads against withdrawal at Salerno, p. 69; p. 73; p. 76; on to the Pacific, p. 76; Bucklew writes him in Pacific asking for a job, p. 122;

COOK, Admiral Charles: p. 185-6;

DANANG: Bucklew inspects the situation there, p. 335-6;

DEYO, VADM Morton Lyndholm: p. 108; p. 116;

DUNCAN, Admiral Charles K.: Chief of BuPers - a help in achieving a career program for Special Warfare, p. 405;

DYER, Admiral George: p. 70-71;

EISENHOWER, General Dwight D.: President of Columbia University, p. 192-3;

FAHRION, Adm. Frank George (Spike): in command at Little Creek during most of time spent there by Bucklew, p. 29; relieves Adm. Briscoe as ComPhibLant, p. 198; p. 199; p. 209-11; p. 220;

FELT, Admiral H. D.: CincPac - special study group on Vietnam calls on him for instructions enroute to Saigon, p. 322-3; he asks them to report back on problems, recommendations, p. 323; p. 330-; p. 347; p. 352;

FORT PIERCE, Florida: Bucklew sent there after Normandy to train Scout and Raider candidates, p. 119;

GAETA, Italy: p. 74;

GANTZ EXPEDITION: under command of Lt. Comdr. Saxe Gantz; destination of Bucklew was the Amoy area; destination of others including Gantz, other parts of coast, p. 132 ff; final recommendation of Bucklew, etc. of the coastal area as possible place for invasion, p. 134;

HALL, Admiral John Lesslie, Jr. (Jimmy): p. 96; p. 99; p. 106-7; p. 118;

HARKINS, Lt. Gen. Paul D.: p. 325; p. 330-1; p. 348;

HOLMES, Admiral Ephraim (Eph) Paul: problems with him and repairs to BJU boats, p. 215-6; in 1963 he directed Bucklew to coordinate various units into the Naval Operations Support Group, p. 218; p. 317-18; sends Bucklew to Vietnam as member of study team under RADM Paul Savidge, p. 321-2;

quizzes Bucklew on the Vietnam Report (Bucklew Report), p. 352; p. 376;

HONG KONG: p. 309-10;

HOOPER, VADM Edwin B.: becomes commander, Amphibious Group One, p. 291; p. 293; p. 296; p. 308; p. 309; p. 311;

INDONESIA: p. 305-6;

ISLE OF WIGHT: training in preparation for reconnaissance of Normandy Coast, p. 82; p. 87; sand samples from the beach, p. 87-9;

JARRELL, VADM Albert E.: in command of Naval Forces Korea, p. 267 his diverse command relationships, p. 268-9;

KAI, Admiral Liu Kwan: C-in-C, Nationalist Chinese Navy, p. 299; p. 301; requests Bucklew and his wife to stop in Taiwan enroute home - as official guests of Chinese navy, p. 315-6;

KIM, Captin Se Won: Director of Naval Intelligence for the Korean Navy, p. 229 ff; p. 255-9; p. 263-6;

KIRK, Admiral Alan G.: p. 99; p. 107;

KOREA: Bucklew assigned to Korea to work with CIA, p. 224; p. 229 attached to the Naval Advisory Group in Korea, p. 229; his tour comes to end in July, 1958, p. 267; discussion of complexity of the North/South Korean problem, p. 245-250;

KOREAN NAVY: p. 262-3;

KUNMING, China: border town - supply station for U.S. Naval Group, China, p. 128; p. 131; entire group of Scouts assembled in Kunming, p. 143; p. 146;

USS LEEDSTOWN (ex-SANTA LUCIA): transport carrying landing craft for North African invasion, p. 37 ff; ship sunk by Germans, p. 41-2;

LITTLE, Lou: coach at Columbia University - Bucklew spends four years at Columbia working on a doctorate and coaching for Little, p. 25ff; p. 194-5; p. 197;

LITTLE CREEK: Bucklew back in the Navy in June 1951 - spends four years at Little Creek p. 29 ff;

LODGE, The Hon. Henry Cabot: U.S. Ambassador to South Vietnam - his relations with General Harkins, the MAAG, p. 325;

LST: for accounts of LST actions, performances, etc. see entries under:
    SICILY
    and
    SALERNO

McNAMARA, Robert S.: his visit to Danang - his order for SWIFT boats, p. 398-9;

MILES, VADM Milton E. (Mary): Adm. Conolly refers Bucklew to him for work in the Pacific, p. 122; his headquarters in Chungking, p. 128; mission assigned Bucklew and his men - reconnaissance of China coast, p. 128 ff; p. 145; Miles arrives in Shanghai (after armistice) - asks Bucklew to find headquarters building, p. 155 ff; names Bucklew as billeting officer, p. 158; story of Miles and his banquet for 7th fleet officers, p. 159 ff; Bucklew's price control job, p. 162 ff; Bucklew sees Miles in Washington, p. 191-2;

MOON, RADM Don Pardee: p. 104;

MULBERRY: artificial harbor used at Normandy, p. 103-4;

NAVAL ADVISORY GROUP - Korea: p. 224; Bucklew attached, p. 229; Bucklew's mission - account of various missions and efforts against the enemy, p. 230 ff.

NAVAL OPERATIONS SUPPORT GROUP:
    see entries under:
    SPECIAL OPERATIONS GROUP

NAVAL RESERVE: Bucklew joins the Naval Reserve in 1930, p. 7-8;

NORMANDY: Bucklew and four others go from Bizerte to England - preparatory to NORMANDY, p. 77; Bucklew and Andreason put under command of Capt. Ted Wellings, p. 81; Bucklew sent to a British unit on Isle of Wight for reconnaissance training, p. 82; British insisted they be sent to Escape and Evasion School, p. 83-5; Bucklew and Andreason train U. S. personnel, p. 92; the first UDTs sent over, p. 94 ff; Bucklew's last operations on Normandy coast, p. 105-6; Bucklew's experience with certain personnel under his command, p. 108-11; Bucklew tells about submerged tanks, the first to land on Normandy beaches, p. 112-4;

impressions of D Day on Normandy, p. 114 ff; devastation wrought by Deyo's shore bombardment, p. 116; Bucklew writes report on lessons learned at Normandy for Scout and Raiders, p. 117-119;

NROTC: Bucklew teaches in the program at Columbia University, 1950-51, p. 26 ff; p. 29 ff;

OVERLORD: Bucklew and Andreason in Falmouth - the Admiral in command shows them (Dec. 1943) the early plans for the Normandy invasion, p. 79; their reconnaissance for the training area - Slapton Sands, p. 80, p. 90-91; also: entries under:
<u>NORMANDY</u>
and
<u>ISLE OF WIGHT</u>

PANMUNJAM: Armistice Commission at, p. 243 ff;

PATTON, General George: a picture of him in action on the Normandy beachhead, p. 106-7;

USS PHILADELPHIA: burns out guns in Salerno bombardment, p. 69;

HRH PRINCE PHILIP: training on the Isle of Wight (Dec. 1943), p. 82;

USS PUEBLO: p. 217-8;

RHEA, President Syngman: p. 250-1; p. 261;

RICKETTS, Admiral Claude V.: p. 212;

RIVERO, Admiral Horacio: his opposition to Special Operations in the Navy, p. 202-3; p. 339;

ROCKY SHOALS: special amphibious exercise (1958) on California coast off San Simeon; Bucklew served on Joint Intelligence Staff (Army/Navy) and Adm. Speck was joint naval commander p. 270 ff;

ROMMEL, General Erwin: German general at Normandy, p. 96-7;

RUGGIERI, Lt. Rocky: partner with Bucklew in China assignment, p. 131; p. 140-41;

SACO (Sino-American Cooperation Organization): was headed by Admiral Miles (American component) and Gen. Tai Li (Chinese component), p. 142; p. 167; a summary statement on SACO, p. 170; p. 191;

SALERNO: the role of Scout and Rangers, p. 63 ff; story of Bucklew in the kayak canoe for initial landing, p. 65 ff; Adm. Conolly wins over Gen. Clark's attempt to withdraw - the day for naval bombardment of beaches and one more attempt at landing, p. 69 ff;

SAVIDGE, RADM Paul S.: heads study group sent to Vietnam by Admiral Holmes to report on conditions there, p. 321-2; Savidge becomes ill and brought home - Bucklew takes over, p. 324 ff;

SCOUT AND RAIDERS: assemble in Ft. Pierce, Florida where they set up a base early in 1943, p. 46 ff; Bucklew and several others join British Combined Operations Group at Malta to reconnoiter coasts of Sicily, p. 50 ff;

SEAL TEAMS - IN VIETNAM: the state of the SEALS when Bucklew took command, p. 361-2; requirements, training, p. 362-3; p. 367; the Vietnamese SEALS, p. 369-70; obtaining approval for SEAL operations in Vietnam - the frustrations and delay, p. 371-3; lessons learned through improvisation, p. 374-5; U.S. SEAL advisors with Vietnamese teams, p. 377-78; p. 393-4; p. 439;

SHANGHAI: Bucklew delegated to act as escort to General Tai Li and take him to Shanghai after Japanese surrender, p. 152 ff; immediate postwar problems in Shanghai, p. 175-192;

SICILY: Scout and Raiders - reconnoiter coasts p. 50 ff; training under Conolly command with mission to see that troops land on the assigned beaches in Sicily, p. 57; Bucklew's comments on the techniques used - the exceptionally brave Raider who stationed himself under the occupied pill-box, p. 59-60; after Sicily Raiders back to Bizerte to train for Salerno, p. 61;

SINGLAUB, Gen. Jack: p. 335-6;

SPECIAL OPERATIONS GROUP: Bucklew named by Admiral Holmes to form Special Operations Group (UDTs, SEALS, BOAT SUPPORT, etc.), p. 318; p. 321-2; Bucklew sent to Vietnam with Adm. Savidge to conduct survey, p. 321; name of group changed to Naval Operations Support Group at behest of VCNO, p. 358-9; a consolidation of five different small commands, p. 359; p. 396;

SPECIAL WARFARE AND SPECIAL OPERATIONS DIVISION of CNO: (Op. 343) Bucklew assigned as head of this office in late 1966, p. 403 ff; the development of a career program in Special Warfare, p. 403 ff; the incentives found in hazardous duty pay, p. 414; cooperation with the Marines, p. 415; cooperation with the Army, p. 416; comments on the abilities of the Italians, Israeli, British, etc. p. 418-20; the SEA LAB project, p. 423-4; Salvage and Special Operations, p. 424-5; comment on the growing importance of this type of warfare, p. 434; Special Warfare and public relations, p. 438-9; p. 440-2;

TAI LI, General: p. 142; Bucklew ordered to escort the General to Shanghai after the Japanese surrender, p. 152 ff; a thumb-nail biographical sketch of him, p. 165-6; p. 174-5;

TAIWAN: amphibious operations of Amphibious Group One, P. 300-04;

TAYLOR, VADM Rufus: p. 226; Intelligence Officer for Adm. Callahan in FE, p. 229; p. 234; p. 258; p. 295;

TONKIN GULF: the story as told from the point of view of the SEALS, p. 368;

TORCH OPERATION: p. 39-41;

TUNNEY, Gene: his WW II program - Bucklew is enrolled, p. 32-34;

UDTs: Rangers train first contingent of UDTs to arrive from states for Normandy operation, p. 94-6; p. 112; p. 219-222; intelligence gathering in southern area of Gulf of Tonkin, p. 296; p. 380; p. 425-6; p. 428-9; p. 442;

VAN FLEET, General James A.: p. 228-9;

VIETNAM: Special Study Group sent by Admiral Holmes - caused by concern over infiltration of the Viet Cong, p. 322 ff; group stops in Pearl Harbor for indoctrination by Adm. Felt's staff, p. 322-23; begin study of situation in Saigon, Savidge becomes ill, Bucklew ordered to take over, p. 324 ff; reasons for the military impass, p. 330-1; his comments on the Vietnamese Navy, p. 337-40; observations on the Cambodian border, p. 344; useful comments to the study group by an Army Intelligence Officer, p. 344-5; the SWIFT boats and the Norwegian NASTY (USS OSPREY), p. 346; comments on the personnel who comprised the group making the report and their special contributions, p. 350-1; reception of the report in Pearl Harbor and Washington, p. 352-4; Bucklew uses the term 'counter-insurgency' to delineate U.S. activity in Vietnam, p. 433; p. 446-9;

WEDEMEYER, General Albert C.: Chief of Staff to Gen. Chiang kai-chek in Shanghai, p. 160; p. 162;

WELLINGS, RADM Ted: p. 107; p. 118;

WESTMORELAND, General Wm.: p. 331; relieves Gen. Harkins, p. 336-7;

XAVIER University: Coach Crowe persuaded Bucklew to attend, p. 6-7; completes his four years at Xavier and then coaches there, p. 12; in charge of scholarships and student funds, p. 12-13; after WW II returns to Xavier (1946), p. 21; becomes dissatisfied with pressures, etc. and goes on to Columbia University, p. 22-23;